Land Rover
Series One to Freelander

Other titles in the Crowood AutoClassic Series

AC Cobra	Brian Laban
Alfa Romeo Spider	John Tipler
Alfa Romeo Sports Coupés	Graham Robson
Aston Martin DB4, DB5 and DB6	Jonathan Wood
Aston Martin and Lagonda V-Engined Cars	David G Styles
Audi quattro	Laurence Meredith
Austin-Healey 100 & 3000 Series	Graham Robson
BMW 3 Series	James Taylor
BMW 5 Series	James Taylor
BMW 7 Series	Graham Robson
BMW M-Series	Alan Henry
BMW: The Classic Cars of the 1960s and 70s	Laurence Meredith
Citroën 2CV	Matt White
Citroën DS	Jon Pressnell
Datsun Z Series	David G Styles
Ferrari Dino	Anthony Curtis
Ford RS Escorts	Graham Robson
Jaguar E-Type	Jonathan Wood
Jaguar Mk 1 and 2	James Taylor
Jaguar XJ Series	Graham Robson
Jaguar XJ-S	Graham Robson
Jaguar XK Series	Jeremy Boyce
Jeep – From Bantam to Wrangler	Bill Munro
Lamborghini Countach	Peter Dron
Lotus and Caterham Seven: Racers for the Road	John Tipler
Lotus Elan	Mike Taylor
Lotus Elise	John Tipler
Lotus Esprit	Jeremy Walton
MGA	David G Styles
MGB	Brian Laban
MG T-Series	Graham Robson
Mini	James Ruppert
Morris Minor	Ray Newell
Porsche 911	David Vivian
Porsche 924, 928, 944 and 968	David Vivian
Range Rover	James Taylor and Nick Dimbleby
Rolls-Royce Silver Cloud	Graham Robson
Rolls-Royce Silver Shadow	Graham Robson
Rover P4	James Taylor
Rover P5 & P5B	James Taylor
Rover SD1	Karen Pender
Saab 99 and 900	Lance Cole
Sunbeam Alpine and Tiger	Graham Robson
Triumph 2000 and 2.5PI	Graham Robson
Triumph Spitfire & GT6	James Taylor
Triumph TRs	Graham Robson
TVR	John Tipler
VW Beetle	Robert Davies
Volvo 1800	David G Styles

LAND ROVER
Series One to Freelander

Graham Robson

The Crowood Press

First published in 2003 by
The Crowood Press Ltd
Ramsbury, Marlborough
Wiltshire SN8 2HR

www.crowood.com

© Graham Robson 2003

All rights reserved. No part of this publication may be reproduced or transmitted in any form or by any means, electronic or mechanical, including photocopy, recording, or any information storage and retrieval system, without permission in writing from the publishers.

British Library Cataloguing-in-Publication Data
A catalogue record for this book is available from the British Library.

ISBN 1 86126 558 1

Acknowledgements
In condensing everything I have every learned, driven, read and heard about Land Rovers, I have drawn on more than forty years of Solihull experience. This includes past interviews with personalities as various as Tom Barton, William Martin-Hurst, Tony Gilroy, Spen King – plus an almost endless list of contacts in, and around, Solihull. However, when I came to compile this new volume, I was helped by several very important people: Gavin Green, Mike Gould and Judy Maiden, of Land Rover in the UK; Lynne Slovick, of Land Rover North America; Gary Anderson, Editor of *British Car* in the USA; and James Taylor, Editor of *Land Rover Enthusiast*. Although many photographs came from my own archive, I am grateful to James Taylor/*Land Rover Enthusiast* for loaning me some vital detail shots, to Gary Anderson for letting me have pictures of his Freelander drive in Iceland, and to Judy Maiden for letting me use the ultra-modern aerial photograph of Solihull, 2002.

They know, and I know they know, that this job might not have been completed without their help, and I am extremely grateful.

Typeset by Focus Publishing,
11a St. Botolph's Road,
Sevenoaks, Kent TN13 3AJ

Printed and bound in Great Britain by Bookcraft, Midsomer Norton

Contents

Evolution		6
Introduction		7
1	Rover's First 4×4: the Original Land Rovers	8
2	Series II and IIA (1958–71)	34
3	Series III (1971–85)	55
4	Ninety and One-Ten: Coil Springs, New Engines – a Thorough Update	76
5	Defender – and Still They Come	96
6	Discovery – With Thanks to the Range Rover	110
7	Discovery II: The Second Generation	134
8	Freelander: New Structure, New Engines, New Thinking	148
Appendix	Oddities, Militaria and Specials	172
Index		190

Evolution

Spring 1947	Design work began on the original Land Rover, using the US Jeep as inspiration.
April 1948	Land Rover (later known as Series I) originally shown to the public, at the Amsterdam Motor Show, with 80in wheelbase chassis, 1,595cc petrol engine, and pick-up body.
Early 1952	Engine enlarged to 1,997cc.
1954	Long-wheelbase version (107in) introduced, and short-wheelbase increased to 86in at the same time.
October 1956	Wheelbase increased by 2in, both versions – to 88in and 109in, respectively.
June 1957	Introduction of optional 2,052cc diesel engine.
April 1958	Series II model range replaced Series I. Petrol engine enlarged to 2,286cc.
September 1961	Series IIA model range replaced Series II models. Diesel engine enlarged to 2,286cc.
April 1967	Addition of petrol six-cylinder 2,625cc engine option for long-wheelbase models.
September 1968	Introduction of special '1-ton' (payload) version of 109in wheelbase model. Lightweight/ strippable body version of 88in model made available.
October 1971	Series III model range took over from Series IIA.
March 1979	Introduction of petrol 3,528cc V8-engined 109in Land Rover.
March 1983	Introduction of new-generation One-Ten (110in wheelbase) with coil-spring suspension. V8 and four-cylinder engines, and five-speed transmission. Replaced the 109in Series III.
January 1984	Introduction of 2,495cc diesel engine, to replace 2,286cc type.
June 1984	Introduction of new-generation Ninety (wheelbase actually 92.9in). Available with four-cylinder engines. A direct replacement for the 88in Series III. V8 engine made available from May 1985.
September 1985	2,495cc petrol engine replaced 2,286cc type.
October 1986	Introduction of 85bhp turbo-charged version of 2,495cc diesel engine.
September 1989	Introduction of original Discovery range, using 100in wheelbase frame from Range Rover, plus V8 or turbo-diesel four-cylinder engines.
	Ninety and One-Ten range renamed Defender – Defender name officially launched in 1990.
September 1990	Five-door Discovery and fuel-injected V8 engine available for first time.
Summer 1992	Limited-edition Defender 110 Station Wagon announced for sale in North America – the first 'classic' Land Rover to go there since 1974.
September 1992	ZF automatic transmission became optional on V8 fuel-injected Discovery.
April 1993	Option of 136bhp/2ltr twin-cam petrol engine for Discovery.
Autumn 1993	Discovery V8 engine uprated to 180bhp/3.9ltr.
March 1994	BMW took control of the Rover group (from British Aerospace), and immediately began a large investment programme in new models.
	Launch of facelifted Discovery and of North American Specification model.
Autumn 1997	Introduction of all-new Freelander range. Transverse engines, with estate car or soft-back body styles.
Autumn 1998	Introduction of second-generation Discovery range, with new TD5 five-cylinder turbo-diesel engine, or 3.9ltr V8.
December 1998	New TD5 five-cylinder turbo-diesel engine standardized in Defender chassis.
September 2000	BMW 2ltr Td4 turbo-diesel replaced Rover L-Series engine in Freelander; 2.5ltr V6-engined Freelander went on sale.
December 2001	Freelander introduced for sale in North America.
March 2002	Introduction of facelifted Discovery II, with nose like that of new third-generation Range Rover.

Introduction

I have been a dedicated follower of Land Rover's 4×4s for many years, and whenever I get the chance of more 4×4 experience, I enjoy it. It helps, of course, that I live miles from a big city, so wherever I travel in the countryside I see these amazingly versatile machines hard at work.

Even so, times have changed enormously since I first wrote about Solihull's finest. In those days there were leaf-spring Land Rovers, but no other variety. Now, in the early 2000s, Solihull produces four completely different product lines, and the bush telegraph suggests that other, and more exciting products, may be on the way.

There was, and always will be, a fascinating story to be told. So much, however, has happened at Solihull since 1948 that we did not quite see how we could squeeze a 'Complete Story' into one book! However, after Crowood's fine book about the Range Rover had been published, we realized that the story of Solihull's 4×4s could be completed by adding a new volume, and surveying all the other models that have accompanied it. It is still a large and impressive list.

This book, therefore, covers classic Land Rovers, Defenders, Discovery types and Freelanders, but not Range Rovers, and we think there is a great deal of logic in that. Range Rover, after all, is a marque all on its own, while all the others are Land Rovers of one type of another, and badged accordingly. It is a fascinating story covering more than fifty years, for it starts at a time of post-war shortages, and reaches the affluent 2000s. In the beginning, the factory could produce perhaps 10,000 4×4s a year, but by the early 2000s we had reached a time when annual Solihull production was approaching the 200,000 mark.

This, incidentally, is not just a nuts and bolts story, for the corporate history – who owned who, when and why – is also important. When the Land Rover was unveiled, the parent company was independent, but by the 2000s Land Rover was a subsidiary of Ford. Along the way there had been links with British Leyland, with the British Government and with BMW: the miracle is that Land Rover's own character has never been lost.

If you are like me, there always seems to be an excuse for driving one of these cars. To celebrate his gap year, my son crossed the Sahara desert in a petrol-engined One-Ten. I was one of the first journalists to get a Discovery stuck in a narrow gateway in the West Country – and felt a fool. I even got a secretive MoD press officer to tell me what the forward control 101in model was really all about.

There has, also, been a personal downside – like discovering that my garage door was not high enough to accept a Discovery, nor yet being able to persuade my wife that she needs a V6-engined Freelander more than the hot hatchback she loves so much: but I am working on that.

1 Rover's First 4×4: the Original Land Rovers

The Land Rover is now one of those British artefacts, which seems to have been around for ever. Along with red phone boxes, Minis, and London taxicabs, a Land Rover is now an institution. Not so. Either we Brits have very short memories – or we really do think that every worthwhile feature of our lives arrived after 1945.

Land Rovers, in fact, have now been on sale since 1948, but there was little sign of such four-wheel-drive machinery before the Second World War. Until then, four-wheel-drive was confined to big trucks, and the only machinery that went willingly off the highway was a tractor.

Then came the War, then came the Jeep – and the rest is history. Farmers who never knew that they had needed four-wheel-drive machinery, soon discovered that they could not manage without a 4×4. The new Land Rover was one the first to satisfy that need and – more than fifty years on – it still does.

Although times, fashions and trends have changed dramatically since then, Land Rovers have regularly shifted their stance to remain desirable. More than three million Land Rovers of all types have now been built – that milestone being passed in 2001 – and the pedigree continues to evolve.

Inspiration

First there was an empty factory, and then there was an unmanageable farm. Luckily for all of us, Maurice Wilks was involved in both of them. The factory in question was at Solihull, and run by Rover, while the farm was owned by Maurice Wilks, in North Wales.

Solihull – Origins

Although Rover began by building bicycles, motorcycles and then cars in Coventry, it was invited to join the British Government's 'shadow factory' scheme in 1936. As a result, Rover was delighted to take over the running of a brand-new factory in Acocks Green, south-east of the centre of Birmingham. To follow that, in 1940 it took over the running of a second, much larger, 'shadow' factory at Solihull.

Solihull built Bristol Hercules and other aeroplane engines until 1945, after which it was emptied. Because Rover's traditional car-making factory in Coventry had been badly bombed, Solihull was then transformed into a car-producing plant, the first private cars being completed in December 1945.

Land Rover assembly began at Solihull in 1948, and for the next thirty years this site was gradually but persistently expanded to accommodate all Rover, Land Rover and Range Rover assembly. From 1980 (and under British Leyland control) Solihull also became the home of Triumph TR7/TR8 sports car assembly, but after 1981 this model was phased out, and Rover car assembly was moved to the old 'Morris Motors' factory at Cowley, near Oxford.

Henceforth, Solihull concentrated on Land Rover and Range Rover assembly, which it continued to do into the early 2000s. By that time the business had been taken over from BMW by Ford, but it was BMW which had financed the development of a state-of-the-art press shop which not only serviced Land Rover's needs, but also supplied major steel pressings for the new Mini project.

Time for a very short history lesson. Set up in Coventry in the nineteenth century, Rover had started by building pedal cycles, then motorcycles and, finally, (from 1904) motor cars. The cars were distinctive, but the company sometimes struggled to survive. It was only after the Wilks brothers – Spencer and Maurice – joined the management team that stability was assured.

By the mid-1930s, Rover was not only profitable once again, but well-regarded, particularly in Whitehall. Invited to join the Government's 'shadow factory' scheme (a major initiative to increase the production of aircraft engines), Rover soon came to manage two large new factories. One was at Acocks Green and one at Solihull – both locations being in the south-eastern suburbs of Birmingham, though all its private car assembly remained in Coventry. At first these concentrated on the building of Bristol Pegasus and Hercules aero-engines, and later the manufacture of V12 Rolls-Royce Meteor engines (for tanks) also took place.

Rover worked flat out on military contracts throughout the Second World War. Unhappily, although neither of the shadow factories was hit, the Coventry (car manufacturing) plant was badly hit by bombing., and could only be patched up on a temporary basis. Accordingly, when peace

> **Maurice Wilks**
>
> The Wilks brothers – Spencer and Maurice – did much to save Rover from oblivion – twice. In the 1930s they revived the Coventry-based car company's fading reputation, and re-established its fine quality image. Then, in the 1940s, they approved the development of the Land Rover, originally as a stop gap to help fill up the massive ex-military 'shadow factory' at Solihull.
>
> Maurice Wilks was the younger brother. An engineer by training, he started his working life with the Hillman company in Coventry, became Rover's chief engineer in 1930, then directed the company's technical fortunes for the next three decades.
>
> As related in the main text, it was his personal need for an all-can-do four-wheel-drive machine on his farm in Wales that inspired him to approve development of the original Land Rover. Although he later became more remote from the sharp end of vehicle design, he never lost his enthusiasm for those magnificent machines.
>
> Following in the footsteps of his elder brother Spencer ('Spen'), he became Joint Managing Director of Rover in 1957, Managing Director in 1960 and (after his brother retired) Chairman in 1962.
>
> He died, suddenly, in September 1963, yet because he had been involved in Rover for so many years, everyone was astonished to realize that he was only 59 years old.

In 1947, Maurice Wilks (left) and Robert Boyle were the two principal characters behind the design of the original Land Rover. This posed picture shows a general layout of an 80in Land Rover chassis on the drawing board.

arrived in mid-1945, Rover was faced with major problems – and major opportunities. The old factory in Coventry, which had been bursting at the seams in the late-1930s, now needed major rebuilding, and was thought to be too small for Rover to expand into the future. Solihull and Acocks Green, on the other hand, were rapidly emptied as aircraft and tank engine contracts came to an end – and were then offered to Rover for its own civil work.

Spencer Wilks and his co-directors therefore swallowed the Brave Pill and elected to concentrate its post-war efforts at Solihull (for cars) and at Acocks Green (for remaining military contracts, and for component machining) – and to sell off its Coventry premises. Rented at first, Solihull would eventually be purchased outright, and become Rover's headquarters.

That was the opportunity – but the immediate problem was to keep the business busy. One consequence of post-war material shortages, and the government's interventionist policies, was that the supply of sheet steel was to be strictly rationed, with the majority to go to those concerns who guaranteed to export their products.

Although Rover's immediate post-war ambition was to produce about 15,000 fine cars every year, on its previous record the company found itself unable to guarantee a large percentage of exports, and the cars it was ready to make all used pressed steel bodywork. Not even an enterprising scheme to develop a new small car – the M-type – which featured aluminium panels and box-section chassis members, could plug the gap.

Financial problems, if not immediately, then certainly in the medium term, stared Rover in the face. A large factory and a big workforce could only be sustained if there was enough for them to do. Something – anything, almost – was needed as a stopgap. What was needed, the Wilks brothers concluded, was a new product that would sell well, that could be put into production quickly, and that would require the absolute minimum of capital investment.

Stopgap

Other sources have suggested that it was the Land Rover – always the Land Rover and nothing but the Land Rover – that provided the stopgap. In fact a variety of projects, mostly to be aimed at the agricultural, off-road and construction markets, were all concerned in that frenetic period. Rover, for sure, was jealous of the way that Standard's Sir John Black had pulled off a deal to manufacture Ferguson tractors at Banner Lane, Coventry, in what was another otherwise redundant ex-Government shadow factory.

Although Rover could not secure an instant manufacturing deal of that calibre, it became convinced that there was a huge pent-up demand, all over the world, for the mechanization of the land. Horses were giving way to engines –

Steel Rationing

If Britain's immediate post-war supply of steel sheet had not been so controlled, the Land Rover might never have been conceived. In 1945, with the war recently won, and with a new Government committed to a philosophy of central planning and of rebuilding the nation's shattered stock of housing and industrial buildings, there were huge overseas debts to be reduced.

One way to deal with this, the economists decided, was to make sure that much of Britain's industrial production was exported. 'Export or Die' was the politicians' slogan, which told its own story. As far as the motor industry was concerned, the allocation of steel sheet for car-making was to be rationed, with most supplies going to those who could export the most.

Rover could not secure enough steel to fill up its Solihull factories (and would surely have hit financial trouble if that had persisted), so the decision to provide the Land Rover body with aluminium panelling was a stroke of genius. As far as the Government was concerned, the Land Rover was an ideal post-war export product. Not only was it the sort of machine for which every recovering country was screaming (so exports were guaranteed), but it used aluminium bodywork to fulfil that need.

Almost from the day it was conceived, therefore, the Land Rover's future was assured – and we can all thank the rationing of steel for that!

and much of the world, it seemed, was ready to swap horses and nose bags for engines and petrol cans.

In the end, and almost by chance, it was chief engineer Maurice Wilks who provided the vital spark. For some years the younger Wilks, though a dedicated engineer, had also owned a 250-acre estate on the Welsh island of Anglesey. Most of the time this mixture of farmland, woods and sand dunes had to be managed for him, but whenever possible he liked to get personally involved.

Later in life he admitted that he began to need an all-can-do machine to do everything for him. It had to pull a plough, to haul logs, to carry livestock, to drive machinery (through a power take-off) and to have the sort of traction that could deliver on any and every surface, up or down the steepest of gradients, in and out of water. As a thinking engineer, he realized that he would need something almost as strong as a tractor, and with four-wheel-drive.

His first purchase was an ex-military Ford V8-engined half-track (too big, too bulky, not versatile enough) – but his second was one of the ubiquitous Jeeps, which the Allied forces had been using with conspicuous success since 1941. Jeeps had provided vital 'soft skin' transportation all around the world, in every battlefield. In the Pacific, in the deserts, and in Europe, they provided amazing service.

Now comes the fairy tale. Spencer Wilks, visiting his brother in Anglesey, sampled the Jeep, then asked Maurice what he proposed to do when it finally fell apart: 'Buy another one,' said Maurice. 'there isn't *anything* else I can buy.' In a Hollywood movie, no doubt, that sentence would have been followed by a flash of sunlight, a clash of cymbals on the soundtrack and by the arrival of a rapt expression on the Wilks brothers' faces. Matters might have been more prosaic in North Wales, but even there, it seems, they both realized the significance of that occasion. In every way, it seems, this crystallized their thinking. Not only could this be the ideal gap-filler, but it could be built with aluminium – not steel – bodywork.

Wilks' Jeep, it seems, was bought as ex-military surplus (thousands of vehicles, some as small as

Is this a Jeep, or is it an original 1947 Land Rover? The two chassis were amazingly similar, for the Land Rover was effectively a copy of the American layout. This, in fact, was a Jeep – the location of the rear axle dampers being a perfect identification point.

> **The Mighty Jeep**
>
> Rover has always admitted that the Land Rover was inspired by the Jeep, that famous and incredibly versatile four-wheel-drive machine, which achieved great things for all the Allied Forces in World War Two.
>
> Originally it was the US Army that issued a requirement for a light, go-anywhere, four-wheel-drive machine, which could transport up to 600lb/272kg of men, ammunition, supplies, petrol or medical equipment over any surface.
>
> Bantam produced the first prototypes for the Jeep, but it was Willys-Overland and Ford-USA who would make almost all the 647,000 military-specification models produced from 1940 to 1945. Like the Land Rover, which would follow, the Jeep's attraction was not only its amazing capabilities – nothing except Jeep-deep water would stop it – but its rugged build, and its ability to accept overloads that its sponsors could never even have considered at the design stage.
>
> Like the Land Rover, which it inspired, the WW2 Jeep featured an 80in wheelbase chassis, and had permanent four-wheel-drive, with rock-hard leaf-spring suspension.
>
> The name of 'Jeep' came, apparently, by popularizing this amazing little car's GPW military acronym (General Purpose Willys), and by the time it became a truly mass-production machine in 1941, it weighed much more than the Bantam prototypes, though its payload had also rocketed to 800lb/363kg.
>
> Once the fighting was over, Ford no longer built Jeeps, but Willys took over the design, adapted it, improved on it, rapidly turned out civilian versions, and it is descendants of that company that builds four-wheel-drive machinery in Toledo, Ohio, to the present day.

bicycles, some as large as tanks, were auctioned off in 1945 and 1946), and came to him totally without warranty. Yet it was cheap, cheerful – and did almost everything that he could ask. But it was designed, above all, as disposable transportation, and was always liable to wear out.

Immediately after that momentous weekend, Maurice Wilks returned to Solihull, gathered his design team around him, and got a new project under way. Christening it a Land Rover, he instructed his team to find a better alternative to the Jeep – to develop a new 4×4 machine,

The original Land Rover prototype of 1947 had a centrally-mounted steering column and wheel – an interesting idea that was never taken forward. There is more evidence of Jeep-like styling around the rear quarters than would survive into production machines.

Rover originally saw the Land Rover as an all-can-do agricultural machine. Here is a 1947 prototype, on test, in typical conditions.

which could go anywhere, do almost everything and – most important of all – to be ready in double-quick time to get Solihull buzzing with activity.

Five section leaders were set to work. Tom Barton (an ex-Whittle gas turbine engine designer, who would become 'Mr Land Rover' in future years) once told me that:

> Maurice Wilks wanted us to design a vehicle very like the Jeep, but it had to be even more useful to a farmer. That was the point – it was to be a proper farm machine, not just another Jeep. He wanted it to be able to drive things, to have power take-offs everywhere, and to have all sorts of bolt-on accessories, and to be used instead of a tractor at times....

Engineer Gordon Bashford (who was one of Rover's unsung 'packaging' geniuses) was sent out to a vast army surplus dump in the English Cotswolds, where he bought two Jeeps. Both

Corrosion Proof? Not Quite

Although most of the original Land Rover's body shells was in aluminium sheet (its trade name, Birmabright, defined where the supplies came from, not the qualities of the alloy), this did not make the machine corrosion proof.

Any Land Rover that had a tough time, out in all weathers, and often up to its axles in mud, water, ice or sand, attracted corrosion to its steel chassis – and to the steel parts of the shell which held the aluminium pressings together.

The moral of this story, therefore, is that Land Rovers rot away just like any other motor vehicle. Body panels, however, survive a very long time – it's everything else that needs attention at restoration time.

were immediately stripped down to their components, and much of this 'big-boys' construction kit' was then used in building up the very first Land Rover prototype. The original Land Rover, in fact, took shape around a refurbished Jeep chassis frame, but later examples used all-Rover-sourced components.

No frills around the original 80in/1.6ltr or 86in 2ltr Land Rovers, this being a ready-for-completion example.

In later life, Bashford was always totally open about the process:

> It is no coincidence that the wheelbase and the basic dimensions were all repeated in the Land Rover, as I based my original package around the jeep. In the very first vehicle we used a lot of Jeep material, and almost automatically that meant we could use the same important dimensions.
>
> The machine I laid out at first had no doors (these were going to be optional extras), no trim, no hood as such – and it even had a central driving position and steering, with chain drive to a steering box on the appropriate side of the scuttle!
>
> The body, such as it was, would be made out of aluminium. That was partly because of the sheet metal [steel] shortage, and partly to give the best possible corrosion protection. It helped a lot when we came to forming the panels, because aluminium alloy is that much easier to work.

And so it was that the first Land Rover, the 4×4 that set the standard for all post-war civilian machines, took shape. Once the team had elected to use the Jeep as their 'mule', it was logical that they should also adopt the same basic mechanical layout. The engine was front-mounted, there was a central gearbox, a transfer box behind it, propeller shafts leading to front and rear axles, those axles being mounted on extremely stiff half-elliptic leaf springs.

Land Rover and Jeep – a Comparison

Land Rover engineers cheerfully admit that they followed the Jeep layout when designing the original S1 model. Except that the Land Rover had marginally better interior equipment, and more stowage space, the two machines were remarkably similar. Here is a brief comparison of their layouts:

	Land Rover (1948)	**Jeep (1941–5)**
Wheelbase (in)	80	80
Length (in)	132	133
Width (in)	60	62
Wheel track (in)	50	48
Engine	1,595cc, 55bhp (gross) @ 4,000rpm	2,199cc, 60bhp (gross) @ 3,600rpm
Transmission	Four-speed gearbox, transfer gears, and low-ratio step-down	Three-speed gearbox, transfer gears and low-ratio step-down
Axle ratios	4.88:1 (soon changed to 4.70:1)	4.88:1
Tyre size	6.00-16in	6.00-16in.
Suspensions	Live axles, half- elliptic leaf springs	Live axles, half- elliptic leaf springs
Unladen weight (lb)	2,520lb	2,315lb

The ride, of course, was rock hard, but that was thought to be no bad thing – hence one of the most-quoted Land Rover aphorisms of the time: 'Off road performance is limited by the comfort of the driver ....'. The company's reasoning being that if they gave their new model a soft ride, it might encourage drivers to press on even harder and faster over rough ground, and damage the chassis.

Fifty years on, there seem to be many different ways of providing four wheel drive to a vehicle with a front-mounted engine, but in the late 1940s only one method – what we might call the 'classic Jeep' method – was used. The engine and main gearbox was mounted conventionally. Behind the gearbox there was a transfer box, which not only moved the drive shaft alignment sideways by several inches, but also incorporated a centre differential, and a separate set of drop-down gears to give a second set of ultra-low 'crawler' ratios.

Drive shafts were then led forward from output flanges on the transfer box, to the front and rear axles. Since these were offset, it also meant that the differentials and final drives of both axles had to off-centre, by several inches.

Comfort – Who Needs It?

Have you ever wondered why early Land Rovers had such a bone-shattering ride? Simple, really – that's what Land Rover intended it to be. Design chief Tom Barton used to smile broadly when asked to explain, and say something like this:

> Hard springs mean that in rough going the driver is bounced out of his seat at high speeds. That means that he can't control the Land Rover, and he slows down a bit. So the hard springs limit the shocks put in to the chassis ....

...which was good for the fatigue life of the Land Rover, if not for that of the driver's liver!

Building Blocks

To cut down on capital investment costs, the chassis design was as simple as Rover could make it. For a major, long-term, project, they would have designed a box-section assembly which required massive press tools and jigging equipment for it to be built in quantity, and then hired in a specialist company like Rubery Owen or John Thompson to do that job for them.

For the Land Rover, Gordon Bashford and Chief Planning Engineer Olaf Poppe, devised much simpler assemblies. Instead of producing chassis with monstrous pressings and channel sections, they arranged for box sections to be created by utilizing four long strips of sheet steel, and welding their edges together into long seams! At a casual glance this looked as if it would not be durable enough, but it most certainly was – the same production fixture, built up in 1947–8, was modified and evolved, but remained essentially the same, and was used on all short-wheelbase leaf spring Land Rovers for the next thirty-odd years!

There was no money available to develop a new engine, so this had to come out of Rover's existing 'parts bin'. Simply, for 1948, the company was preparing to use variations of a new type – to be manufactured as a 1.6ltr 'four' or a 2.1ltr 'six' in its P3 passenger cars. The choice, therefore, was 'Hobson's Choice' in the end, for the 'six' was too large, too heavy and too expensive. Accordingly, the original Land Rover was built with the same engine – the same, not only in capacity (1,595cc), but even with the same 50bhp net rating, though it had a slightly lower compression ratio. This, in itself, was a major advance on the Jeep, which used a lusty but old-fashioned side-valve power unit.

The main gearbox (though with a different change mechanism) was the same as that of the P3, with synchromesh only on top and third gears, and was backed by the newly-devised transfer gearbox with provision for a change to low-ratio driving. On the original cars, too, four-wheel-drive was permanent, with a freewheel (Rover knew all about these, for they featured on

Early production 80in Series I types already had the familiar layout, with the fuel tank mounted under the right-side seat. In this case, the optional power take-off and the rear propeller shaft to drive it, have been fitted for demonstration purposes.

Land Rover Series I (1948–58)

Layout
Ladder-style chassis frame, with choice of mainly-aluminium body styles. Front engine/four-wheel drive, sold as pick-up, van, estate and various special types.

Engines
Type   Four-cylinders, in-line

1948–51 (petrol)
Capacity   1,595cc
Bore and stroke   69.5 × 105mm
Valves   Overhead inlet valve, side exhaust valve
Compression ratio   6.8:1
Carburettor   Solex
Max power   50bhp @ 4,000rpm
Max torque   80lb ft @ 2,000rpm

1952–8 (petrol)
Capacity   1,997cc
Bore and stroke   77.8 × 105mm
Valves   Overhead inlet valve, side exhaust valve
Compression ratio   6.8:1
Carburettor   Solex
Max power   52bhp @ 4,000rpm
Max torque   101lb ft @ 1,500rpm

1957–8 (diesel)
Capacity   2,052cc
Bore and stroke   85.7 × 88.9mm
Valves   Overhead valves
Compression ratio   22.5:1
Fuel injection   CAV
Max power   51bhp @ 3,500rpm
Max torque   87lb ft 2,000rpm

Transmission
Type   Four-wheel-drive (or rear-wheel drive, from 1950), with choice of high or low range
Gearbox   Four-speed manual gearbox, synchromesh on top and third gears
Clutch   Single dry plate, coil springs
Ratios   Top   5.396
                    3rd   8.039
                    2nd   11.023
                    1st   16.165
                    Reverse 13.743:1

High range step-down ratio 1.148:1
Low-range step-down ratio 2.89:1
Final drive ratio   4.70:1
(4.89:1 on very early 1948 types)

Suspension and steering
Front   Live axle, by half-elliptic leaf springs, telescopic dampers
Rear   Live axle, by half-elliptic leaf springs, telescopic dampers
Steering   Worm and nut
Tyres   6.00-16, or 7.00-16in., cross-ply
Wheels   Steel disc, five-bolt-on fixing.

Brakes
Type   Drum brakes at front, drum brakes at rear, hydraulically operated
Size   10.0 × 1.5in. front drums, 10.0 × 1.5in. rear drums

Dimensions (in/mm)
Track   Front   50/1,270
                Rear   50/1,270
Wheelbase   (Original) 80/2,032
                (From 1954) 86/2,184
                (From 1956) 88/2,235
Overall length (Original) 132/3353
                (From 1954) 140.7/3,574
                (From 1956) 140.75/3,575
Overall width   61/1,549
Overall height From 70.5/1,791
Unladen weight From 2,594lb/1,176kg
                (From 1954) 2,702lb/1,225kg
                (From 1956) 2,740lb/1,243kg, 195lb/88kg extra with diesel engine

Optional long-wheelbase types:

(1954–6)
Wheelbase   107/2,718
Overall length 173.5/4,407
Unladen weight From 3,031lb/1,375kg

(1956–8)
Wheelbase   109/2,769
Overall length 173.5/4,407
Unladen weight From 3,080lb/1,397kg, 195lb/88kg extra with diesel engine

The original late-1940s Series I was a compact machine. In retrospect, we can see that there was not much space behind the seating area for much to be carried.

Rover P3 – Donating Parts to the Land Rover

Look carefully at the layout of the original Land Rover, and you will find much that has been donated from a very different type of machine – the elegant P3 saloon. Rover's first post-war private car, coded P3, was a development of those 1930s machines, which had done so much to established Rover's 1930s reputation.

The P3, also launched in 1948, was available with a new type of 1,595cc four-cylinder or a closely-related 2,103cc six-cylinder engine. These were mated to a four-speed manual gearbox, and a spiral bevel rear axle. For the Land Rover, the design team was able to pick up the 1,595cc engine (in exactly the same tune), the same gearbox (though without the free-wheel of the private car) and the same basic axle, which was also much-modified for use at the front end too.

Nowadays, of course, pundits would call this 'building block' engineering, and claim it as modern thinking. Not so. Well over half a century ago, Rover knew exactly how to trim their development problems – and their investment bills.

---

the passenger cars) between the transfer box and the front propeller shaft to eliminate any wind-up which might develop.

The very first prototype of 1947, was unique in many ways. Not only did it use the Jeep chassis frame, but it also used an old-type 1,389cc Rover '10' engine – and it was fitted with a strange seating arrangement. The driver sat in the centre of the chassis, with seats on each side of him, the steering wheel and column was centrally positioned, and on the engine bay side of the bulkhead there was then chain drive to link the column to a steering box and steering linkage fed down the side of the engine! A good idea at the time? Maybe, but it did not survive beyond the first car.

The body shell, essentially built up from flat aluminium sheet, or the very simplest of aluminium pressings, was meant to fit together like a construction outfit, for Land Rover always intended to make it in several different guides – of which a closed-cab pick-up and a van derivative were first. Estate cars and all many of further combinations would follow. There was provision only for three-abreast seating, comfort and padding being minimal. The fuel tank was under the seat on the right (British drivers' side) of the car. The facia/instrument panel was simple in the extreme, for the fit, finish and 'styling' was all rudimentary. So what! This was meant to be a working machine.

The most complex body panels (for which press tools were needed) were those for the bonnet, and for the contoured top surfaces of the wings – almost every other panel was essentially flat, and most were fixed to their neighbours by brackets or hinges, many being small pressings or steel forgings.

The very first prototype was on the road by the summer of 1947, and was followed by a handful of others. Rover's Board gave approval for production in September 1947, after which an evaluation/testing batch of fifty further vehicles was sanctioned though only forty-eight were completed. Introduction to the public was set for the Amsterdam Show of April 1948 (Geneva in March would have been ideal, but Rover was concentrating on its new P3 saloons at that major exhibition, and did not want to muddy the publicity waters. Headlamps were mounted inboard, initially behind a mesh screen/radiator grille.

At this stage, of course, no-one could call it the SI. It was only in 1958, when the Series II was introduced, that it became a SI – for it was, and would remain throughout the 1950s, merely *the* Land Rover.

Land Rover on Sale

When the new Land Rover first appeared in April 1948, it was still not quite ready for deliveries to begin. Assembly lines were still being laid down at Solihull, and supplies of chassis frames and body panels were not yet assured. Incidentally, there was still the problem of making enough machines to keep Solihull busy. Although Rover initially proposed to build a mere fifty vehicles every week, it thought that it could sell up to 5,000 in a year of this 'stopgap' model. In December 1947 the result of applications for sheet steel supplies to produce chassis frames meant that only about 1,000 could be produced at first.

Happily, no sooner had the Land Rover's export potential become clear than the British

HUE 166 was developed to production specification, and was the very first pilot-production machine built in 1948. After being in private ownership for many years, it later came back into company ownership. Note the three-abreast seating.

Government's stifling limits on material supplies were eased, and production could build up. In the first full financial year of production (September 1948 to August 1949) 8,000 Land Rovers would be built, a figure that would be doubled in the year that followed.

Even though few Land Rovers would be sold in the UK at first, the new model was immediately given a price of £450. There was no purchase tax (which was high, and severe, on private cars at this time) because it was rated as a commercial vehicle. Many features – such as passenger seats, a spare wheel, doors, sidescreens and the canvas hood weather protection – were scheduled as extras.

This did not go down at all well, so Rover changed its policy. From October 1948, by which time the 'extras' had all been standardized, the price had risen to £540. Even so, a cabin heater was not available at all until 1950, and many other features (such as the power take-off and winch) were still listed as optional extras.

Although the Land Rover really had no direct competitors in the British market, it is worth recalling a few private car prices of this period. The new Austin A40 Devon was listed at £442, the Ford Prefect at £371, and the brand-new Standard Vanguard at £544. The Rover P3 '60' (which used the same engine as the Land Rover) was listed at £1,080.

From late-1948 the sensational new Morris Minor was listed at £359. The Land Rover, therefore, was by no means cheap, though there is no doubt that it offered astonishing value for money.

The demand for this new-fangled machine was enormous – and not only among farmers. It was almost as if the marketplace went out of its way to invent new ways of using the Land Rover's unique blend of capabilities. Not only

John Ferguson's excellent cutaway drawing shows off the mechanical layout for which the Land Rover became famous. Early examples used a 1.6ltr version of Rover's modern overhead-inlet/side-exhaust engine. This example has the optional power take off attachment fitted to the rear bumper.

R01, the original pilot-build example, which later found a home in the Heritage Collection at Gaydon, shows off the basic specification that became so familiar – 80in wheelbase, pick-up style, with a canvas tilt behind it. The design was so carefully packaged that there was little 'fresh air' in the layout: the obvious place to mount the spare wheel was on top of the bonnet.

did the new machine have amazing traction, but it was agile. Not only could it climb up and down the most forbidding inclines, but it could turn its hand to almost everything. It was an ideal bridge between the tractor and the private car, and for some purposes it was more suitable than either variety. Even so the company, one feels, was occasionally surprised by the use to which a Land Rover could be put.

Within months it was clear that the Land Rover would not need to be a stopgap. In the first place, it had been seen as a machine that could keep Solihull busy while Rover private car assembly built up. By the end of its first year, the Land Rover was already outselling the Rover motor car, and even in the 1960s (after the arrival of the fast-selling P6 2000 saloon) this incredibly versatile 4×4 was dominant at Solihull. Any intent to drop the 'stopgap' had been abandoned a long time ago.

Perhaps it was *Motor* magazine, which, in the early days, summed up the attraction so perfectly:

> It combines the go-anywhere properties already mentioned with many of the qualities of the light tractor, plus the added scope offered by a portable source of power which is available for operating plant actually mounted on the vehicle, or for driving external farm or industrial machinery ....

Interestingly enough, although Land Rover originally published many evocative pictures – of Land Rovers hitched up to their own ploughing kit, to towing seed-harrowing machines, to pulling massive rollers, and to other related 'tractor' duties – the clientele did not actually use their machinery for such tasks. Although Land Rover had not made a fatal mistake, it was a mistake. Many farmers already owned a tractor, so they did not need a Land Rover to double those duties – the Land Rover's great advantage was that it could do everything for which a tractor was not suitable, *and* it could be treated as a rather rough-and-ready car as well. Maybe it was not the ideal sort of machine to choose for a shopping trip, or for a long journey – but some Land Rovers did that too.

Thus it was that Land Rovers came to be used for carrying livestock, animal feed, and materials – sometimes across country, often on tracks, and sometimes on sealed roads. When equipped with trailer hitches – and most of them were – they could be used for towing anything on wheels. Anything? Yes – from animal trailers to compressors for building sites, from up-market horseboxes

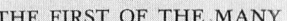

Years later, Land Rover issued this charming montage of HUE 166 pictures, showing the 80in Land Rover from all angles, tilt up, tilt down, rear door closed or rear-door open. The Series I was always a versatile machine.

to slurry wagons, and (in military guise) for rapidly transporting weapons of war (including fully-fledged artillery) from depot to flash-point.

In the next ten years, therefore – 1948–58, without a single downturn in demand – Rover's incredible 4×4 built up its reputation. All around the world (in almost every country that traded with the West, but especially in the Commonwealth nations, which still owed commercial allegiance to the UK), the Land Rover made its mark. Coffee growers in Kenya, mining engineers in Canada, farmers in Australia, oil prospectors in the Middle East, and farmers everywhere, made their choice. And as those sales increased, Rover was at pains to build a sales and service distribution network to support them.

So, where was the competition? For years, in fact, there was none from North America and none at all from the Far East. Later, as everyone now knows, Japanese manufacturers led by Toyota and Nissan would join in the battle for 4×4 sales, although Jeep made no attempt to take their share.

The Jeep situation is instructive. Although production of 'civilian' Jeeps got under way rapidly in 1945–6, the American company concentrated almost entirely on building one type of machine (which was an evolution of the military machine) for some years – and sold almost all its output in the USA. Although Jeep soon began producing well over 100,000 4×4s a year (a figure that slipped back rapidly in the 1950s) – mostly four-cylinder, but also six-cylinder engined, mostly 80 or 81in wheelbase, but some 104in wheelbase types – they do not seem to have pushed as rapidly down the versatility route, nor as aggressively into the commercial sector. In particular, they did not develop a diesel power unit.

Jeep, of course, had its own enormous North American market sector to satisfy (and there was enormous respect, and obvious sentiment, tied up there), and since USA car manufacturers had very little desire to go looking for exports, these machines rarely appeared overseas in developing countries. That, and the 'Imperial Preference' which seemed to apply in many of the 'British Empire' countries, all helped to leave Land Rover on its own.

Theme and Variations

If you were to park a 1957–8 S1 alongside an early 1948 example, they would look almost alike. Except that the headlamps had come out into the open, there had been no style changes. Under the skin, however, it was a different story. This is where a Land Rover fanatic always has a field day. By 1958 there had been five different wheelbase lengths, three different engines, one style modification, one major transmission update, the launch of an unsuccessful estate car type, and the launch of several different variations on the original body shell theme. Not only that, but in the UK there was even a long-running legal dispute about the Land Rover's motoring status – was it an agricultural vehicle or was it a car?

In the meantime, annual production built up steadily – from 8,000 in 1948–9 to 20,135 in 1953–4, and all the way up to 28,656 in 1957–8, the year in which the Series II model finally arrived.

With more space, I could cover each change and improvement in glorious detail, yet the most logical approach, I hope, is to cover model development year by year, thus showing how the Land Rover theme evolved. For although the *looks* of the machine changed very little in ten years, the engineering progress made was enormous.

October 1948

This was the point at which Rover made its only real marketing mistake with the new model. The very first body variant to be revealed was a light-alloy bodied estate car, and it was a flop. Not because it was ugly, not because it was not as versatile as the original pick-ups, but simply because it was too expensive.

Here was a machine that was too well-equipped, too wind-proof and too car-like to call itself an agricultural machine, so Rover had to market it as a private car. Not only was the

By the 1970s the workaday Series I had become a collectors' piece, so Tony Hutchings took time and trouble to restore his pilot-production example to better-than-original condition.

body style more obviously costly to build, but Purchase Tax then had to be paid. The result was a machine that was certainly no faster than the original pick-up (it weighed 400lb/181kg more than the original pick-up) – but it was priced at £959, which was almost double that of the basic model.

Today, maybe, that does not sound too bad. In 1948–9, however, you could have chosen a Jaguar 1½ltr saloon for £952, a Jowett Javelin for £819, a Riley 1½ltr for £863 or a Sunbeam-Talbot 90 for £991. No contest really. Which was a pity, for the station wagon's two-door body, which was constructed by Salmons–Tickford (in a factory that would later become the home of Aston Martin), looked smart and purposeful. It had a one-piece windscreen, full-frame passenger doors with wind-up windows and a two-piece tailgate (upper and lower sections, hinging up and down, respectively).

Inside the cabin, it was configured as a seven-seater, for there were pairs of inward-facing seats on each side of the rear compartment, which sat rather uncomfortably atop the wheel arches. Useful? For sure – but far too expensive, and this explains why only 641 such machines were sold before the model was finally withdrawn in 1951.

1950
Now the addition of special features to the chassis began. The 'Compressor' and 'Welder' special types had obvious special duties to perform, but neither of these were popular. From February 1950 it was possible to buy the 4×4 with a removable metal hardtop, which converted it into a van (a truck cab version would not be ready until 1952), and from May the style was altered slightly, with the reshaping of the front grille so that it surrounded, rather than covered, the

The Tickford-bodied station wagon of the late 1940s was not a success, mainly because of its much higher price. It is important to this story, though, as the first all-enclosed Land Rover ever built.

Opposite *How would you like your Land Rover? This is how the company showed off the various aspects, and possibilities, of the original 1948–53 examples.*

LAND ROVER
80" MODEL
1948 ... 1953

WITH ALL-WEATHER EQUIPMENT

FITTED WITH TRUCK CAB

SHOWING REAR SEATING

Land Rover assembly, at Solihull, at a very early stage, and I suspect these are pilot production examples, for the definitive assembly line is still being laid down towards the right of this picture.

headlamps. From this moment, therefore, the Land Rover achieved its classic proportions – which not be altered until the headlamps moved outboard, on to the front wings, in the 1970s.

(Did you know, incidentally, that intrepid travellers could – and did – use this steel mesh grille as a griddle when setting up their own barbeque in remote conditions!)

This was also the year in which the new-generation P4 (private car) gearbox and set of gears was fitted inside the Land Rover gearbox and, more importantly, it was the year in which the four-wheel-drive system was changed. In place of the original freewheel (which was eliminated), the engineers fitted a simple dog-clutch instead: not only did it became possible for the 4×4 to become a 4×2 at the movement of a lever, but it also gave full engine braking on the over-run.

1952

Early in the year (though the changes began to be phased in at the end of the previous summer) the chassis received its first major boost, when the original 1,595cc engine was replaced by a 1,997cc power instead. With no increase either to the physical size of the engine, nor to its weight, this provided a tiny boost in peak power (50bhp net to 52bhp), but a sizeable increase in peak torque – 101lb ft at 1,500rpm instead of 80lb ft at 2,000rpm.

This – the ability to slog away at low engine revs, rather then screaming the engine at much higher speeds – was exactly what Land Rover owners needed, especially as the best methods of maintaining and retaining grip with this chassis had now become apparent. Unhappily for the factory, this seemed to make their customers ever more adventurous, and to assume that the Land Rover could achieve everything, and scale the most impossible barriers!

Superficially, and certainly by studying the specifications, this looked as if there had been a simple enlargement of the cylinder bores – from 69.5 to 77.8mm – with a 25 per cent increase in size and a 26 per cent increase in torque, and so it was, but even more change was on the way.

For a couple of years, this engine would be unique to the Land Rover (this particular version was never fitted to a P4 private car). It was only from the autumn of 1953 that a shake-up of the P4 range saw a much-changed 60bhp version of the 1,997cc engine added to that range. The two types, however, differed considerably, as the P4 '60' featured an aluminium cylinder head, whereas the Land Rover kept its cast iron head.

1954

Now it was time to make the Land Rover even more versatile. Right from the start, the customers had regularly overloaded their

Rover's First 4×4: the Original Land Rovers

Another neat little possibility was the enclosed pick-up cab version. This machine was built in 1951.

machines, and were demanding more space. This, then, was the year in which the seemingly inexorable stretching of Land Rover capabilities began. With what sounded like a simple 6in lengthening of the wheelbase, the company provided a much improved machine. The 86in model not only included an extra 6in between the axles, which usefully lengthened the loading platform, but there was the added bonus of a further chassis frame stretch of 3in at the tail. In total this gave 9in extra length.

Sounds easy to incorporate? Well, no ... not only did the simple chassis tooling need to be changed, but an extra-length propeller shaft, new springs and dampers, and associated changes to the rear body panelling all had to be incorporated. The new 86in model was about 100lb/45kg heavier than before.

But that was only the beginning. Next to start flowing down the assembly lines at Solihull was a 107in wheelbase version – only originally available as an open pick-up. This, of course, had a lengthy loading platform. Not only that, but to 'balance' the new design, the rear end was lengthened yet again – making the loading platform no less than 41in longer than that of the original machine of 1948.

The original Series I Land Rover driving compartment and facia/instrument display was starkly trimmed, to say the least. No trim on the floor, no seat adjustment, and the tiniest possible instruments – even so, there was a huge demand.

All in, this meant that the 107in machine weighed much more, and could carry much more. Its unladen weight was from 3,031lb/1,375kg (compared with 2,594lb/1,176kg), and its official payload was now a sizeable 'three persons plus 1,500lb/680kg'. Not that this left the clientele satisfied. Almost immediately they began to overload the larger chassis – and Land

Rover was often horrified to see what its pride and joy was asked to carry.

Now, at least, the load space was large enough to carry the sort of payload which it deserved, and one version that shortly became available was a ten-seater station wagon for carrying workmen (nowadays we might call it a 'crewbus') – and it was this sort of machine that caused the authorities to bring test cases, to argue whether or not such Land Rovers were commercial vehicles, buses or private cars, and whether or not commercial speed limits should be applied.

As every Land Rover enthusiast surely knows, it was the 'Kidson case', heard in front of the Lord Chief Justice Goddard in the Appeals Court in 1956, which decided that a Land Rover was a dual-purpose vehicle. This meant that the Land Rover could be (and now, officially, was) all things to all men – the happy situation which has persisted ever since then.

1956

By this time, the British Army had made a strategic decision to dump its Austin Champs and to adopt the Land Rover as its standard 'lightweight' 4×4. Lightweight? Yes, well, after you have considered the Alvis Saracen troop carrier, and the Centurion tank, anything else counts as 'lightweight'.

Only two years after the original long-wheelbase Land Rover appeared, the company was ready to stretch the design even further. This time an extra 2in were added to the length of the chassis, making the Land Rover finally available in 88in or 109in wheelbase lengths – dimensions that were to remain fixed for the next three decades, until the mid-1980s. It was puzzling that the extra was not devoted to providing more space for the occupants, or for extra

Completion of the first 100,000 Land Rovers – actually in mid-1954 – was a real landmark. Could any of those present at this Solihull occasion know that descendants of the Series I would still be on sale in the twenty-first century?

By the mid-1950s, Land Rover advertising was getting cocky, as this posed shot in the Warwickshire countryside confirms....

....as does this excellent Brockbank cartoon!

Rover and Standard – Merger Talks

If the merger talks which Rover held with Standard in 1954 had succeeded, the Land Rover might have ended up using a Standard diesel engine, which had been designed for the Ferguson tractor. Not only that, but in export markets the Land Rover could have been sold alongside the Ferguson tractor – and that really could have been a 'dream ticket'.

Rover and Standard started talking about a merger in March 1954. Not only was a great deal of industrial logic involved (and the two businesses were less than 15 miles apart), but there were family connections – Spencer Wilks was related by marriage to Standard managing director Alick Dick!

In the long term, neither Rover (of Solihull) nor Standard (of Coventry) was really a large enough business to generate enough money to secure its future. But perhaps there were possibilities of getting together, for Standard (and Triumph) did not build cars that were in competition with Rover. Further, Standard was currently building huge numbers of Ferguson tractors under a very profitable arrangement, which the previous managing director Sir John Black had made with Harry Ferguson.

The immediate logic of such a merger would have been to let the Land Rover and the Ferguson tractor co-exist alongside each other, and to develop a formidable marketing partnership for the future. In overseas territories the two products were being sold by separate distributors or subsidiaries; A joint approach would have been a seductive possibility.

Standard had only recently put a new diesel engine into production for the Ferguson tractor – at the time it was a 2,092cc/40bhp power unit, which developed 85lb ft of torque at 1,500rpm, and was capable of much more – and they were also building their own rugged wet-liner 2,088cc petrol engine for the Vanguard. For Rover, as possible partners, the attraction of the Standard diesel engine was that it already existed, which meant that they would need no huge design, development or capital expenditure programme to produce their own diesel for the Land Rover. In the beginning it was clear that the Standard diesel would not easily fit the Land Rover, but modifications were surely possible ?

Talks got under way in a good atmosphere – until, that is, Rover discovered that Standard had already had brief discussions with Willys-Overland (the deadly rival, which produced the world-famous Jeep 4×4). Then there were the questions of relative profitability, whether a new joint company should be set up to run both businesses, and who should become the new 'Top Dogs'.

It was personalities, rather than practicalities, which finally killed off the deal. And if you've ever wondered why the old Solihull office block used to have a brass plate outside the main entrance bearing the legend 'Allied Motors Ltd' – you now have an answer.

30 Rover's First 4×4: the Original Land Rovers

Left Land Rover owners do not come more famous than this – Britain's wartime Prime Minister, Sir Winston Churchill, bought this Series I example for use on his estate at Chartwell, in Kent.

Below The first long-wheelbase (107in) Series Is arrived in 1954. This was typical of the load-carrying they were expected to do.

The 107in station wagon of the mid-1950s was a capacious load-carrier, though Land Rover clearly wanted customers to see how the body shells were bolted together.

load-carrying, but was effectively located in the engine bay, to provide that important bit more space.

But why? We would have to wait until the following year to find out ….

June 1957

Although the Series I was already approaching its ninth birthday, there was still time for one major innovation before the whole design was updated – the introduction of a new diesel engine. This was the reason for the enlargement of the chassis, which had already taken place, for it was substantially larger than the ageing 1,997cc petrol engine.

At this time such small-capacity diesels were still rare, and because Rover could see no use for such a unit in any of its private cars, its development had to be tackled purely for use in the Land Rover. One reason for the merger talks with Standard (see the panel on page 29) was that Rover might then have been able to use the new and rather bulky Ferguson tractor diesel (which would, in any case, have necessitated a longer wheelbase). It would have saved millions of pounds in investment, but that pipe-dream was soon abandoned.

For Rover, the design and, in particular, the manufacture of an all-new engine was to be a major operation but, as we now know, in future this would pay handsome dividends, in that hundreds of thousands of such units (and their developments) would be fitted to the ever-widening range of Land Rovers. In 1957, too, we did not realize that the company had not only designed a new diesel, but a new engine family, for a conventional petrol-powered version was also envisaged, and would follow in 1958.

The Land Rover's optional diesel was new from end-to-end, and top-to-toe, there being no link with any previous Rover power unit (nor in fact with any rival engine). In particular, the unique and rather expensive-to-build

Above *The first chassis/wheelbase 'stretch' came in 1954, and was mainly intended to provide a much larger loading/carrying space behind the seats. The basic layout of the famous 4×4, however, was not disturbed.*

Below *The original, all-new, Land Rover diesel engine, a 2,052cc four-cylinder unit, was introduced in 1957. Diesel-power then became an important asset in the Land Rover range.*

2-litre Diesel Engine

1957–1961

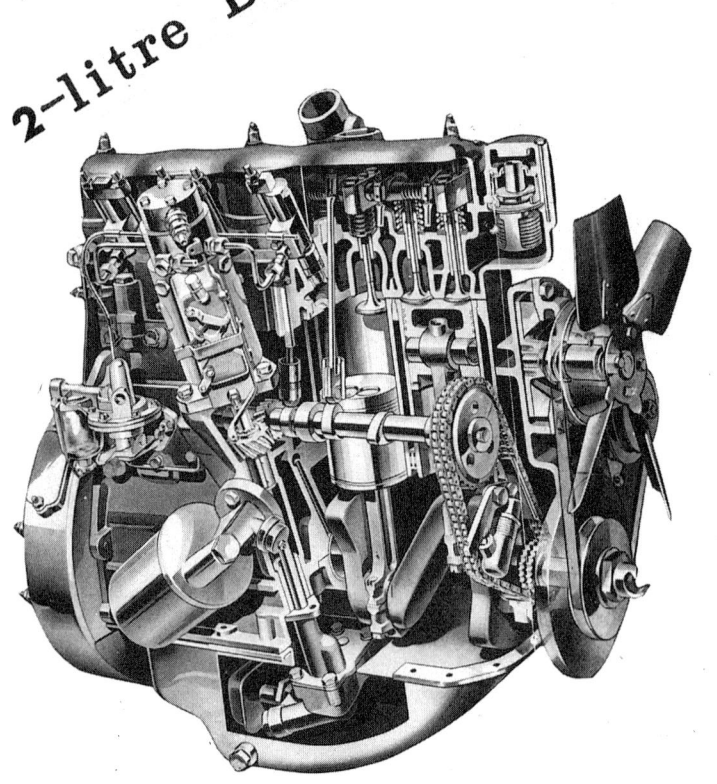

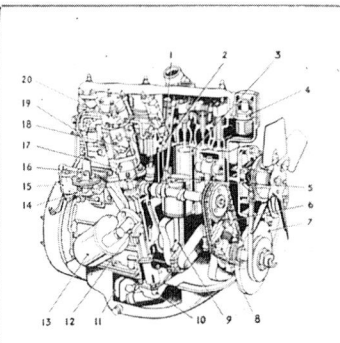

1. Pintaux Injection Nozzle.
2. Ricardo Comet V Combustion Chamber.
3. Wet Cylinder Liners.
4. By-pass Thermostat.
5. Roller Tappets.
6. Rubber Damper Pad.
7. Crankshaft Vibration Damper.
8. Hydraulic Timing Chain Tensioner.
9. Oil Jet to Cylinder Walls.
10. Oil Pump.
11. Gauze Strainer.
12. Oil Pressure Warning Light Switch.
13. Large Capacity Full-Flow Oil Filter.
14. Hand Priming Lever.
15. Sediment Bowl.
16. Fuel Lift Pump.
17. Stop Lever.
18. Accelerator Lever.
19. Glow Plugs.
20. C.A.V. D.P.A. Injection Pump with Mechanical Governor.

Rover's First 4×4: the Original Land Rovers

In the 1950s, Land Rover spent time dabbling with the 'Road Rover' project, where the chassis of a P4 saloon was modified, then clothed in this Land Rover-like estate car body shell. It never went in to production – though is said to have inspired the birth of the Range Rover.

inlet-over-exhaust-valve layout of the car-related petrol engine was completely discarded.

We now know that serious design on Land Rover's own-brand diesel did not begin until after the merger talks with Standard were abandoned. This meant that Tom Barton's team not only had time to develop their own special features, but to look at the best features and detail of their rivals. The Standard/Ferguson diesel, and the latest from Perkins (of Peterborough) were certainly on that list, but there was no question of slavishly copying what was already evident.

Land Rover's new engine had 'wet' cylinder liners (which means that the drop-in liners were in direct contact with the power unit's cooling water) and this was clearly provided with an eye to speedy and straightforward engine rebuilds 'in the field', a long way from the factory. What is fascinating to me is that the Ferguson engine, which had clearly been studied, featured 'dry' liners (in contact with the cylinder block casting), whereas the Vanguard petrol engine from which that drew inspiration had slip-fit 'wet' liners. Confusing, or what?

Here, therefore, was a robust, rock-solid and conventional diesel power unit of 2,052cc, with a cast-iron cylinder block, cast-iron cylinder head, a robust three-bearing crankshaft and CAV (a Lucas distributor) fuel injection. Engine-breathing specialists Ricardo had provided their Comet V type of pre-chamber combustion chamber layout, and the new engine was conservatively rated at 52bhp at 3,500rpm, this being allied to a creditable 87lb.ft. of peak torque at a mere 2,000rpm.

(This, let us never forget, was a normally aspirated diesel. The days of turbo-diesels with colossal low-speed torque outputs were still a long way in the future.)

From this moment – and after nine years of gradually increasing production and sales – the Land Rover reached maturity, not only offering petrol and diesel engines, but a choice of wheelbase lengths, a wide choice of body styles, and what looked like an endless list of optional equipment. The 'stopgap' of 1948 had become the dominant model in Rover's line up, and looked likely to hold that title for years to come.

Now, though, it was time to think about refreshing the entire design, and in 1958 the company did just that. Ladies and Gentlemen, please welcome the Series II Land Rover.

2 Series II and IIA (1958–71)

For years and years, Land Rover was in that happy position of being able to sell as many 4×4s as it could make. With waiting lists for some models, and Solihull's production lines as busy as the business could tolerate, it would have been easy to sit back, accept the orders that flowed in, and do little to up-date the product. So why rush to change the original type?

Rover, fortunately, was led by wise men. Spencer Wilks and his co-directors, while sober, cautious businessmen (if you need to check out their character, look at the type of Rover private cars that were being manufactured at this time – it will tell you a lot), were always ready to look out into the wide world. What they saw was, on the whole, very reassuring. Apart from Jeep (which, in the mid-1950s, was producing about 65,000 vehicles a year), they still had no real competition. Alfa Romeo and Fiat had both built heavier, more complex 4×4s, originally for their own military market. The Alfa never reached the civilian market, while Fiat's Campagnola (launched in 1951) was civilianized, yet sold only 3,000–4,000 examples a year.

This happy time could not last for ever, and as early as 1954 Rover was alarmed to hear that Willys-Overland (Jeep, that is) had already

Series II Land Rovers arrived in 1958, looking very similar to their predecessors, though with a touch of 'barrel-side' in the styling, and with more obvious attention to shape and equipment. This 109in pick-up has been specially kitted-out for crop-spraying.

considered setting up a European base for its own very successful machines. Although this came to nothing, it was just one of several dust storms on Land Rover's horizon.

Then, in the mid-1950s, rumours began to spread throughout the British motor industry that Land Rover might finally have to face a domestic rival. Ford, you might have thought, would want a 4×4 to sell alongside its tractors, but never did anything about it. On the other hand Britain's largest car-making combine, the British Motor Corporation (BMC), was more ambitious.

By the mid-1950s, BMC had already produced a limited number of FV1800 4×4s for the British military, eventually 'civilianizing' them as the short-lived Austin Champ. Yet both these were much larger, heavier and not as versatile as the Land Rover.

Now, it seemed, they thought they could do better – and set out to produce a head-to-head competitor. How did Rover learn this? Originally because several Land Rover engineers were enticed away from Solihull, to BMC's HQ at Longbridge, to start a new design. Tom Barton was invited but wisely turned down the offer.

In the beginning, it seems, it was David Brown Industries (the same 'David Brown', incidentally, who had taken control of Aston Martin and Lagonda), which dabbled with the idea of building a 4×4. This Yorkshire-based business was already prominent in the tractor market, and poached Land Rover staff to make studies – but nothing came of this. 'Later,' Tom Barton told me, 'Colonel Pogmore, my boss, was invited to join BMC at Longbridge to look after the design of the new Austin Gipsy, and he asked me if I would go with him!'

Although tempted, Barton was happy to stay where he was – and rightly so – for he would rise yet further in the Land Rover hierarchy, always concentrating on the improvement of this

---

Austin Gipsy – Big Competition?

When BMC launched the new Gipsy 4×4 in 1958, Land Rover seemed to be facing real, head-to-head, competition. It was not until the early 1960s, when the Gipsy's flaws had been exposed, that Solihull could breathe again.

Before the Gipsy, Austin (later the dominant partner in the BMC) had built 13,000 Champs, which were big, heavy 4×4s based on a military 4×4, which originally had a Rolls-Royce B40 engine. This was far too expensive to be a civilian success. Indeed, by the mid-1950s, the British forces had started dumping their still-modern Champs in favour of Land Rovers.

(A total of 33 B40-engined Land Rover prototypes were built and supplied to the British Army for assessment, these having a slightly stretched 81in wheelbase.)

The Gipsy, which followed, was meant to be a direct competitor for the Land Rover and (as mentioned in the main text) was designed by engineers poached from the Solihull team. Unhappily for BMC, but to Solihull's great relief, the Gipsy suffered from major problems in service – for it had an all-steel body (which rusted) and all-independent suspension by rubber-in-torsion 'Flexitor' units, which were not durable enough.

Early examples, which looked remarkably similar to the Land Rover, went on sale in the spring of 1958. At first, all types had an 90in wheelbase, were available only as open-cab pick-ups, and came with a choice of 62bhp/2.2ltr petrol or 55bhp/2,178cc diesel engines. Modifications (simplifications, in some cases), then followed steadily, for hard tops, vans, closed-cab pick-up trucks and fire-tender derivatives were all added. A long wheelbase version (at 111in this was even longer than that of the latest Land Rover) followed in 1960, which always had a beam rear axle and leaf spring suspension.

Flexitor independent suspension was abandoned completely in the early 1960s, and for a time there was even a rear-drive-only version of the pick-up.

Land Rover's Tom Barton summed up succinctly: 'There was a lot wrong with the first Gipsys – it was if they had been designed by people who didn't understand the sort of life a 4×4 had to lead …. Funnily enough, by the time the Gipsy was dropped in 1968, it was a good product. We were quite relieved to see it go ….'

In fact, the Gipsy was not a commercial success, with sales never even approaching 5,000 units a year. By 1968, when Rover joined Austin in the British Leyland combine, the Gipsy was already moribund – and was immediately killed off. Total production was 21,208.

Typical Land Rover weather, and typical Land Rover life-style – this 109in van of the 1960s is delivering fodder to the cattle in the depths of winter.

consistent theme, until he finally retired in 1980. A complacent company (such as BMC, incidentally, always seemed to be – but not Rover) might have shrugged off the defections, and the threat to its marketplace, but Rover seems to have treated it as a wake-up call.

With well over 150,000 Land Rovers already built by mid-1956, Rover seems to have thought it was time to take a fresh look at the design. There was always plenty to consider, for the engineering team (and the sales force, which seemed to come under continual pressure from all sides) always had an on-going 'shopping list' of changes that could be made.

A decade of on-going experience, and a flurry of new features, were all stirred into a new derivative, the Series II, which appeared in April 1958. And, just to forestall the appeal of the new Gipsy, well before the Series II was ready, Rover put out a series of adverts stating that: 'When better Land Rovers are made, the Rover company will make them.'

By the time the Series II took over, more than 200,000 of the original type had already been delivered. It was no wonder that *Autocar* would greet the newcomer with the words: 'Every so often, automobile manufacturers produce a design which is a winner from the start – the basic conception is right, and though detail alterations may be called for, in general the vehicle is exactly what is required.'

What to Do?

Since the chassis (and, therefore, the available loading space) had only recently been lengthened – those relatively novel 88in/109in wheelbase dimensions were to stick around for many years to follow – little further was immediately planned in that department. The engine line-up, however, needed attention. Not only was 'the competition' – the latest Jeep power unit – now offering 72bhp, but every time a special-application Land Rover was built, it seemed to weigh more than ever!

And more, perhaps – was it even time to consider up-dating the looks of the famous machine? Because the team intended to widen the wheel tracks, which would place the tyres outside the line of the wings, was it now time for a real novelty – to let the stylists have a look at the Land Rover's shape?

For management, the chance to unleash Rover's stylists on the Land Rover – or, at least, to allow them to look at the 'stopgap' (which was already approaching its tenth birthday!) – came at an ideal time, for the studio was just easing back from a peak of passenger-car activity. On the basis that the stylists would not be allowed to demand private-car levels of investment in new panel shapes, this could be interesting.

The styling department (these days we would call it 'design'), was small but accomplished, and was then run by David Bache. He had already completed some excellent work on the freshening-up of the existing P4 saloons, and was also just finalizing the new, and rather larger, P5 model range. Along the way, the department had also dabbled with what would now be called 'cross-over' estate car types called Road Rover, the first of which had been built, as a one-off, in 1952.

First, though, it was necessary to settle the new model's mechanical base. The latest chassis frames – 88in and 109in wheelbase types – were retained, as was the rock-hard leaf-spring suspension, and the well-proven four-wheel-drive layout. Both front and rear wheel tracks were increased by 1.5in/38mm, and at the same time improvements to the steerable front hubs allowed them to articulate further, which meant that the turning circles tightened – by 3ft on the 88in model, and 5ft on the 109in chassis.

This was the moment, too, when Land Rover introduced a new and dedicated type of petrol engine – a conventional overhead-valve 2,286cc power unit, which would find a home in future 4×4s until 1985 (a life of 27 years), and which would then be enlarged for further use. Except that it was a conventional 'dry-liner' engine (the diesel had slip-fit 'wet' liners), it was closely related to the diesel, which had been new in 1957; it could be machined on many of the same fixtures, for the two engines had always been designed as a matching pair.

Although it was time, at last, to discard the old-type petrol engine, a limited number of early-specification Series II Land Rovers actually used

The best way to demonstrate Land Rovers at county shows was to make them do impossible things. Land Rover's salesman demonstrates this Series IIA example to Lord Stokes, whose Leyland combine took control of Land Rover in 1967.

Series II and IIA (1958–71)

it – this being a perfect way of using up old stocks!

The new petrol engine was considerably more powerful than the old, as the comparison in the table makes clear.

Comparison Between Old and New Petrol Engines

Engine	Power @ rpm	Peak torque @ rpm
1,997cc petrol	52 @ 4,000	101 @ 1,500
2,286cc petrol	70 @ 4,250	120 @ 1,500

From the mid-1950s, and on all Series II models, there was a more modern type of facia/instrument panel, and when the six-cylinder version appeared in 1967, it was up-rated yet again. But there was still no sign of any padding, or of what we might call 'creature comforts'. A Land Rover, after all, was a working machine.

Layout
Ladder-style chassis frame, with choice of mainly-aluminium body styles. Front engine/four-wheel drive, sold as pick-up, van, estate and various special types.

Engines
Type   Four-cylinders, in-line, except for six-cylinder 2,625cc model

Petrol
Capacity   2,286cc
Bore and stroke   90.47 × 88.9mm
Valves   Overhead valves
Compression ratio   7.0:1
Carburettor   Solex
Max power   70bhp @ 4,250rpm
Max torque   124lb ft @ 2,500rpm

To 1961 (diesel)
Capacity   2,052cc
Bore and stroke   85.7 × 88.9mm
Valves   Overhead valves
Compression ratio   22.5:1
Fuel injection   CAV
Max power   51bhp @ 3,500rpm
Max torque   87lb.ft @ 2,000rpm

1961–71 (diesel)
Capacity   2,286cc
Bore and stroke   90.47 × 88.9mm
Valves   Overhead valves
Compression ratio   23.0:1
Fuel injection   CAV
Max power   62bhp @ 4,000rpm
Max torque   103lb ft @ 1,800rpm

1967–71 (six-cylinder, petrol)
Capacity   2,625cc
Bore and stroke   77.8 × 92.1mm
Valves   Overhead inlet, side exhaust valve
Compression ratio   7.8:1
Carburettor   SU
Max power   83bhp @ 4,500rpm
Max torque   128lb ft @ 1,500rpm

Land Rover Series II and IIA (1958–71)

Transmission
Type	Four-wheel-drive, or rear-wheel drive, with choice of high or low range
Gearbox	Four-speed manual gearbox, synchromesh on top and third gears
Clutch	Single dry plate
Ratios	(1958–67)
Top	5.396
3rd	7.435
2nd	11.026
1st	16.171
Reverse	13.745:1
	High range step-down ratio 1.148:1
	Low-range step-down ratio 2.89:1
Final drive ratio	4.70:1
Ratios	With 2,625cc six-cylinder engine, and all models from 1967
Top	5.396
3rd	8.09
2nd	11.98
1st	19.43
Reverse	16.30
	High-range step-down ratio 1.148:1
	Low-range step-down ratio 2.35:1
Final drive ratio	4.70:1

Suspension and steering
Front	Live axle, by half-elliptic leaf springs, telescopic dampers
Rear	Live axle, by half-elliptic leaf springs, telescopic dampers
Steering	Recirculating ball
Tyres	6.00-16 cross-ply
Wheels	Steel disc, five-bolt-on fixing

Brakes
Type	Drum brakes at front, drum brakes at rear, hydraulically operated
Size	10.0 × 1.5in front drums, 10.0 × 1.5in rear drums (With 2,625cc engine) 11.0 × 3.0in front drums, 11.0 × 3.0in rear drums

Dimensions (in/mm)
Track	Front	51.5/1,308
	Rear	51.5/1,308
Wheelbase	(Short)	88/2,235
	(Long)	109/2,769
Overall length	(Short)	142.4/3,617
	(Long)	175/4,445
Overall width	64/1,626	
Overall height	From 77.5/1,969	
Unladen weight	(Short wheelbase) From 2,900lb/1,315kg	
	(Long wheelbase) From 3,294lb/1,494kg	
	(Long wheelbase, 2,625cc) From 3,459lb/1,569kg	
	On four-cylinder models 1,95lb/88kg extra with diesel engine	

(1968–71)
Wheelbase	Special 109in 'One Ton' version incorporated
Ratios	High-range step-down ratio 1.53:1
	Low-range step-down ratio 3.27:1
Tyres	9.00-16in
Unladen weight	From 3,886lb/1,762kg

Another important milestone reached – in November 1959, when the 250,000th Land Rover was produced. George Farmer is next to the near-side door, and Maurice Wilks is immediately on his left.

However, although this indicated a 35 per cent increase in peak power, it did little to improve the Land Rover's on-road performance, for top speed rose from 58mph to 67mph, hardly a startling improvement. Blame this, for sure, on the aerodynamic qualities, which were no better than the average barn door, or cliff face.

Although the Series II's general proportions were much the same as before, David Bache's team made a real attempt, with budgetary limits, to civilize it in detail. In so many details, it had changed from being a stark-and-capable go-anywhere machine into one that was still all-purpose, but which looked more like an on-road device at the same time.

Although the inner body structure was not changed at all from the Series I, most of the skin panels came in for attention. Increasing the track widths, fore and aft, meant that the outer wing pressings had to be modified, so these became slightly more shapely, and rounded along their top edges; door skins were altered to match. The bonnet panel, too, was slightly re-shaped – wagons and longer-wheelbase versions even getting a slightly rounded front edge too – while new front indicator and tail lamps were added.

Styling also persuaded the Wilks family that 'modesty skirts', which were totally without function, except to 'finish off' the side view, should be added.

Inside the front compartment there were pendant pedals for the first time, while seat cushions and backrests with interior springing became standard. The doors finally got simple interior trim panels, the sliding side-screens became glass instead of Perspex, and on some models it was now possible to fill the fuel tank without first moving the doors and seat cushions to expose the neck.

Civilization of Solihull's famous 4×4 model, in effect, was setting in. Though the new Series II was no less capable than before – in fact, with so much extra power from the petrol engine, it could perform an enormous number of extra duties – it was just that important bit more up-market than the original had ever been.

By the mid-1960s, when the Series IIA was in full flow, Land Rover was able to boast that they were producing the 'World's Most Versatile Vehicle'. This impressive line up was captured in about 1966.

Naturally there was a price penalty for all this innovation, but this did not seem to stifle demand. Compared with the £450 once asked for the original 80in Series I in 1948 (or the £540 asked after the early price increase), Series II prices began at £640. It made no difference, for demand continued to boom.

Rover, quite simply, had made the Land Rover indispensable. At this time, not only was the basic chassis more useful than that of the Jeep – it was more overtly a working machine and not what we would now call a 'life-style' accessory – but it was already available in such profusion. Even at this point, with new types still to be developed, there were already two wheelbases and two types of four-cylinder engine. Available body types spanned an open-top pick-up, to a truck cab, to a van, to an estate car – and there was a mountainous list of options that could be specified for any or all of these types.

The provision of military derivatives was becoming more important, for the Australian army standardized their requirements in 1959, the Swiss in 1960. Not only that, but from 1957 a Technical Sales Department (later to be re-named the Special Projects Department) had been set up, the better to deal with the demand for special off-production-line derivatives. Ambulance and fire-tender conversions were the more obvious candidates for approval by this Department – there would be many more.

The Land Rover achieved so many new targets that it would have been possible to celebrate new peaks at Solihull almost every week. The quarter millionth Land Rover was built in November 1959, while more than 30,000 Land Rovers were built in 1959–60, and production continued to grow.

As ever, the changes continued to flow. Once established in mid-1958, the Series II would carry on unstoppably until September 1961, at which point the Series IIA took over. Yet it would then be a further ten years before a Series III type came along. Here were the major events of that period:

Autumn 1958

Six months after the original launch of the Series II models, the old-type (Series I) 107in station wagon was finally phased out, to be replaced by a superficially similar 10-seater Series II 109in wagon. Yet not only did this have a 2in longer wheelbase, but it had the more rounded Series II style instead of the stark and angular Series I type. Because it had more obviously complete bodywork than before, and seemed to look much more car-like than its predecessor, it was once described by another noted Land Rover historian as 'almost elegant'.

It was at about this time that the last of the 2ltr engined types (as Series IIs, in any case, these only being available on the 88in wheelbase) was completed. Thereafter, all four-cylinder types - petrol or diesel – would be from the same basic family for many years to come.

This was also the point at which a business set up by MSA (Metalurgica de Santa Ana), for the manufacture of Land Rovers at Linares in Spain. At first these were no more and no less than locally-assembled machines built from Solihull-supplied kits, but after a very slow start, this operation gradually began incorporating more and more local components.

By the 1970s, what I might call the 'Santana Land Rovers' had begun to look, and actually to be, rather different from the Solihull variety. The Spanish company, for instance, retained a leaf-sprung chassis for years after Solihull had abandoned it. With different styles, different engines and different transmissions, these Santana models really fall outside the scope of this book.

September 1961

The Series II evolved into the newly-designated Series IIA without visual changes, but with the arrival of an important new version of the diesel engine. This was the time for the diesel to be enlarged to 2,286cc and given a dry-liner cylinder block (which made it virtually the same as that of the petrol engine, with which it shared many machining and assembly facilities) and to rationalize the complete range. With 11bhp extra, and another 16lb ft of peak torque, this was a big step forward.

Certainly the line-up of Land Rover engines had advanced a lot in a short time. The table below shows a comparison between the last of the Series I types, and the first of the Series IIAs.

It is the extra low-speed torque, rather than peak horsepower, that made such a difference.

\multicolumn{3}{c}{**Comparison Between the Last of the Series I and the first of the Series IIA**}
Engine	Power @ rpm	Torque @ rpm
1997cc Series I	52 @ 4,000	101 @ 1,500
2286cc Series IIA	70 @ 4,250	124 @ 2,500
2052cc Diesel Series I	51 @ 3,500	87 @ 2,000
2286cc Diesel Series IIA	62 @ 4,000	103 @ 1,800

When Spencer Wilks retired, Maurice Wilks became chairman and this character, William Martin-Hurst, became Rover's managing director. A great enthusiast for all things motoring, he was also the inspiration behind the purchase of the V8 engine from General Motors. That is a 109in Series IIA station wagon to his right.

May 1962

To take advantage of Great Britain's complex Purchase Tax laws, this was the point at which a twelve-seater version of the Station Wagon was launched, as an option to the ten-seater. Ten-seaters had sideways facing rows of seats in the back, whereas twelve-seaters had a mix of sideways and forward-facing seats instead – and in all cases leg room and knee room was at a premium.

So, why all the upheaval, merely to provide two extra seats? In the UK the reason was that a ten-seater was defined as a private car, and Purchase Tax was payable, whereas a twelve-seater was recognized as a bus, and was free of tax! The result, for economy-minded buyers, was that they could buy an installation with two extra seats and (in 1962) pay £950 instead of £1,293. Crazy? Maybe so, but it was only HM Government who could complain.

September 1962

For years the company had been under great pressure to make further increases in Land Rover load-carrying capacity. One ambitious project, to provide a new design with a walloping 129in wheelbase, tipped the design over the edge into out-and-out truck territory, and would have absorbed too much investment capital to put into production, so nothing came of it (five prototypes were built), but the idea of developing a forward control device showed a lot more promise.

The original Forward Control Land Rover, which was previewed in 1962, retained the basics of the existing 109in wheelbase frame. The whole of the cab and controls, effectively, were carried forwards and (relatively speaking) upwards, the three-seater cab and load floor being mounted on an extra pressed-steel chassis sub-frame. The engine and transmission, however, kept its

Series II and IIA (1958–71)

original position – which meant that the engine was between/behind the seats – and the gearchange mechanism could best be described as lengthy and willowy! Heavy-duty front and rear axles were specified – for the company had ideas for more conventional Land Rovers which would also need them.

Massive 9.00-16in tyres were standardized, the ground clearance was no less than 10in/254mm, and the quoted maximum payload was 3,360lb/1,524kg – double that of a normal-control equivalent – though this could rarely be carried in poor territory. It was delivered from Solihull only as an open-backed truck with drop sides.

Even so, this liberated more carrying space behind the truck cabin, which was obviously good for carrying larger and heavier loads. However, although Rover loudly claimed that up to 75 per cent of existing chassis components had been carried over, this was strictly a 'best-we-can-do' compromise model, so much heavier (900lb/408kg) than the normal-control equivalent that it was only offered with the more powerful 2,286cc petrol engine.

Stable Interlude

For the next four years, however, Rover seemed to ease off on the development of new Land Rovers, and appeared to concentrate on building more and more of the models they already have. The fact was, of course, that Rover also had a line of private cars to nurture – and this was a time when they took precedence.

Nor was this just another new model. Not only was Rover preparing to launch a new medium-sized car – the 2000, which was also known as the P6 – but Solihull was being extensively rebuilt to accept it. A brand-new assembly building, known as North Block, was being erected alongside the existing complex. And more was on

This was Solihull from the air in the mid-1960s, after the new North Block (at the top of the picture) had been completed, to build Rover 2000s. Land Rovers were – and still are – assembled in the original, massive, 'shadow factory' building in the centre of the complex. Those were the days when about 50,000 Land Rovers and 25,000 Rover cars were being produced every year – by the early 2000s the site had expanded considerably, with annual production exceeding 200,000 a year!

the way – once the first version had been put on sale, Rover planned to expand the range: all the signs were that the new P6 would soon begin to sell as fast as the Land Rover had ever done.

Or would it? Although P6 was undoubtedly a commercial success, we now know that it rarely sold more than 20,000 cars a year. To this, Land Rover enthusiasts would say – Peanuts! – and they would be right: 37,139 4×4s were sold in 1961–2, 42,569 in 1963–4 and no fewer than 47,941 in 1965–6. Along the way, actually in April 1966, the 500,000th Land Rover was completed – and this was only the beginning.

September 1966

Only four years after the original forward-control model had been introduced, it was replaced by a look-alike – but one that was altogether more capable than before. Although the wheelbase only went up by an inch – from 109in to 110in – and the style was virtually unchanged, here was a more solid machine, which could carry more and which offered a choice of engines.

Allowed to re-assess the entire design, but not change the basic drop-side packaging or the three-seater cabin, Solihull's engineers made many improvements. On the new machine, the chassis frame was little changed. Improvements included the use of 4in wider wheel tracks, the fitment of a front anti-roll bar and (because a larger and bulkier engine option was planned) the front axle had to be moved forward by 1in – which explains the new wheelbase dimension.

This time, too, there were to be three different engine options – the $2\frac{1}{4}$ltr petrol unit (only for export markets), the $2\frac{1}{4}$ltr diesel unit, and (for the very first time on a Land Rover), an 83bhp version of the P4 passenger car's six-cylinder 2,625cc engine.

The new 'six' was by no means 'new' – for it was effectively the final derivation of the 'six' first used in the P3 private car of 1948, and an even larger, 2,995cc, version already existed. This 'six' shared its basic architecture (including the overhead inlet and side exhaust valves) with the

Donald Stokes (later Lord Stokes) made his name as a truck salesman at Leyland Motors, before being drafted in to revitalize Standard-Triumph. Later, as the Leyland Group grew and grew, he became chief executive, and was responsible for the agreed take over of Rover (which included Land Rover) in the winter of 1966–7. Within a year, of course, he also became the king-pin of the ill-fated British Leyland colossus.

four-cylinder power units that had powered the Land Rover from 1947 to 1958. In truth it was already quite an elderly power unit, for Rover was already involved in tooling up to produce the later, legendary, light-alloy V8. This would be a replacement for the 'six', and would feature at Solihull for the rest of the twentieth century.

Although re-engineering the '109' into the '110' had involved a weight penalty of 141lb/64kg, it also produced a more capable machine, which could now carry a payload of up to 3,360lb/1,524kg in almost all conditions.

Although this was a solid, unpretentious machine, it fell rather uneasily into a little-explored hinterland between light trucks and large 4×4s. According to Land Rover, it sold

In 1967 the original six-cylinder-engined 109in Series IIA Land Rover was announced. This chassis picture shows that the engine fitted very comfortably, and it also shows just how sturdy the chassis frame had become.

steadily, if not excitingly, for the next six years – but after it was withdrawn in 1972, there seemed to be no marketing need to replace it.

April 1967

It was only a matter of months before the six-cylinder i.o.e.v. (overhead inlet, side exhaust valve) engine of the Forward Control machine found another home – this time in a more conventional Land Rover. Offered only in the 109in wheelbase chassis (neither marketing nor engineering specialists could see the worth of applying such a lengthy and costly power unit to the shorter version of this chassis), it produced a rather different mix of characters.

Requests for more powerful Land Rovers had been pouring in from customers for years – not only from those who merely wanted to go faster on sealed surfaces, but from those who wanted to be able to carry more passengers or payload. Although the famous six-cylinder had always been available, as it were, in the company's 'parts bin', because of the way that it was constructed and detailed, it was always going to be a costly addition to the specification.

Earlier, too, there had always been a problem of engine supply, for all the available six-cylinder power units that could be made, had been needed for use in P4 and P5 private cars. From 1964, however, the P4 had been dropped (which, incidentally, liberated some space inside the assembly buildings), and from 1967 the P5 would inherit the new ex-General Motors V8.

Suddenly there was some spare capacity. By the mid-1960s, in any case, with annual Land Rover sales approaching 50,000 a year – that figure would be exceeded for the first time in 1968–9 – perhaps this was an ideal time to think about making the marriage. The 'six' had already appeared in several sizes – 2,103cc, 2,230cc, 2,625cc, 2,638cc and 2,995cc – all of which shared the same machining and assembly lines, and all had gone through several mid-life updates. Even so, it was the available horsepower, rather than cubic capacity, which would govern the final choice.

This is where the classic 'product planning' compromise was reached. Choosing the 2.2ltr type would be to gain little – in high-compression private-car guise it produced 80bhp – whereas it was surely going over the top to pick the 3.0ltr type, which produced up to 134bhp. The choice of the 2,625cc 'six' – with either 104bhp or 123bhp in its final car-type – almost made itself.

For use in the Land Rover, of course, the engine could be de-tuned. Not only did the engineers not need the high figures just quoted, but they wanted to tailor the unit to load-hauling, and to the doubtful quality of petrol available in some countries. The Land Rover-style 'six', therefore, would have its compression reduced to a mere 7.8:1 (or even 7.0:1, where requested), which compared with the 8.8:1 in the P4 110.

Other changes – to the camshaft timing, and related details – meant that the new Land Rover application produced just 85bhp at a leisurely 4,500rpm. In any case, the carburation and manifolding associated with the high-output car-specification 'six' would not fit into the engine bay without fouling some of the existing fittings, including RHD pedals. In the UK, for instance, this meant that it could run on Regular Grade (in later years we would call this '2 Star') petrol.

Amazingly, this engine fitted easily into the existing engine bay – which, hitherto, had only accommodated four-cylinder power units – for the Land Rover had always been very generously packaged in this area. The intermediate gear ratios were revised – this new set-up then being adopted for other versions of the design. In general the transmission and the overall gearing were basically unchanged, as was the rest of the chassis. Larger (11 × 3.0in) front drum brakes were fitted, to look after the increase in performance.

This advance, of course, came at a cost – but a remarkably restrained one. The twelve-seater Station Wagon, for instance, already cost £1,013 with the four-cylinder petrol fitted, but only £1,073 with the more powerful 'six'; as already explained, there was no British Purchase Tax applied to this 'bus'.

To see what the media thought of this new model, I turned to *Autocar's* test of July 1967. Although off-road enthusiast Stuart Bladon wrote the report on a twelve-seater Station Wagon, even he had to admit that there was still not enough 'road', and still perhaps too much 'tractor' in the balance of virtues:

> Those familiar with the Land Rover will find the extra torque of the bigger engine most noticeable .... Once the car is on the move, the noise level of the engine increases a lot, and from being so quiet on tickover it produces considerable power roar which makes one feel that about 50mph is fast enough .... The driver soon gets used to it and turns a deaf ear.
>
> The suspension is very hard, and on ordinary roads the ride is far too bumpy for comfort, but when pounding over really rough going it absorbs huge bumps and pot holes impressively well.
>
> Pitting the vehicle against what seemed near-vertical hills showed dramatically how well it will climb in the lowest of its eight available ratios, and it came as quite a relief when the wheels eventually lost their grip on the rough gravel and it would climb no further ....

The six-cylinder Land Rover was announced in 1967, and used a smaller and de-tuned version of the engine, which was still in use in the Rover P5 3ltr range. This engine, of course, was a close relative of the original petrol engines which had powered Land Rovers from 1948 to 1958.

Series II and IIA (1958–71)

In the end, though, there was the usual amazement that always surrounded a Land Rover's go-anywhere capabilities and:

> The revised Land Rover is still very much a utility vehicle, specifically designed for hard use and exacting conditions. The 6-cylinder option is well worth its extra cost for the much-improved hill climbing and better performance which results ....

That improved performance, incidentally, saw a 73mph top speed, allied to 0–60mph acceleration in a still leisurely 29 seconds. The bad news was that overall fuel consumption plummeted to a mere 13.8 miles per Imperial gallon.

Below Land Rover styling changed steadily, but slowly, over the years. This shows the difference between HUE 166 (the first pilot-build car of 1958), and one of the last Series IIAs of the late 1960s/early 1970s. The most recent change had been to relocate the headlamps outwards, into the front wings – for until 1968 all Land Rovers had been built with headlamps on either side of the central grille.

Spring 1968–February 1969

It was almost twenty years after the launch of the original Land Rover that the first significant change to the front-end style was introduced. Before then, the headlamps had always been inboard – on either side of the radiator grille aperture – but now it was time for them to be to relocated. New safety-related regulations were sweeping the world towards the end of the 1960s – some of them defining how near the outside of the vehicle the lamps had to be – though such rules did not yet apply to the UK market.

Accordingly, Land Rover arranged to make a change. The headlamps were relocated, outboard, to the front of the front wings, with side lamps and turn indicators flanking them close to the extremities of the wings. In place of their previous position, the grille was slightly restyled, and featured extra brightwork flanking the main area, all covering extra cooling-air slots in the front panel.

This change was fed in progressively at Solihull, first for Land Rovers destined for

Above By the 1960s almost everyone contemplating an expedition in hostile territory equipped themselves with Land Rovers for transport. Although these machines could put up with amazing abuse, they often came back looking battered and bruised.

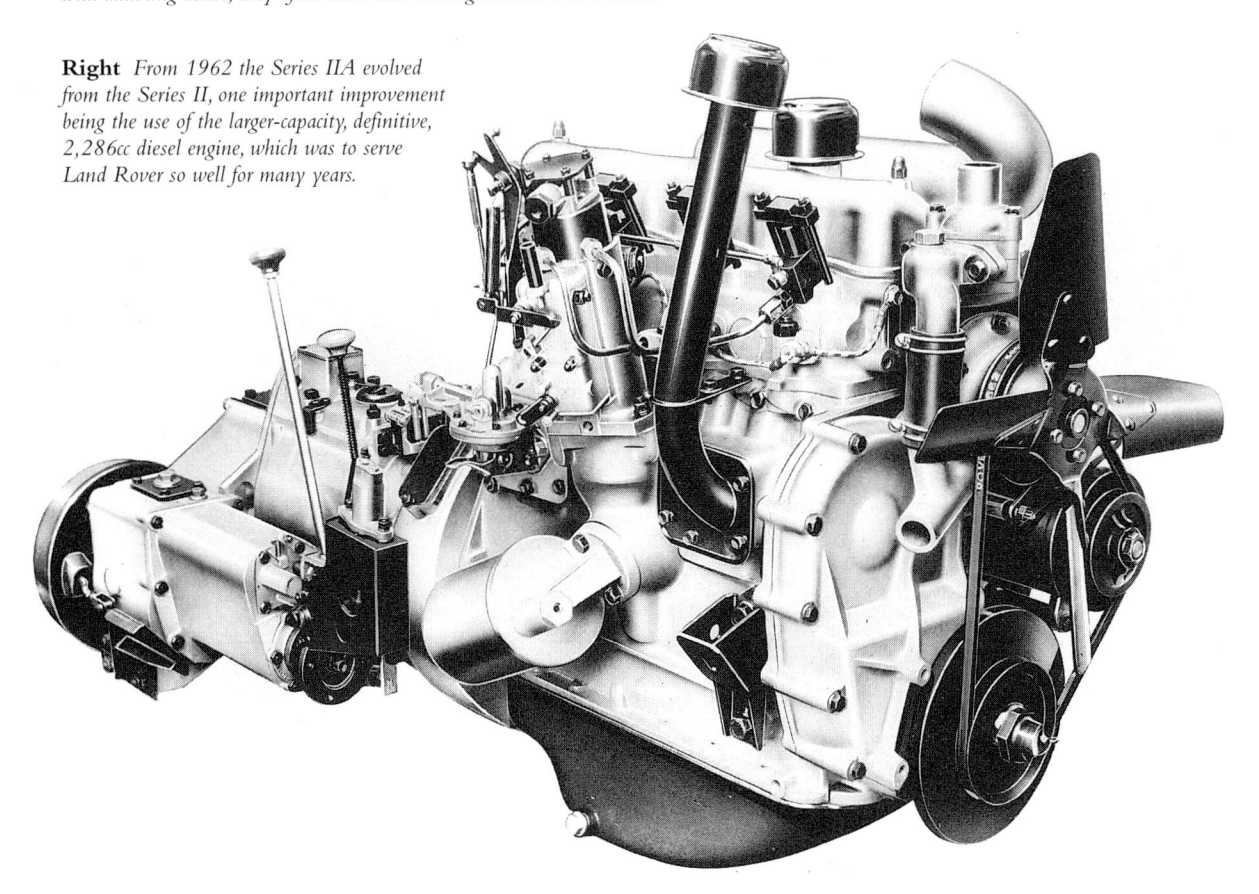

Right From 1962 the Series IIA evolved from the Series II, one important improvement being the use of the larger-capacity, definitive, 2,286cc diesel engine, which was to serve Land Rover so well for many years.

The first-ever forward-control Land Rover was previewed in 1962, a massively up-graded 109in wheelbase device in which 75 per cent of existing chassis material was retained. At first the only engine available was the 2,286cc petrol power unit.

the USA and for Australia, next for Europe and finally (and only when existing stocks of plain wing pressings had been exhausted) for domestic market cars. The changeover was completed in February 1969.

September 1968

Finally it was time to take advantage of the increased power and torque of the six-cylinder engine, by launching a heavy-duty 109in model with an extra payload capacity. Called the 'One Ton', which told its own story, this defined a model that could carry up to 2,240lb/1,016kg – a very worthwhile 25 per cent advance on existing examples.

To produce this type, of course, it had not merely been a case of writing a new brochure. The new package included the more massive front and rear axles, which were already standard under the Forward-Control type, the One Ton also used that machine's lower-ratio gearbox and transfer box arrangements, it sat higher on its springs, and ultra-fat 9.00-16in tyres were standard. Not only that, but there was heavy-duty

Series II and IIA (1958–71) 51

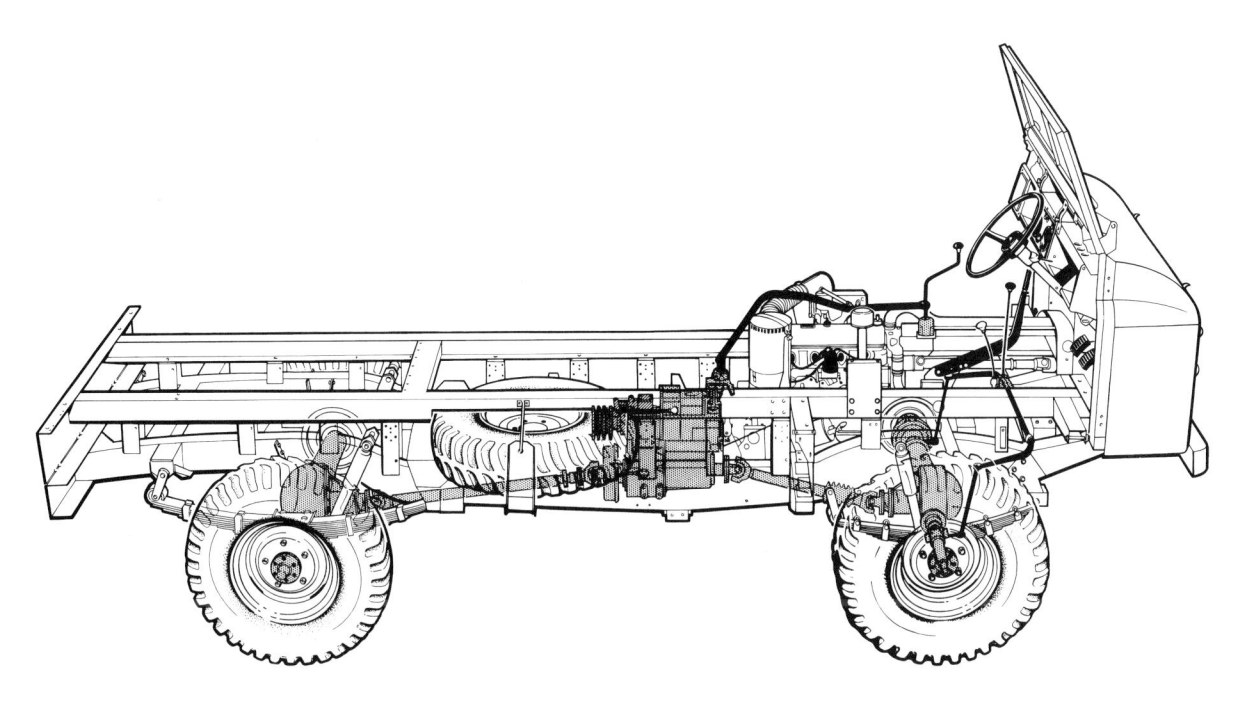

Above *This is the chassis layout of the revised, 110in wheelbase, forward-control Land Rover, which came along in 1966, and was available with petrol or diesel four-cylinder, and the 2,625cc six-cylinder petrol power units. The engine position in the chassis was as for normal-control vehicles – it was merely the cab itself, the seats, the steering and the other controls which had been moved forward. Function before beauty, and function before comfort, however.*

Below *Complete with its generous ground clearance, and its massive tyres, the 110in forward-control Land Rover was able to clamber over the most forbidding obstacles.*

Above *The definitive forward-control model, complete with 110in wheelbase, was made between 1966 and 1970. With wider wheel tracks than the original 109in type, and with more power, it had a certified payload of 30 hundredweight/3,360lb and, at the time, had the largest loading space/platform of any Land Rover in the range.*

Left *This was the stark, but functional, layout of the two-seater cabin of the 110in forward-control model. The driver and front-seat passenger sat up very high, while the engine was between and behind the seats. The noise level in the cabin can be imagined.*

suspension, servo-braking and a lower-ratio steering box to reduce the efforts needed by the driver.

All in all, it was a very specialized model (though amazingly capable), and only 308 would be produced before the Series IIA gave way to the Series III.

The Final Years

By the late 1960s, demand for Land Rovers was higher than ever before and, as usual, the Solihull factory was doing its best to satisfy that. Because there were so many derivatives of this model – not only in wheelbases and engine types, but in body types, and in special versions too – to push up production beyond the 1,000-a-week mark was always going to be a labour-intensive business.

There were limits, too, to the capacity of the factory facilities, which were beginning to look rather old-fashioned (how much longer, for instance, would it make sense to fabricate short-wheelbase chassis frames from long, thin, flexible, strips of sheet steel?), and Rover's directors had already realized how much capital they would have to find to fund a replacement model. Perhaps this explains that when a takeover approach from Leyland Motors arrived in the winter of 1966–7, that it was accepted in such a friendly manner.

From then until 1971, in fact, the Series IIA had to soldier on, on its own, much loved, but little changed. On the other hand, Rover novelties included the arrival of the first V8-engined Rover cars (the P5B $3\frac{1}{2}$ ltr in September 1967 and the P6B 3500 in April 1968), the cataclysmic formation of British Leyland (Spring 1968) and – memorably – the launch of the related, but almost entirely different, Range Rover in June 1970. Commercially and finally, these were all more taxing.

Another milestone to be celebrated – this being when the 750,000th Land Rover was completed in June 1971, only months before the Series IIA (this type) gave way to the much-modified Series III. Tom Barton (in dark suit, close to the front left corner) leads the cheers; managing director A.B. Smith is on the extreme right of the frame.

Above *Her Majesty The Queen has used specially prepared and equipped Land Rovers on many occasions. This much-modified SIIA was seen at Stoneleigh.*

Right *Underground, overground – it did not matter where there was a problem, because the Land Rover could usually deal with it. This was a late-model SIIA, c.1969/1970, with an 88in chassis, and a basic van body.*

Even so, the traditional Land Rover line was not neglected. In a typical year, nearly three-quarters of production would be directed at export markets. And, which markets? Really, every country in the world with which free nations could trade. No single destination dominated. The 'Top Ten' for Land Rover exports in 1969 are shown in the table on the right.

Annual sales exceeded 50,000 units for the first time in the financial year 1968–9 (50,561), a figure that would then be dwarfed in 1970–1 (56,663), this being close to the peak of demand for this, the original design of Land Rover.

Even so, and although the Series IIA had come close to the end of its run, there was still time for one more anniversary to be celebrated. This time it came in June 1971, with the completion of the 750,000th Land Rover. As I have already pointed out regarding earlier land marks, not bad for a 'stop gap'.

This, though, was very close to the end of the line for the Series IIA. The arrival of a much-revised, though familiar-looking range, to be called Series III, was imminent.

The 'Top Ten' for Land Rover Exports in 1969	
Australia	5,005
South Africa	2,327
Persian Gulf nations	2,026
French West and Equatorial Africa	1,907
Tanzania	1,426
Iran	1,423
Nigeria	1,272
USA	1,222
Malaysia	1,218
Angola	1,052

3 Series III (1971–85)

The next big move – from Series IIA to Series III – followed in 1971. Was it overdue? Should the change have occurred earlier? Not according to the Land Rover's sales figures, which were booming as never before.

One problem was that Land Rover assembly had to share the same 1940s factory buildings as Rover P4 and P5 passenger car assembly. At one point, indeed, to give everyone more living space, thought had even been given to moving Land Rover final assembly to a new plant at Pengam (near Cardiff), where Rover components would eventually be made.

Rover, in any case, had been far too busy to tackle a Land Rover update any earlier. Not only had the company been busy launching new V8-engined versions of its existing passenger cars, but it had also taken the big step of launching the original Range Rover, which took 4×4 technology to a new level. There are only so many hours in a week, and only so many men on a pay roll – and the Series IIA – 'Old Faithful', as it were – had to await its turn.

There was also a further, major, influence. By the end of the 1960s, of course, Land Rover had become one of the many components of the

The new Series III range was announced in 1971, and was visually distinguished by this smart new grille. Headlamps had been in the wings, for all markets, since 1969.

sprawling new British Leyland conglomerate – incidentally, it was one of the few truly profitable companies in the group at this time. Once British Leyland had been founded, innumerable studies had been made of the incredibly wide range of vehicles thus brought together, and for a period of months much innovation was frozen.

By 1969, however, the 4×4 conundrums had all been solved. First, and foremost, the Austin Gipsy was dropped, which cleared that particular 4×4 field for Land Rover. Next, final investment approval was given to the new '100in Land Rover', which we all now know as the Range Rover. And, finally, Rover was cleared to bring forward plans to expand 'classic' Land Rover capacity to 1,400 vehicles a week, together with a package of improvements to the range, which could then be re-launched as the Series III.

What's New?

Although Tom Barton's engineering team was encouraged to look at any, and every, possible improvement to the existing models, apparently they did not consider making wholesale changes – not, that is, at this stage. The appearance, in particular, was scrutinized, inspected from all angles and found to be just what Land Rover owners still wanted – so little was altered.

I am reminded of the time in the late 1950s, when Volkswagen was already making hordes of Beetles, and when they consulted the legendary Italian stylist, Pininfarina, about making changes, the Italians, it is said, walked round and round the car, studied it, drove it, considered it, then came back with their recommendations: 'Enlarge the rear window'.

The same, in a totally in-house way, was done for the Land Rover. Study after study, and report after report, considered the style of the latest Series IIA, and in the end just one external change was made – to the front grille.

When the headlamps had been moved outboard in 1968–9, the change to the front grille had been strictly utilitarian, for the metal mesh had merely been enlarged to fill in the newly-available space. For the new Series III, there was

Layout	Ladder-style chassis frame, with choice of mainly-aluminium body styles. Front engine/four-wheel drive, sold as pick-up, van, estate and various special types.
Engines	
Type	Four-cylinders, in-line, except for six-cylinder 2,625cc model
Petrol	
Capacity	2,286cc
Bore and stroke	90.47 × 88.9mm
Valves	Overhead valves
Compression ratio	8.0:1
Carburettor	Zenith
Max power	70bhp @ 4,000rpm
Max torque	120lb ft @ 1,500rpm
Diesel	
Capacity	2,286cc
Bore and stroke	90.47 × 88.9mm
Valves	Overhead valves
Compression ratio	23.0:1
Fuel injection	CAV
Max power	62bhp @ 4,000rpm
Max torque	103lb ft @ 1,800rpm
Six-cylinder, petrol	
Capacity	2,625cc
Bore and stroke	77.8 × 92.1mm
Valves	Overhead inlet, side exhaust valve
Compression ratio	7.8:1
Carburettor	Zenith–Stromberg
Max power	86bhp @ 4,500rpm
Max torque	132lb ft @ 1,500rpm
Transmission	
Type	Four-wheel-drive, or rear-wheel drive, with choice of high or low range
Gearbox	Four-speed manual gearbox, synchromesh on all forward gears
Clutch	Single dry plate

Series III (1971–85)

Land Rover Series III (1971–85)

Ratios	Top	5.396
	3rd	8.05
	2nd	12.00
	1st	19.88
	Reverse	21.66
	High range step-down ratio 1.148:1	
	Low-range step-down ratio 2.35:1	
Final drive ratio	4.70:1	

Suspension and steering

Front	Live axle, by half-elliptic leaf springs, telescopic dampers
Rear	Live axle, by half-elliptic leaf springs, telescopic dampers
Steering	Recirculating ball
Tyres	(Wheelbase 88in) 6.00-16 cross-ply (Wheelbase 109in) 7.50-16in cross-ply
Wheels	Steel disc, five-bolt-on fixing
Brakes	
Type	Drum brakes at front, drum brakes at rear, hydraulically operated
Size	(Wheelbase 88in) 10.0 × 1.5in front drums, 10.0 × 1.5in rear drums (Wheelbase 109in) 11.0 × 2.25in front drums, 11.0 × 2.25in rear drums

Dimensions (in/mm)

Track	(Wheelbase 88in) front and rear 51.5/1,308	
	(Wheelbase 109in) front and rear 52.5/1,333	
Wheelbase	(Short)	88/2,235
	(Long)	109/2,769
Overall length	(Short)	142.4/3,617
	(Long)	175/4,445
Overall width	66/1,676	
Overall height	From 77/1,956	
Unladen weight	(Short wheelbase) From 2,953lb/1,339kg (Long wheelbase) From 3,301lb/1,497kg (Long wheelbase, 2,625cc) From 3,459lb/1,569kg On four-cylinder models 1,44lb/65kg extra with diesel engine	
Wheelbase	Special 109in 'One Ton' version incorporated	
Ratios	High-range step-down ratio 1.53:1 Low-range step-down ratio 3.27:1	
Tyres	9.00-16in	
Unladen weight	From 3,886lb/1,762kg	

109in V8 Land Rover (1979–85)

Specification basically as for other 109in Land Rovers, with following exceptions.

Engine
(V8 petrol)

Capacity	3,528cc
Bore and stroke	88.9 × 71.1mm
Valves	Overhead valves
Compression ratio	8.1:1
Carburettor	Two Zenith–Stromberg
Max power	91bhp @ 3,500rpm
Max torque	166lb ft @ 2,000rpm

Transmission
Same basic gearbox but:

	High-range step-down ratio 1.336:1 Low-range step-down ratio 3.321:1
Final drive ratio	3.54:1

Brakes

Size	11.0 × 3.0in front drums, 11.0 × 2.25in rear drums

Dimensions

Front and rear track	52.5/1,333mm
Unladen weight	From 3,396lb/1,540kg

This was the new facia/instrument display of the Series III models, looking much more finished, and much less spartan than that of earlier types. Still not luxuriously detailed though – and still easy to sponge down!

to be a new silver-grey injection-moulded ABS grille, not only featuring mesh as before, but headed by a bolder 'shield' with six intermediate bars. Equally important was the use of a new type of badge, simpler but equally emphatic, rectangular instead of oval.

And that, apart from a new grilled air intake for the fresh-air heater (in the left-side front wing) was as far as the exterior style changes went. Changes in the cabin were more sweeping, though they did not do more than move the Land Rover into more modern times. For the very first time, the Land Rover would have its instruments in front of the driver's eyes – which meant that the facia display (complete with safety padding above and below) would be 'handed' for the very first time.

No-one, in fairness, had ever claimed that a Land Rover was meant to have a pretty, nor visually attractive, facia/instrument style. Function – in all weathers, and in all underfoot conditions, was more important. Original Series Is had used a small, simple, central, oval board, with three small dials and a few switches. By the mid-1950s, the panel and its instruments were larger, but still starkly trimmed, and though Series II and IIA types were a bit smoother and neater than that, they were still functional, and definitely not beautiful.

Now, for the Series III, here was a new layout, where the large-diameter speedometer, and a circular combination of instruments, were placed in front of the steering wheel, and therefore in the driver's line of sight, these being flanked by a series of well-labelled switches. A single column steering stalk controlled the indicators and headlamp flasher, and a steering column lock was fitted to machines destined for territories that demanded this as a legislative requirement. Across the rest of the facia was a large shelf.

This was part of a wholesale change to the

Land Rover introduced this instrument pod for the new Series III model of 1971. For the time being, that 90mph speedometer was still well capable of measuring any four-cylinder example's top speed!

This nicely trimmed three-abreast seating package was an optional extra on the original Series III Land Rovers. It makes the rest of the cabin look positively pre-historic.

general layout and equipment of the bulkhead, for the new facia style included space for auxiliary instruments (and for a radio – if one could hear it over the transmission and wind noise!) to be added in a centre panel under the shelf. There was a series of new fresh-air vents atop the screen rail, and now, for the very first time, there was a $4\frac{1}{2}$ kW fresh-air heater to replace the old 3 kW recirculating-air type of the Series IIA.

Even though there were many mindless observers (some in high-profile positions in the media) who counselled wholesale changes to the running gear, these were also rejected. According to Rover's commercial staff – particularly the sales and service personnel based overseas – it was not styling or technical novelty that was needed, but even more reliability, even more flexibility and even more of a chance to provide the *exact* Land Rover, which every customer demanded. Rover, in any case, wanted to get as much of a financial return from its existing layout as possible.

For the Series III, the most important technical innovation was the introduction of a new transmission. Not only was a new and robust four-speed all-synchromesh gearbox specified, but all derivatives were matched to a 9.5in diaphragm spring clutch. The old-type gearbox, which was car-related from old generations of Rovers, had always lacked synchromesh on second and first gears, and was finally laid to rest.

The new and robust design was specific to the Land Rover (it was never fitted to a Rover private car, nor to the Range Rover, which also had a brand-new transmission of its own). Inside its cast-iron casing was a new four-speed cluster, in

Series III (1971–85)

which all gear wheels had helical teeth and all were constantly in mesh. At the same time, a much lower-ratio reverse gear was chosen and gear lever movements (from gear to gear) were considerably shortened. The result was a much quieter-running transmission, one that was more suited to the increasingly civilized character of the latest leaf-spring Land Rovers.

Compared with the Series IIA types, there were few immediate engine changes. Although the six-cylinder engine was slightly uprated (from 83bhp to 86bhp, and from 128lb ft torque to 132lb ft), the existing four-cylinder petrol and diesel types carried on as before. This was the moment, however, when the drum brakes were upgraded somewhat and made more resistant to fade, and when a brake servo was standardized on all Station Wagon and six-cylinder types.

Other upgrade details included the fitment of more sturdy drive shafts, a tougher rear axle, more sturdy suspension mounting details and the use of the Lucas alternator instead of the less powerful direct-current generator.

Prices of Series III models were a little higher than those of the last Series IIAs, but these 4×4s still offered remarkable value for money. The basic line up of British retail prices is shown in the table.

Although British inflation had now started to creep upwards – it would soar over 20 per cent a year in the mid-1970s before trending downwards once again – this never seemed to hit the

Comparison of British Retail Prices

88in	Four-cylinder petrol	£1,002
88in	Four-cylinder diesel	£1,135
109in	Four-cylinder petrol	£1,185
109in	Four-cylinder diesel	£1,318
109in	Six-cylinder petrol	£1,263
88in	Station Wagon/ four-cylinder petrol	£1,511 (this, of course, included Purchase Tax)
109in	Station Wagon/ twelve-seaters/ four-cylinder petrol	£1,4663
100in	Range Rover	£2,134 (which included Purchase Tax)

The 109in truck-cab type was one of the most basic varieties of Series III models – and sold in very large numbers.

One of the many derivatives of the versatile Series III design was this seven-seater station wagon body, on the 88in wheelbase chassis.

sales prospects of the Land Rover. Labour problems, caused by the increasingly militant trade unions within British Leyland, hit the productions much more seriously and much more often. This explains, perhaps, why Land Rover assembly sagged from 52,445 in 1971–2 (the final year in which the Series III was announced) to 45,169 in 1973–4, though Range Rover output went up from 5,510 to 8,604 in the same period.

Before long the Series III range became the acknowledged staple of Solihull's existence, for although Range Rovers were more glamorous, and the passenger cars more technically and stylistically interesting, they were never as numerous as this amazing 4×4. Although it would be more than seven years before another engine option became available, and twelve years before a new-generation Land Rover appeared, there always seemed to be some new development, fitment, or option to keep the marketplace interested.

From 1972, in any case, a new type of big and brawny forward-control Land Rover would appear – this not only having the Range Rover's V-8 engine, but being specifically built for the use of the British Army. This model is described more fully in the Appendix.

Overdrive

Overdrive gears – usually housed in separate casings which bolted directly to gearboxes – had been pioneered on North American cars in the 1930s, but became popular in Europe in the 1950s and 1960s. By raising the overall gearing of a product, they might have done nothing for the performance, but usually provided more restful cruising, and an improvement in fuel consumption.

But, did the Land Rover need an overdrive, even as an option? For many years the engineer-

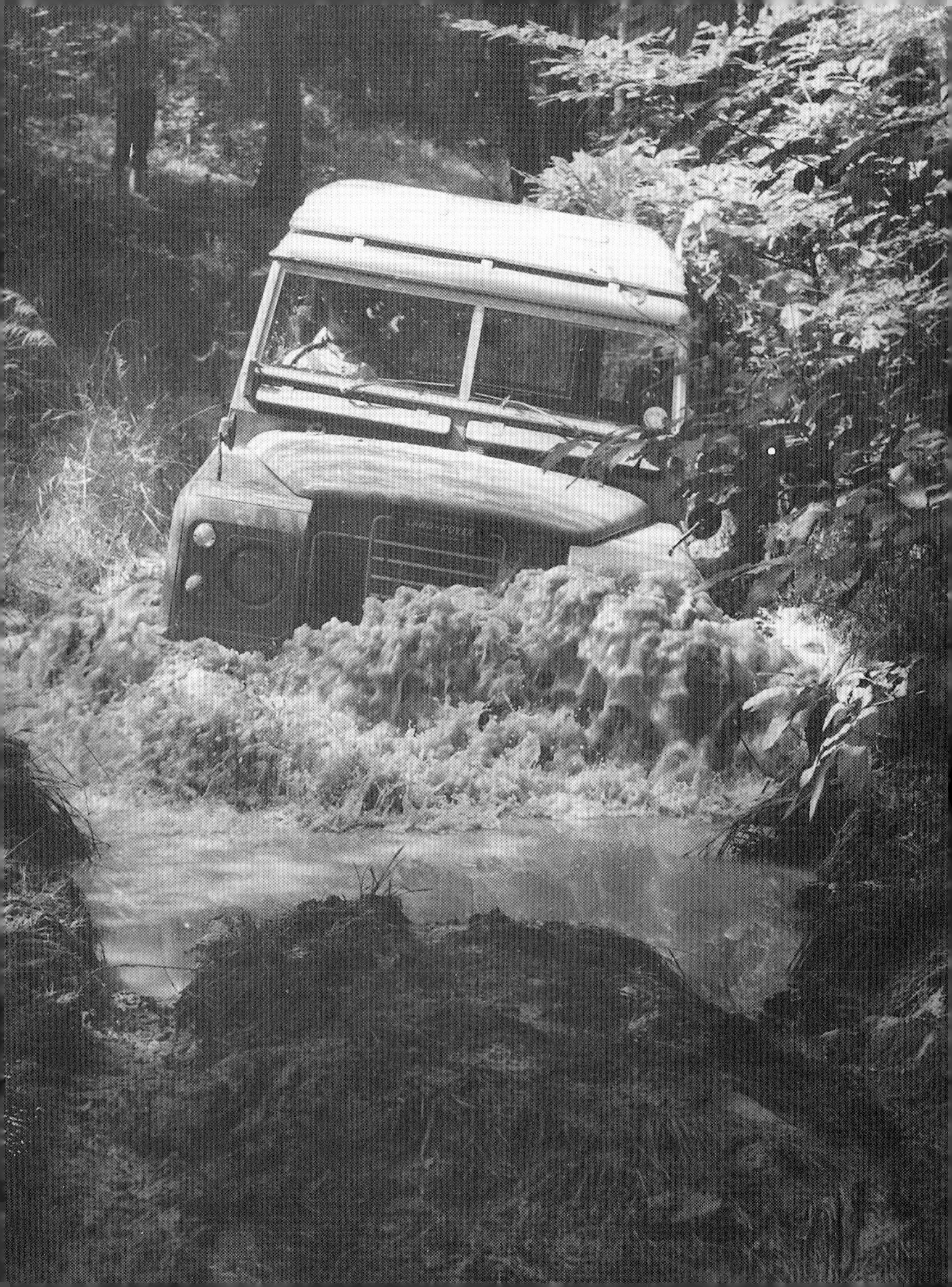
LAND-ROVER

Above Britain's police forces bought Land Rovers in big numbers – though surely not as pursuit vehicles! This 109in Series III, complete with van body, has many special 'police' features, including the large loudspeaker behind the front number plate.

Opposite Happy as a pig in fertilizer – this sort of going is what Land Rovers had always been designed to tackle. So, what if they leaked…it was only muddy water!

ing team thought not – for a Land Rover, in the early years, it was much more important to provide ultra low, rather than higher, gearing, and who needed an overdrive to bounce over rough tracks, and unmade countryside?

By the 1970s, when more and more people were buying Land Rovers with Station Wagon bodies and with six-cylinder engines, that perception began to change. – when they were driving these cars along good, metalled, highways at 60mph, the rather rough-and-ready four-cylinder engines would be turning over at 4,000rpm. The noise can be imagined. Was an overdrive now justified?

By the early 1970s, Rover thought it was, though the alternative of designing a new five-speed main gearbox (with an 'overdrive' fifth gear) was not pursued. That major advance was still a decade into the future. Over the years, several established Rover suppliers had dabbled with the overdrive concept – a separate 'bolt-on' overdrive – and all of them had come up against the same packaging problem. By definition, an overdrive casing would have to be fitted behind the main gearbox, either behind or ahead of the transfer gearbox.

Too much additional length would push the front end of the rear propeller shaft perilously close to the stout, immovable chassis cross-member, and it might also disturb the alignment of that shaft to the rear axle itself. A short and compact design was therefore essential.

Chief engineer Tom Barton therefore posed this conundrum to several of his already-established accessory/special-equipment suppliers. A number of promising schemes were submitted, but in the end it was Fairey Winches Ltd (who already supplied bolt-on winches for fitment to

Land Rovers) who seemed to have the best solution. In particular, they must have endeared themselves to the company by utilizing Rover 2200 synchromesh components in their own casing!

Fairey's neat little installation was launched in August 1974, conveniently close to the end of the first energy crisis, and just ahead of the vast increase in petrol prices that followed, and which would make better fuel efficiency very desirable. In effect it was a neat and compact two-speed gearbox with a light alloy casing, which bolted on to the back of the main gearbox, but ahead of the transfer gearbox, and which required an extra change speed lever to be mounted on the transmission tunnel.

Making this an approved accessory option at once (the cost in 1974, including British VAT, was £110), it provided a 27.9 per cent boost in overall gearing. Because of its position in the transmission, overdrive could theoretically be set into operation on all forward gears and reverse – though this was naturally not recommended.

Land Rover claimed that it could be fitted on to any Series II, IIA and (then current) III Land Rover in about three hours. With the overdrive control lever pulled back, the 2200 synchromesh and dog clutch components had no effect on the overall gearing. With the control lever pushed forward, the 2200 synchromesh and dog clutches were locked to the particular gear which operated the two-speed mechanism.

Fairey Winches claimed that optimum use of their overdrive could result in fuel savings of up to 17.8 per cent at a steady 40mph. In round figures, this often translated into savings of at least 3mpg, and even with British petrol costing only about 75p/gallon at the time (happy days!), this meant that the fitting soon paid for itself.

Because twelve-seater vehicles can be classified as commercial vehicles, Land Rover was able to sell many of this variety of Series III station wagon. If all twelve seats were filled by adults, though, the Land Rover was at the limit of its payload capacity.

Although it was possible for overdrive to be selected, or cut out, when the Land Rover was on the move (the synchromesh cones could certainly cope with it), most people seemed to make their choice even before moving off from rest.

Planning Ahead

By the mid-1970s, the Land Rover's reputation was so well-established that the company could begin to plan ahead, with confidence, a whole series of future derivatives. The use of the modern light-alloy V8 was obviously one possibility, as was an adaptation of the five-speed gearbox now developed for the Rover 3500 passenger car – but much more, surely, was possible?

Development, in fact, had not stood still at any point, as Tom Barton once told me in a mid-1970s interview:

> Nothing from the first Land Rover, not a single component or casting, is still used in the latest Series III machines. Nothing, that is, except for one or two standard nuts and bolts.
>
> Everything else – chassis, engine, transmissions and bodywork – has changed completely over the years. It has all happened very gradually, as you can see from the records. One year we might alter chassis and wheelbase lengths, another year there would have been a major engine change or new engine option, and at another time we would have gone in for a minor re-style.

However, although the brand itself was healthy at this time, Land Rover was continually being dragged down by the problems of its parent company, British Leyland. First of all, the directors of this monstrous manufacturing group seemed to find it almost impossible to rationalize the ramshackle organization that had grown up. Far too many models were being made, labour relations were awful (especially within the Austin-Morris Division), and many parts of the business were not profitable.

As far as Rover was concerned, corporate upheaval seemed to be ongoing. From 1972,

Assembly at Solihull in the 1970s, in much more modern conditions than had been present when the Land Rover was originally put on sale. This appears to be an early V8-engined model.

Series III and its Competitors

When the Series III arrived, it faced real competition. By this time, other manufacturers, particularly in the Far East, had seen the potential of an expanded 4×4 market, and were anxious to take a share. By mid-1972, the Austin Gipsy might have been abandoned but the world's price lists now included the following:

Ford Rural (Brazil)

International Scout (USA)

Jeep (USA)

Nissan Patrol (Japan)

Toyota Landcruiser (Japan)

Toyota Bandeirante (Brazil)

A crowded marketplace? Companies like Isuzu, Lada and Mitsubishi, who still had to make their play, did not agree. For Land Rover, in the years that followed, the struggle for market share was going to get more and more fierce.

Left *Even in the 1970s, robotization had not been introduced to the Land Rover assembly lines. Here, a simple sling, and manpower, was employed to mate the station wagon roof to the main body shell.*

Below *This shot of assembly at Solihull shows that building Land Rovers has always been a 'constructional toy' process. This left-hand-drive example is presumably going to a European market, for that is a kilometre speedometer in the instrument pod.*

British Leyland decided that Rover should get together with Triumph in a new Rover–Triumph operation, which soon meant that the Land Rover (and Range Rover) brand was neglected. In 1974, too, Land Rover withdrew completely from the American market – they would not be back for another decade. Where new models were concerned, Rover–Triumph had so much on its hands in bringing the new TR7 sports car and the new executive hatchback Rover 3500 to market, that the 4×4 operation had to run on 'automatic pilot' for some time.

That, on its own, was bad enough, but in the aftermath of the first energy crisis (or 'oil shock', as it came to be known in some quarters), British Leyland began to lose money – lots of money. At the end of 1974, chairman Lord Stokes was forced to go to the Government, cap in hand, for financial assistance – and for a time it even looked as if the entire monolith would come crashing down.

By the spring of 1975, the result was that the Government had taken over as British Leyland's owners. Effectively, it had become a nationalized concern and a distinguished adviser, Lord Ryder, was charged with making sense of the business, and the fundamental failing – that this business was, quite simply, too large, and too cumbersome – was swept aside.

For a time, therefore, Land Rover carried on as before, the lines regularly being paralysed by strikes from other factories, or from major suppliers. This was not a period of which any part of the organization – unions or management – wants to remember, for there were human failings in all directions.

Even so, there was time for one short celebration, on 17 June 1976, when the company built what it supposed to be its millionth Land Rover. As with all such celebrations, this was slightly bogus, as with overseas CKD assembly now going ahead in several countries, and with the Santana concern making more and more vehicles in Spain, who knew which the 'millionth' actually was? In any case, a $2\frac{1}{4}$ltr petrol engined 88in station wagon, nominated as the 'millionth' was actually built two weeks early, and loaned out to

> **Spen King**
>
> Although Spencer King's mother was a member of the extended Wilks family (which included both Spencer Wilks and Maurice Wilks, his uncles) Charles Spencer King ('Spen' to almost everyone who knows him) never needed any family connections to help him on his way: by almost any measure, he is an engineering genius.
>
> Educated at Haileybury public school, apprenticed to Rolls-Royce, and an early student of gas turbine engine technology, Spen arrived at Rover in 1946, then concentrated on gas turbine engine development for some years. By the 1950s he was running a special projects department, then moved across to mainstream car engineering in 1961.
>
> It was Spen who invented the Range Rover in 1966 (the amazing four-wheel-drive machine, which gave its suspensions to the Nine/One-Ten Land Rovers, and its chassis to the Discovery), before he was spirited away (by British Leyland) to run the Standard-Triumph engineering division in 1971.
>
> When Rover was merged with Triumph, Spen took overall charge of the technical departments of both companies, before moving up to higher, corporate, appointments within British Leyland in 1975.

various media concerns for filming, before being re-positioned on the very end of the final assembly line for the photographs to be taken!

The first million Land Rovers, therefore, had been built in 28 years. At the time, of course, no-one realized that annual sales would gradually (but slowly) began to tail off, nor that no new radically-re-engined new-model Land Rover would appear until 1983.

Although the glossy new-fangled Range Rover was well into its stride by this time, the original-type Land Rover (or Defender, as we would come to know it from 1989) now had to face up to more and more competition. This came from Japanese competitors, particularly in some of what the British had always assumed to be its 'traditional' export territories.

Not that the Government – Land Rover's ultimate owners – showed much common sense at this time. Soon after he took over as British Leyland's chairman at the end of 1977, Sir

Series III (1971–85)

Michael Edwardes received a particularly stupid letter. As he noted in his famous book *Back from the Brink*:

> I particularly remember a long letter from the then Secretary of State for Trade, Edmund Dell, complaining at poor Land Rover deliveries and now that a new Chairman was at the helm, could he be assured that all this nonsense would come to an end forthwith?
>
> I replied that all that stood between us and proper deliveries of Land Rover was £250 million of capital expenditure to modernise the Land Rover factory at Solihull and double its production capacity. It might just take a few months to set in motion. Perhaps a year or two would solve the problem ....

It was typical of British politicians that Edmund Dell never apologized for his demand, and that Sir Michael's request for extra investment funds took ages to be approved. The miracle, however, is that in spite of the serious lack of support they got from the Government, some dedicated planners continued to look ahead, and what became known as the 'Hodgkinson Plan' (Mike Hodgkinson was appointed managing director of Land Rover in 1978) eventually gained approval.

Under this scheme, in mid-1978 Land Rover Ltd, for the first time an operating company of its own, was to be allocated £280 million to transform the business for the future. Within five years, it was hoped, not only would several new models be finalized and put into production, but the factories would be modernized, and production capacity would be expanded to 2,700 4×4s every week.

Some of this money would be allocated to modernizing several Rover satellite factories, and some would go to setting up a new engine manufacturing plant in part of the Solihull 'North Block' (which had originally been erected for the assembly of Rover 2000 passenger cars in the 1960s, but now lay empty). Two extra Land Rover assembly lines were somehow fitted in to the confines of the historic old 'aero engine', which was itself expanded as far as possible. Even so, the concentration of all Land Rover operations into the Solihull facility was still only a pipe-dream, and would not take place until the 1990s.

Stage 1, as it was christened, would cost £30 million, and would encompass an interim expansion to a capacity of 1,500/4×4s a week, plus the launch of a new V8-powered Land Rover. The whole project, sometimes called Stages 2 and 3, would involve the design and development of entirely new chassis – which would be very different from anything previously seen under this badge.

Twenty-five years of Land Rover production is covered by this 1973 study of two vehicles, both of which have the basic type of canvas tilt. On the right is a 1973 Series III, while on the left (closest to the camera) is 'Old No.1', the first pre-production car built at Solihull in 1948.

A great occasion – Solihull in 1976 when the millionth Land Rover was ceremonially driven off the assembly line. By the end of the Century, total production was up to the 1.5 million mark.

Land Rover V8

When the company finally put a V8-engined model on sale in March 1979, it was following, rather than leading, the trends. Ever since Rover had put its V8-engined cars on sale in 1967 and 1968 – and especially after the appearance of the Range Rover in 1970 – Land Rover fanatics had been sizing up the power unit, to see whether it could be fitted into the Land Rover chassis.

Private conversions, usually using much of the running gear from the altogether larger Range Rover, had already been carried out before Land Rover Ltd got round to tackling its own 'official' version. The new machine, which would soon replace the six-cylinder engined derivative, was merely a first step into the company's future. To quote Tom Barton:

> For quite some time ... we kept on getting feedback from overseas territories, particularly from Australia, where it was obvious that the 60mph cruising speed of the Land Rover simply wasn't really enough to match the 80mph speeds some of the Japanese competition could achieve ....

At this point, as on many previous occasions, the engineers were not only constricted by the changes they were allowed to make, but were also super-cautious. Obliged to limit the use of the V8 engine to the long, 109in wheelbase, frame and the same heavy duty axle beams, plus leaf-spring suspension as other top-of-the-range Land Rovers, they then installed a de-tuned version of the 3,528cc V8 engine, linking it to the established Range Rover transmission.

This, the heart and lungs of any Land Rover, was clearly very different – and more modern – than anything that had gone before it. Although the low compression ratio Range Rover engine, complete with its 135bhp peak output, could certainly have been installed, the team chose to de-tune it to a mere 91bhp, and at the same time the peak torque came down from 205lb ft (Range Rover) to 166lb ft (Land Rover V8).

Incidentally, this had been simply achieved, by lowering the compression ratio yet again – down from 8.5:1 (Range Rover) to 8.1:1 (Land Rover V8), and by inserting air-flow-restrictors between the carburettors and the inlet manifolds.

This had been done for several reasons, the most prominent being the need to keep some continuity with the rest of the range – for the $2\frac{1}{4}$ltr petrol engine produced only 70bhp, and the soon-to-be-obsolete six-cylinder version was rated at 86bhp. Another factor, not spelled out at the time but clear to many Land Rover fanatics, was that this would restrict top speeds of the pick up and estate car types to about 85mph. Neither the existing 7.50-16in tyres, nor the existing

---

V8 Engine – General Motors' Orphan

If managing director William Martin-Hurst had not paid a courtesy visit to Carl Keikhafer of Mercury Marine in Wisconsin in 1963 (at first there was rather a vain hope that the American concern might like to buy Rover gas turbines for their pleasure boats), Rover might never have taken on the lightweight V8 engine, which served them so well for more than 30 years.

It was here that Martin-Hurst saw the lightweight V8, asked what it was, learned that it was a General Motors power unit – and that GM had just decided to abandon the design on the grounds that aluminium engines were more costly to build than cast-iron V8s. Martin-Hurst later met with GM bosses, persuaded them to release the engine rights and set about having it re-engineered to UK (and Rover) standards.

In its original North American life, it was launched in 1960, then withdrawn in 1963, having been used in 750,000 cars like the Buick Special, Pontiac Tempest and Oldsmobile F85 Cutlass, but it was not until 1967 that it was re-launched as a Rover power unit in the P5B saloon.

First used in a Rover four-wheel-drive product in 1970 (the original Range Rover), this amazingly versatile V8 went on to become an extremely successful 'building block' in cars as various as the Land Rover V8 and the Rover SD1, the Land Rover Discovery and the Morgan Plus 8, as well as in sports cars like the Triumph TR8 and the various TVRs.

Even after thirty years, this engine was still capable of meeting modern exhaust emission and noise test regulations. By 2001, though, its use was limited to the latest Discovery, the out-going second-generation Range Rover and a selection of TVR sports cars. In the early 2000s, when Land Rover's owners, Ford, was widely expected to introduce new generation Discovery and Defender types, it was thought that this V8 would finally be dropped.

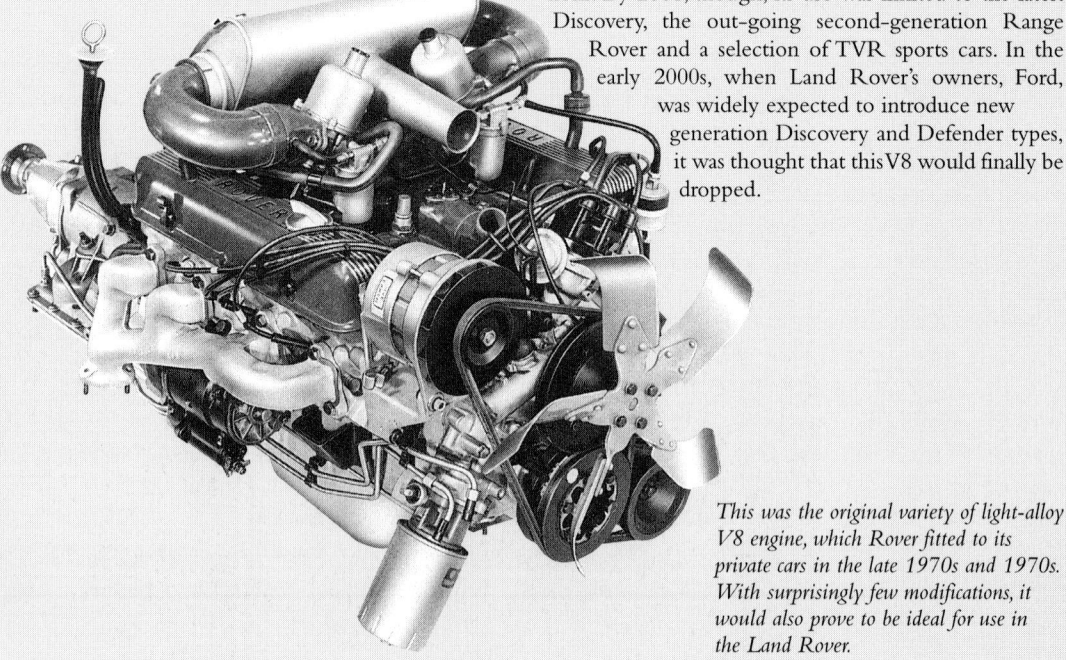

This was the original variety of light-alloy V8 engine, which Rover fitted to its private cars in the late 1970s and 1970s. With surprisingly few modifications, it would also prove to be ideal for use in the Land Rover.

11in drum brakes, would really cope with much more than this. A Land Rover with 135bhp might have been capable of 100mph – stirring stuff, but not quite what the marketing staffs had in mind.

To match the V8's engine, the entire Range Rover central transmission and transfer gearbox, which of course featured permanent four-wheel-drive and a lockable centre transmission, was used. This box was physically larger – and heavier – than the smaller Land Rover transmission that it replaced, but nevertheless fitted in to the existing ladder-type chassis frame without too many problems. At the same time, the axle ratios were changed, to 3.54:1 – this being the very first time a normal-control Land Rover's ratios had been changed in 31 years!

To allow space for the bulky (but not heavy) V8, there was one important change to the style – the first significant one since 1948. In place of the familiar prow, with an inset nose and grille, the front-end panelling was redesigned, not least to allow space for a larger engine cooling radiator to be installed. Now, for the first time, there was a flush full-width front, with a black-painted metal grille, while the bonnet panel had been lengthened and re-contoured to suit. At this stage there were no wheelarch extensions but, if only we had known it, this style was already most of its way to that which would become familiar on the next generation of Land Rovers, in the mid-1980s.

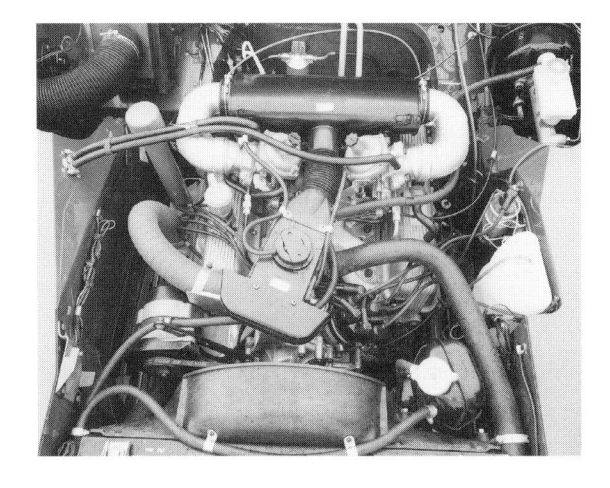

Except that the radiator, and the grille in front of it, had to be moved forward, surprisingly few changes had to be made to the Land Rover to insert the 3.5ltr V8 into the existing engine bay.

The first normal-control V8-engined Land Rover was put on sale in 1979, when it was distinguished by this new front-end style: in most other respects, the body style, and options, were not changed.

Above When fitted with the V8 engine, the truck-cab type of Land Rover became an even more versatile, and capable, workhorse.

Left Twelve seats, a station wagon body, and a lusty V8 engine – a combination which Land Rover found easy to sell in the early 1980s.

Series III (1971–85)

Although this was only a matter of degree, perhaps this was the most 'car-like' of all Land Rovers so far put on sale. Amazingly, although the engine measured 3,528cc instead of the 2,625cc of the old straight six (the use of which would end in 1980), the V8 Land Rover was actually lighter than before – at 3,396lb/1,540kg compared with 3,459lb/1,569kg – and the maximum payload had risen to 2,580lb/1,170kg.

Armed with a new array of ten colour options, the new V8 went on sale in overseas markets at first, but UK deliveries did not begin until August 1980. By that time, the horrendous cost inflation of the 1970s was fast abating, but it is interesting to note the level of British retail prices for Land Rovers at this time. The pick-up bodied version of the V8 cost £7,550, whereas the station wagon price (which included VAT, as a 'private' car) was £8,603. At the same time, incidentally, the cost of a Range Rover was £12,988, and that of a Rover 3500 executive car was £10,159.

Maturity

By the early 1980s, therefore, the original Land Rover mechanical statement had reached full maturity, and the company had few further plans to improve it. Although five-main-bearing four-cylinder engines took over from the original three-bearing types, the range of engine

V8 Land Rover chassis assembly at Solihull, at the crucial 'mating point' where the engine/gearbox assembly was carefully winched into place.

74　Series III (1971–85)

Early in the 1980s, Land Rover introduced a top-of-the-range 'County Station Wagon' with more upmarket trim and equipment. This is a special show-display (what, no roof?) of the seating package.

Open wide, please – for this is the high capacity pick-up derivative of the 109in chassis, which was introduced in 1982. There was a 20 per cent increase in loading area, and a 45 per cent boost in cubic capacity, and with a series of optional related suspension changes the latest device could carry a 3,020lb/ 1,370kg payload.

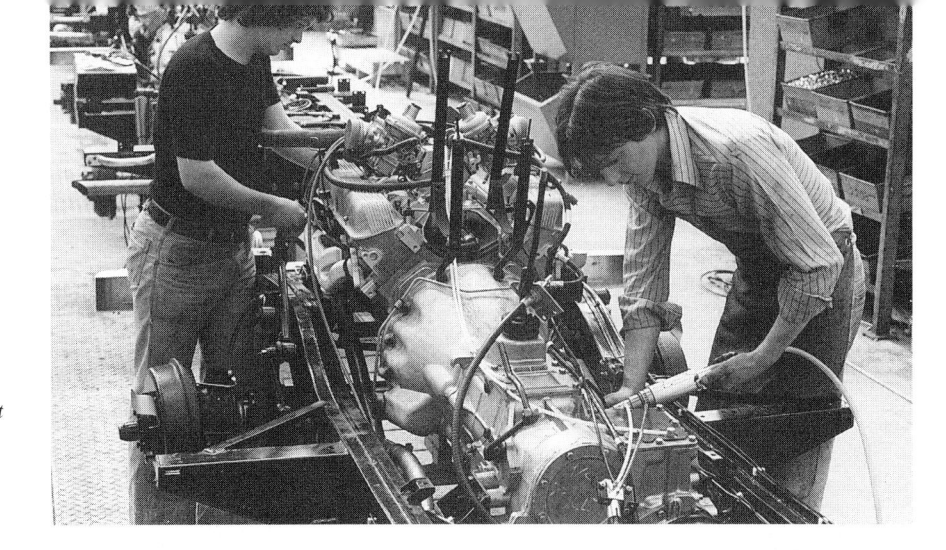

The transmission package of the V8 Land Rover was much more bulky than that normally fitted to four-cylinder and six-cylinder Rovers. It did the job though.

and body options was fully fleshed out, the sales and service network was established all around the world, and the brand had an enviable reputation.

Yet it was already clear that demand for this machine was over its peak. At a time when sales of the plushy Range Rover were trending up towards the ultimate capacity of the Solihull plant – 13,255 would be sold in 1982, which was an average of almost 300 for every working week – the demand for old-type Land Rovers was tailing off. Competition from the Far East was having an effect, which explains, perhaps, why 51,198 Land Rovers were sold in 1980, 41,059 in 1981 and 38,926 in 1982. All the forecasts were that this slide would continue – unless, that is, major changes were made to the machine that well over a million customers had now bought.

Except for the introduction of a 'high capacity' pick-up body for the 109in wheelbase chassis – compared with the existing pick-up, this gave a 20 per cent larger loading area and a 45 per cent increase in cubic capacity, and there was an ultra-wide rear loading gate to suit – and the closely-related County Station Wagon, which was introduced at the same time, was the end of innovation on the leaf-spring chassis.

A brand new family of coil-sprung chassis (the 90 and 110 models) was on the way, and although there was an overlap while existing fleet contracts and the last special derivatives were completed, it was time for a major change. The final UK-built Series III types were not completed until the end of 1985, by which time the coil spring Nineties and One-Tens had been on sale for more than two years, and leaf-spring assembly of much-modified Santana types carried on until 1990.

This was the massive main gearbox/transfer box/transmission brake package of the Range Rover, which was grafted into the V8 Land Rover in 1979.

4 Ninety and One-Ten: Coil Springs, New Engines – a Thorough Update

You could say, and you would be right, that the early 1980s Series III was no more than a lineal descendant of the original Land Rover of 1948. Indeed, it was not until 1983 that the first Land Rover with truly significant technical changes – the use of coil spring suspension – came along. Yet Land Rover's engineers had been thinking about, designing and sometimes actually building new-generation prototypes for at least ten years before the new Ninety and One-Ten models were introduced.

Way back in the late 1970s, when I discussed all such theoretical advances with Tom Barton, he told me as much by saying nothing, as if he had spelt it out. This is an extract from early comment I made on that meeting:

> He [Barton] is a great sketcher, and loves to talk Land Rover with anyone sharing his enthusiasms. It is an instructive experience to sit around a table with him, toss outlandish suggestions into the discussion, and await a reaction. First there is a short silence, then, probably, a twitch at the corner of his mouth, and a tight, secret, little smile, and finally a comment which often begins: 'Well, we actually tried that once, you know …'. You find it almost impossible to produce any suggestion not already considered by the Land Rover design team.

Serious work on replacement Land Rovers, in fact, had started in the early 1970s, soon after the Range Rover was safely put into production. Most work concentrated on the main thrust, of giving the next 4×4 a softer ride and more wheel movement, allied to an even more rigid chassis frame and somewhat more civilized interiors. Clearly, Tom Barton's original theory of keeping the ride rock hard so that cross-country speeds would have to be limited, had been abandoned.

There was always, of course, the question of style. Like the Jeep (yes, sorry, but I must always keep referring to this North American machine), the Land Rover needed to keep a continuity of style as the years passed by. Did that mean that it should never change, that it should change gradually and persistently or that a new style should be developed by David Bache's experts, which merely reflected the old?

Good Ideas

As early as 1972, work began on what the engineers called the 'Series IV' model. This never got as far as the building of fleets of prototypes. New features might have included the use of a punt-type (platform) chassis/inner body structure, a full range of engines (including, of course, the new V8) and longer-travel, taper-leaf, suspension springs to give a more compliant ride.

Once cast aside in 1975, the Series IV was displaced by a project coded SD5. This was the time when Rover–Triumph had begun to use the 'SD' acronym for its new projects, where SD stood for Specialist Division. SD1, incidentally, was the big new Rover 2300/2600/3500 hatchback, which was launched in 1976, while SD2 was the medium-sized project meant to take over from the Triumph Dolomite range, this being cancelled in 1978.

Although it would have retained a separate chassis frame, SD5 had a fresh new style would have looked rather like 'son of Range Rover'. Although it would have retained beam axles at front and rear, the front suspension (but not the

In the late 1970s the SD5 was one of Land Rover's first thoughts on a Land Rover with coil spring suspension. This was a full-size mock, but the project went no further.

rear) would have been by coil springs, Range Rover fashion. This project never got beyond the full-size styling mock-up stage, and by 1977 had been abandoned.

In the meantime, the first Land Rovers with coil spring and radius arm suspension (in place of leaf springs) had already been built, if only on the 'why don't we ...?' basis. The original machine was a real lash-up, with a hybrid Range Rover/Land Rover frame, wide-track Range Rover axles and coil spring suspension, all on a 100in wheelbase, with a rather crudely knocked-about station wagon body. It might have been intended for SUV (sport utility vehicle) usage in the USA, which might explain its equipment – there was a 130bhp 3,528cc V8 engine up front – but that idea was soon abandoned.

Nevertheless, this was the germ that inspired the entire Ninety/One-Ten programme – even though neither of those model names, or types, existed at first. The Stage 2 programme (the V8-engined 109in Series III had been 'Stage 1'), which got under way in 1977, built on all those ideas and added more of its own.

Mike Broadhead (who was currently Tom Barton's assistant, and would take over from him when Tom retired) worked up a series of project notes. It was interesting to see that a 'new' Land Rover would look much like all those that had gone before. Inevitably, too, it would be larger than those earlier machines – longer, wider, heavier and (Land Rover hoped) even more saleable.

In the beginning, Stage 2 took shape around a choice of two wheelbases – 100in and 110in – which were a long way from the 80in of the original model of 1948. Since it was also planned that wheel tracks would be wider (Range Rover dimensions would be used) this would automatically mean that some style changes were essential.

This, in fact, was not a mere facelift, or modification of what had gone before, but was to be a completely re-thought package of running gear. Although the same engine line up was to be retained, there would be a new transmission, new axles, new suspension front and rear, new brakes – and those style changes that have already been mentioned.

To understand this project, overall, I should sort out what evolved in the chassis, and why. Although work on the 100in and 110in wheelbases carried on for some time, Rover management became increasingly uneasy about the shorter of those two types: '100in' had arrived, almost by stealth, in the programme, as this was of

One-Ten assembly at Solihull was well under way before the new model was officially launched in March 1983. Production capacity had been expanded to meet an anticipated leap in orders.

Layout
Ladder-style chassis frame, with choice of mainly-aluminium body styles. Front engine/four-wheel-drive, sold as pick-up, van, estate and various special types.

Engines

Type	All, four-cylinders, in-line – except for V8-engined 3,528cc model

1983–mid-1985 (petrol)

Capacity	2,286cc
Bore and stroke	90.47 × 88.9mm
Valves	Overhead valves
Compression ratio	8.0:1
Carburettor	Weber
Max power	74bhp @ 4,000rpm
Max torque	120lb ft @ 2,000rpm

Mid-1985–90 (petrol)

Capacity	2,495cc
Bore and stroke	90.47 × 88.9mm
Valves	Overhead valves
Compression ratio	8.0:1
Carburettor	Weber
Max power	83bhp @ 4,000rpm
Max torque	133lb ft @ 2,000rpm

1983 only (diesel)

Capacity	2,286cc
Bore and stroke	90.47 × 88.9mm
Valves	Overhead valves
Compression ratio	23.0:1
Fuel injection	CAV
Max power	60bhp @ 4,000rpm
Max torque	103lb ft @ 1,800rpm

1984–90 (diesel)

Capacity	2,495cc
Bore and stroke	90.47 × 97mm
Valves	Overhead valves
Compression ratio	21.0:1
Fuel injection	DPS
Max power	67bhp @ 4,000rpm
Max torque	114lb ft @ 1,800rpm

Land Rover Ninety and One-Ten (1983–90)

1986–90 (diesel)

Capacity	2,495cc
Bore and stroke	90.47 × 97mm
Valves	Overhead valves
Compression ratio	21.0:1
Fuel injection	DPS plus turbocharger
Max power	85bhp @ 4,000rpm
Max torque	150lb ft @ 1,800rpm

V8-cylinder (petrol)

Capacity	3,528cc
Bore and stroke	88.9 × 71.1mm
Valves	Overhead valves
Compression ratio	8.13:1
Carburettor	Two Zenith–Stromberg
Max power	114bhp @ 4,000rpm
Max torque	185lb ft @ 2,500rpm

V8, from late 1986

Carburettor	Two SU
Max power	134bhp @ 5,000rpm
Max torque	187lb ft @ 2,500rpm

Transmission

Type	Four-wheel-drive, with choice of high or low range
Gearbox	Five-speed manual gearbox, synchromesh on all forward gears – all four-cylinder; V8-engined cars from 1985
Clutch	Single dry plate, diaphragm spring
Final drive ratio (all types)	3.54:1
Ratios	Four-cylinder, high range
Top	4.90
4th	5.89
3rd	8.89
2nd	13.57
1st	21.14
Reverse	21.82
	High range step-down ratio 1.41:1 (on 90), 1.66:1 (on 110)
	Low-range step-down ratio 3.31:1
Ratios	V8-cylinder, four-speed, high range
Top	4.72
3rd	7.11
2nd	11.57
1st	19.23
Reverse	17.32
	High range step-down ratio 1.19:1 (on 90), 1.34:1 (on 110)
	Low-range step-down ratio 3.32:1
Ratios	V8-cylinder, five-speed, high range
Top	3.97
4th	4.99
3rd	7.165
2nd	10.88
1st	18.22
Reverse	19.085
	High range step-down ratio 1.411:1 (1.222:1 from introduction of 134bhp V8 engine)
	Low-range step-down ratio 3.32:1

Suspension and steering

Front	Live axle, by coil springs, radius arms, Panhard rod, telescopic dampers
Rear	Live axle, by coil springs, radius arms, A-bracket, optional self-levelling, telescopic dampers
Steering	Recirculating ball (optional power assistance with worm-and-roller)
Tyres	6.00-16in (on 90), or 7.50-16in (on 110) cross-ply
Wheels	Steel disc, five-bolt-on fixing

Brakes

Type	Disc brakes at front, drum brakes at rear, hydraulically operated
Size	11.8in front discs, 11.0in rear drums, with vacuum servo assistance

Dimensions (in/mm)

Track	Front	58.5/1,486
	Rear	58.5/1,486
Wheelbase	(90)	92.9/2,360
	(110)	110/2,794
Overall length	(90)	146.5/3,721
	(110)	175/4,445
Overall width	70.5/1,791	
Overall height	From 80.1/2035	
Unladen weight	(90)	From 3,540lb/1,605kg
	(110)	From 3,799lb/1,723kg

course the Range Rover's dimension – yet a growing number of personalities thought that in the Land Rover context it was really too long, and was straying too far away from the traditional 88in of the Series III types.

Eventually, although work continued on the 100in wheelbase chassis for some military derivatives (it was not widely adapted and was abandoned in the mid-1980s), for civilian purposes it was dropped in favour of a much shorter machine, with a 90in wheelbase. Hence the 'Ninety' – but the story did not end there. Once a 90in prototype had been built, Mike Broadhead decided that more loading space had to be regained: In the end the definitive wheelbase of 92.9in/2,360mm emerged – but to add to the on-going confusion the model was always known – and is known, to this day – as the 'Ninety'.

At this point, I must abandon a strictly chronological narrative, for the Stage 2 vehicles appeared more than a year apart, yet were of essentially identical design. Whereas the Ninety was unveiled in June 1984, the One-Ten was launched earlier, in March 1983. Not only that, but (as I have already noted in the previous Chapter) manufacture of old-type Series III models carried on until the end of 1985. It would not be fair to state that Solihull was in turmoil at this time, but the picture on the final assembly tracks was definitely complicated in the 1983–5 period.

As the Ninety and One-Ten types were essentially of the same design, I shall now analyse their design, jointly.

Chassis Frame

At last, at long last, the old-type edge-welding fixtures for traditional Land Rovers could be thrown away, as here was an entirely new chassis. Inspired, for sure, by the layout of the Range Rover's box-section chassis, this was a monumentally sturdy box-section frame, welded together at the Garrison Street (Birmingham) factory by newly-installed Asea welding robots.

This massive new basis for Land Rover was even more robust than that of the Range Rover, and was no less than 7.5in/190.5mm deep in the centre. Because coil springs were employed in place of leaf springs, the stress paths along this component were completely different from the

The first of the coil-spring Land Rover generation, the One-Ten, appeared in 1983, and demonstrated the complete re-engineering of the chassis, with much experience drawn from the Range Rover family.

On the Ninety and One-Ten models, the advantages of the new coil spring suspension were that the wheel travel had been increased, and the ride softened, though cross-country ability was just as good as ever.

original type – and, all in all, it was an impressive, if heavy, piece of kit.

Although we did not know it at first, the engineers would even find a way of stretching this frame much further, for wheelbase options of no less than 119.6in (Australian-built) examples or 127in (in the UK) were eventually put on sale.

Although it had been inspired by the Range Rover layout, the new types' coil spring suspension was different in detail. As far as the new chassis was concerned, there were stout towers on the front of the frame, immediate above the line of the coils suspending the front axle, while at the rear the coil springs were squeezed between the upswept frame side members, and pads on the rear axle itself.

Suspension and Chassis

Although beam axles were retained, henceforth they were suspended on vertical, large diameter, coil springs. At the front of the car, axle location was by radius arms and a (transverse) Panhard rod, with telescopic dampers actually mounted inside the springs. At the rear, location was by radius arms, an A-bracket, with the dampers mounted separately, ahead of the line of the axle itself, leaning forward and tying up to the chassis side members.

Self-levelling (by a Boge Hydramat strut, as fitted to the Range Rover), was standard on the County-specification Station Wagon version of the One-Ten, and optional on other types. Not only that, but on the County there was also a rear anti-roll bar.

Although no-one would suggest that the new Land Rovers had a ride as soft as that of the Range Rovers, it was much more compliant than before. Not only had the use of internal-friction-free coil springs contributed to that, but there was much more vertical wheel movement than

The Ninety/One-Ten twins both shared a new type of front-end style, complete with a prominent grille, and of course with flared wheel-arches. This was a One-Ten County Station Wagon.

before. There was 7.0in/178mm at the front (a 50 per cent increase over the Series III), and no less than 8.25in/210mm at the rear (25 per cent more than on the Series III). The extra wheel movement, incidentally, meant that a properly-driven Ninety or One-Ten could pick its way across even more difficult terrain without grinding to a halt due to a lack of wheel grip.

Not only that, but because the rear axle was mounted a little further back (relative, that is, to the rear of the frame itself), and much detail work had gone in to ensure no projections, the maximum approach angle (front) had gone up to an astonishing 50 degrees. The departure angle (rear) was less extreme, but still creditable at 35 degrees. The minimum ground clearance was a reassuring 8.5in/216mm.

Recirculating ball steering was retained, and given a new linkage and geometry, which reputedly felt more precise that earlier types, while power-assisted worm-and-roller steering (with a mere 3.0 turns lock-to-lock) became optional. The turning circles, too, were much tighter than before.

For the first time, too, here was a Land Rover with servo-assisted disc front brakes. These 11.8in/300mm diameter units were not only more powerful and fade-free than before, but also had that useful feature of drying out much faster (and regaining their efficiency) after the Land Rover had passed through deep water.

Engines and Transmissions

On original One-Ten models (the Ninety would arrive after the first engine up-grade) there was little advance over the old-type Series III engines, and no novelties, such that many observers guessed that this was only an interim solution to what the engineering team had in mind for the future. The $2\frac{1}{4}$ltr petrol unit got a new Weber carburettor, and pushed out a peak of 74bhp, the $2\frac{1}{4}$ltr diesel was as before, with 60bhp, while the V8 $3\frac{1}{2}$ltr unit was boosted to 114bhp at 4,000rpm.

The real novelty came behind the four-cylinder engines, where a modified version of the Rover–Triumph LT77 five-speed gearbox (it had a special set of internal ratios) became standard. This was a major component already being used in Rover 3500 and Jaguar XJ saloons, had previously been used in Triumph TR7 and TR8 sports cars, and which also found a home in specialist sports cars like the TVR.

Not only was the LT77 amply strong enough to deal with the torque of the current, and planned, four-cylinder engines, but it also featured a geared-up, 'overdrive' top, internal ratio 0.83:1. Because it was linked to the latest LT230 type of two-speed transfer gearbox, it meant that these cars had five high-ratio and five low-ratio forward gears, plus a lockable centre differential and four-wheel-drive was no permanently in operation.

Selectable rear-drive only transmission was still listed, as an option, but was rarely taken up. That option was discarded in 1984.

When the V8 engine was specified, as before it came with the Range Rover type of LT95 four-speed gearbox, which had its own in-built two-speed transfer gearbox. Permanent four-wheel-drive was a feature (there being no rear-drive-only option), along with high-range or low-range.

To top of this major advance, the Ninety and One-Ten types were equipped with new wide-track front and rear axles, these providing the same tread as the Range Rover – 58.5in/1,486mm – a massive increase of no less then 7.0in/178mm, or 13 per cent. This, on its own, ensured more stability, more cornering power on sealed surfaces and (because the tyres were further out from the chassis frame at the front) it also meant that the turning circle could be cut by up to 5ft/1.5m.

Style

Because of the modification described above, it also meant that something drastic would have to be done about the styling of the wheelarches, but as the Rover designers in any case had other things in mind, this was no chore.

Once the SD5 project had been abandoned in 1977, it seems to have been understood that any new Land Rover would not feature a new body style, but would be given a modified and evolutionary version of the existing one. There were three reasons for this – one was that it would emphasize the same features that Land Rovers had always enjoyed (nowadays we might say that it would show off the same 'DNA'), and another

Ninety and One-Ten interiors were considerably more sophisticated than those of the Series III types that they replaced, not only because of their instrument panel layout, but because of the use of a new four-spoke steering wheel. There were even carpets on the floor!

was that there would be considerable carry-over from Series III to 'Stage 2'. The third reason was that it would automatically cut the cost of new body shell investment – and even though Stage 2 had headlined a large sum of money, there were limits beyond which management could not go.

Apart from the changes needed to accommodate the fresh wheelbases – the short-wheelbase type was to be 4.9in/124mm, the long wheelbase type just 1 in/25mm longer than before – there were several other changes to be incorporated. First, the decision to include an adjustable driver's seat, meant that the volume of the driving compartment would have to be enlarged, and this had an effect on the bodywork around it. Second, it was decided to commonize the front-end style of all types, with all engines, and to do this an improved derivation of the flush-fronted Series III V8 was chosen. Front-end panel pressings were not changed, but this time there was a new type of radiator grille, with nine horizontal slats standing slightly proud of the sheet metal.

To accommodate the much wider front and rear axles, Land Rover needed to extend the

As you might expect, the new One-Ten could deal with almost all sorts of going – hard and soft, dry and wet, or any horrid combination of all those. This One-Ten is on test on Solihull's 'jungle' track – a facility which has now been obliterated by new factory developments.

wings to cover the tyres. To do this without spending a fortune on new front and rear wing pressings (which, for styling purposes, would also have meant the reshaping of the passenger doors), wheelarch extensions were chosen instead. Like the rally cars of the day, these looked both functional and trendy – and it was typical of Land Rover that they chose to use flexible, deformable, plastic extensions, which could be leaned against gate posts and other off-road obstructions without suffering permanent damage.

Two other improvements concerned the driver. One was a 25 per cent larger one-piece windscreen – this had been adopted for a combination of stylistic and legislative reasons – and a much more car-like facia/instrument panel. There was also a new type of four-spoke steering wheel, which looked like that of the Range Rover, but was actually unique.

All in all, this was a very impressive reworking of an already well-honed idea, and was well received by the clientele. For a short time, in 1983 and 1984, a mixture of Land Rovers were built at Solihull. The only new-type coil-spring model available from March 1983 to June 1984 was the long-wheelbase One-Ten, which lived alongside the last of the 88in Series III leaf-spring types throughout that time.

The changes – persistent, worthwhile, changes – then began, and would continue until 1989, when these cars became 'Defenders' (see Chapter 5). To avoid confusion I will now cover the stream of improvements in chronological order:

March 1983

Soon after Tony Gilroy took over from Mike Hodgkinson as Land Rover Ltd's managing director – this coming in January 1983 – the new-generation One-Ten went on sale, complete with $2\frac{1}{4}$ltr petrol, $2\frac{1}{4}$ltr diesel and $3\frac{1}{2}$ltr V8 petrol engine options. A variety of body options was topped out by the latest County Station Wagon.

At this time the 88in wheelbase Series III carried on as before.

First you ordered your new Land Rover, then you specified all the options and accessories. Everything shown here – front winch, bull bars, and extra driving lamps, were in the options list in the 1980s.

November 1983

Although this did not directly affect, or influence, the Land Rover product line, the announcement that all 4×4 activities were eventually to be concentrated at Solihull was commercially important. Part of Tony Gilroy's strategy was to comb out all manufacturing inefficiencies, and one part of this was to get rid of uneconomic and far-flung factories.

As things stood up to 1983, although Land Rover assembly was concentrated on Solihull, the manufacture of major components was widespread. As my good friends on *Autocar* magazine commented at the time:

> Land Rover ... suffered badly from the 'sprawl syndrome', a situation in which component supply plants are scattered some considerable distance from the assembly, requiring a high degree of inter-plant transport, which adds costs and wastes time. Add factors such as extra administration costs and rates, and the justification for single site production becomes even easier to make.

The One-Ten County Station Wagon, complete with larger, one-piece, screen, flared arches and special colour flashes, was distinctive and popular in the 1980s.

Land Rover Ltd, in fact, elected to close nine 'satellite' plants, and to shed 1,500 jobs during the 1984–6 period. This, for instance, would mean bringing back the manufacture of chassis frames from Garrison Street (which was close to the Birmingham–Coventry main railway line in the centre of Birmingham), while Percy Road, Perry Barr and Tyburn Road (all in Birmingham), all of which produced transmission components, would also be closed.

Many of these facilities, in fact, had been snapped up cheaply, in a piecemeal manner, during the 1950s and 1960s, in order to expand Land Rover production while the rest of Solihull was building cars. Now that assembly of Rovers cars had finally moved elsewhere (assembly of the SD1 hatchback was moved to another British Leyland factory, at Cowley, near Oxford) and Land Rover activity was actually draining away, Solihull was beginning to echo with empty space.

The key to Solihull's new-found space was what the workforce always called the 'SD1 Block', opened in 1976 for Rover (and, later, Triumph) car assembly, still modern, still massive, but now mothballed and ready for conversion. Gilroy's planners rubbed their hands at the prospects, set to, and forecast that £14 million a year would be saved.

Except for the unfortunate transport drivers, whose trucks would no longer be needed to commute between Victorian-era buildings around the West Midlands and Solihull (that totalled a million truck miles every year), there were really no losers in this strategy, for the workforce was offered the chance to move with the machinery – and most did so.

January 1984

After less than a year, the One-Ten was up-rated when a 2,495cc diesel replaced the earlier 2,286cc engine. The new engine looked almost exactly like the old, and so it was, for it was little more than a long-stroke derivative with revised (DPS) fuel injection. Peak power rose from 60bhp to 67bhp but, more significantly, peak torque rose from 103lb ft at 1,800rpm to 114lb ft at 1,800rpm.

This was the second-phase of a long-term improvement programme – for the change from three to five crankshaft main bearings had already taken place in 1980. However, at the same time as the capacity was increased, an internally toothed camshaft drive belt replaced the roller chain of the original.

June 1984

The new 92.9in wheelbase Ninety model was finally announced, as a short-wheelbase version of the One-Ten. From this time all Land Rovers got one-piece passenger door windows (instead of the historically-familiar sliding windows), and there was a package of trim upgrades to suit.

At first, the Ninety was only available with a choice of four-cylinder engines – petrol or diesel – but this situation would not persist for long.

From this point, Ninety prices started from a low of £6,620 for a working (as opposed to on-road) hard-top model,

May 1985

This was the moment at which a 114bhp 3½ltr V8-powered Ninety went on sale. At the same time the V8 engine for both the Ninety and One-Ten models was matched to a new-type (new, that is, to Solihull) five-speed main gearbox, the LT85, which was already in production at Santana of Spain. Originally designed in Solihull, this had only recently gone into use on Spanish-built Land Rovers

Although it was no lightweight, and still guzzled petrol at the rate of 16mpg (Imperial), a Ninety V8, with the five-speed transmission, could sprint up to 60mph in little more than

As with the previous Series III, there was a high-capacity pick-up version of the One-Ten. Because of the extra-wide loading package, note that there were no flared rear wheel-arches on this derivative.

14 seconds. Not remarkable by current family hatchback standards, but a good deal faster than any previous Land Rover 4×4. Nothing, though, could hide the awful aerodynamics, even of the station wagon – which explains why the top speed was a mere 83.5mph.

September 1985

The time was now ripe for further rationalization of the product line, to make even more sense of the busy engine manufacturing plant at Solihull, and to give a boost to the 'entry-level' Land Rover. Although in 1984 the company's management had denied vehemently that the four-cylinder petrol engine would be enlarged to parallel the newly-introduced 2,495cc diesel, this could best be described as being 'economical with the truth'.

After only 21 months (which means that prototype engines must surely have been on test when the original statement was made), the company announced that the petrol engine was also to be enlarged to 2,495cc. As before, petrol and diesel engines would share the same bore and stroke, much of the cylinder block and crankshaft machining, and would be manufactured side-by-side at Solihull. This was a simple change – the bore was not changed, but the stroke went up from 88.9mm to 97mm – but it brought with it some real benefits (see table).

By the 1980s, Land Rover engine manufacture had been relocated to Solihull, and was a light and airy factory unit. Like soldier ants, this line of four-cylinder power units would be marching – from one horizon to the next – throughout the working shift, for Solihull's assembly lines had a voracious appetite for more components.

Before and After Figures Showing the Benefits of the New Engine

Engine	Peak Power (bhp/rpm)	Peak Torque (lb ft/rpm)
2,286cc	74/4,000	120/2,000
2,495cc	83/4,000	133/2,000

This Ninety may look military, but is in fact a conventional civilian hard top model. In this shot, the large one-piece screen, and the flexible flared wheel arches are particularly obvious.

So, surely this meant that the Ninety and One-Ten models could now look forward to a period of stability (the sort which production chief pray for, but sales and marketing staffs dread)? The one-and-a-half millionth Solihull-built 4×4 (including Range Rovers, of course) was due to be built before the end of in 1985, so surely everything was right in the Land-Rover's world?

In fact, everything was far from right, as annual Land Rover sales, which had slipped from 51,198 in 1980 to a mere 25,562 in 1984, made clear. In particular, there had been a collapse in world-wide military sales. The commercial world, too, had changed, for many hitherto safe 'Empire' markets had been thrown open to competition (especially from the Far East). A host of other factors – including massive increases in energy costs, the adverse movement of currency levels and the economic conditions that followed the two energy crises of 1973 and 1979, and progressive customer over-familiarity with the Land Rover's style – all had an effect.

Early in 1986, too, it did not help that the business soon found itself as a takeover target, for the British Government showed itself to be interested in clawing back some money from its 'investment' in British Leyland. Several big investors (let us call them 'predators') began to prowl around, of which the most serious were General Motors, and Ford, the two largest automotive corporations in the world.

Such was the public outcry, and such was the resistance from the workforce and a mass of Land Rover enthusiasts, that these manoeuvres were not allowed to become serious, and the status quo was restored. It was not until 1988 – when what had now been renamed the Rover Group was sold off to British Aerospace – that Land Rover Ltd found itself with yet another parent company.

In the short term, Land Rover Ltd could do little to affect all this. Because their next major strategic change would be to introduce a new 'gap-filling' model to span the 'classic' Land Rover and the Range Rover (this project would become the Discovery model, to be launched in September 1989), the well-known and original 4×4 would have to soldier on as best it could.

Still a workhorse, still willing, and still no more than matched by its rivals, the Ninety pick-up of the 1980s was an extremely capable 4×4.

Mergers

Although this is a 'product', rather than an 'industrial' book, I ought to sort out who the ultimate owners of the Land Rover brand have been in the fifty-plus years that such cars have been on sale.

In 1948, when Land Rover was new, Rover was still an independent concern.

Late in 1966, Leyland Motors absorbed Rover, in an agreed merger.

In January 1968, the Leyland Group (which included Rover, Triumph and Alvis) merged with British Motor Holdings (BMC plus Jaguar) – the result being the birth of that unwieldy colossus, British Leyland.

British Leyland was nationalized by the British Government in 1975, the car-making side being re-designated Leyland Cars (but still under the same ultimate ownership), and Land Rover continued to be controlled by the state. In the mid-1980s, Jaguar was floated off into private ownership, while the rest of the car-making side became known as the Rover Group.

In 1988, the state sold off the Rover Group to British Aerospace (the country's largest maker of aircraft).

BMW of Germany bought control of the Rover Group from BAe – this purchase also including Land Rover.

In the spring of 2000, BMW decided to sell off most of the Rover Group. It was a complicated deal. The car-manufacturing business at Longbridge was sold off to the Phoenix Consortium. This was soon re-named MG Rover, and would carry on building MG and Rover cars. BMW held on to the Oxford factory (in which to build Minis) – and the Land Rover operation was sold off to Ford Motor Co. Ltd.

From the spring of 2000, therefore, Land Rover became a Ford subsidiary, and an important part of Ford's Premier Automotive Group (a holding company which then included Aston Martin, Jaguar, Land Rover, Volvo and Lincoln).

October 1986

Even so, there was still time for one more significant change, and boost, to the engine line-up. Not only did Land Rover introduce a turbo-charged version of the four-cylinder diesel, but also it up-rated the 3½ltr V8 to what had once only been Range Rover levels.

The engineers already had some experience of turbo-charging (in Spain, Santana had put a turbo 2¼ltr engine on the market some years earlier). Proving that adding a turbo-charger to an otherwise normally-aspirated engine was never simple, the new unit needed a redesigned cylinder block, a cross-drilled crankshaft, new pistons and rings, nimonic exhaust valves, new inlet and exhaust arrangements, an uprated water-cooling system, a viscous-coupled cooling fan, and an oil cooler!

The turbo itself was a Garrett AiResearch T2 type (one of the smallest in that company's wide range), whose integral wastegate limited the extra boost to 10psi. This installation was a great success (see table).

As you might expect, there had been a major improvement in torque. Peak power was up by 13 per cent, but peak torque had rocketed by 31.5 per cent. This gave the turbo-diesel-equipped Land Rover a huge increase in lugging power, and the ability to undertake out-of-the-ordinary tasks.

The introduction of a more powerful 3½ltr V8 engine power unit was achieved by changing the

Before and After Figures Showing the Benefits of the New Turbo-charger

Engine	Peak Power (bhp/rpm)	Peak Torque (lb ft/rpm)
2,495cc (normally aspirated)	67/4,000	114/1,800
2,495cc turbo	85/4,000	150/1,800

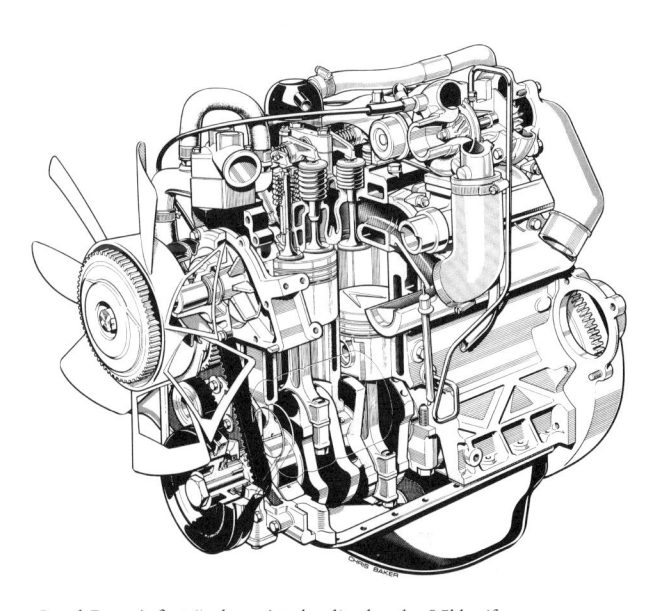

Land Rover's first 'in house' turbo-diesel – the 85bhp/four-cylinder/2,495cc unit – appeared in October 1986. It was a no-nonsense installation which fitted neatly into the Ninety/One-Ten chassis.

Once the coil-sprung Ninety had found its feet, Land Rover also offered it with the V8 engine, this being the first time such a short (and relatively light) Land Rover had enjoyed V8 power. Only in detail was the installation different from that of the original V8 Land Rover shown on page 71.

entire character of the big, light-alloy, unit. SU carburettors replaced Zenith–Strombergs and the camshaft profile was also changed, the revised engine could be revved much higher and develop its extra power beyond the point where earlier Ninety/One-Ten power units would simply have run out of breath.

With 134bhp at 5,000rpm instead of 114bhp at 4,000 rpm, it was now a formidably capable power unit.

Right *The coil-spring suspension layout of the Ninety/One-Ten series was sturdy, and clearly evolved from that of the Range Rover.*

Below *The coil-spring suspension layout, once proven, was retained for the next generation of Land Rovers too – and even on the Defender (this example) it was little changed.*

Forty years of development – and growth – is shown off here, with a Ninety County Station Wagon of 1988 on the right, backed up to the original pre-production Series I 80in model (HUE 166) of 1948. The latest version was larger, heavier, faster, and more capable than the original.

1986 and 1948 – a Comparison

At this point it is worth looking back, with an air of slight disbelief, at 1948, and comparing the original Solihull-built 4×4s with the 1987 models:

In 1948, the original Series I 1.6ltr produced 50bhp, and weighed from 2,594lb.

For 1987, the Ninety offered a choice of 83bhp (petrol), 85bhp (diesel) and 134bhp (V8 petrol), and weighed from 3,540lb.

The original type had a power/weight ratio of 42.5bhp/tonne; for 1987, the Ninety offered 51.7bhp/tonne (four-cylinder) or approximately 80bhp/tonne (V8).

A New Parent Company

By this time, the classic Land Rover found itself rather neglected, and was pottering along, almost on automatic pilot. Out in the wide world, the much more expensive and up-market Range Rover was making all the headlines (fuel-injected V8 engines had recently been standardized, and USA sales began in 1987). Within the factory at Solihull, most of the design and development effort was going into Project Jay – which would become 'Discovery' when it was introduced in 1989.

On the other hand, after the arrival of the turbo-diesel engine, there was really little innovation in prospect for the Ninety or the One-Ten, whose style was settled, and whose market aspirations never seemed to change. For the staff, therefore, it can have been no surprise to see annual sales fall from 31,046 in 1985 to 22,026 in 1986, and again to 20,686 in 1987. By historic standards this was depressing – for Land Rover sales had first surged up through the 20,000 barrier as long ago as 1953, and had been at twice this level (and more) through the 1960s and 1970s.

Then, of course, there was the question of corporate control. Land Rover Ltd, like other subsidiary organizations within the British Leyland/Rover Group conglomerate, had become thoroughly unsettled by all the bids, rumours of sales, part-privatizations, and renaming that characterized the 1980s. In 1988 this intensified.

Britain's Conservative Government came to power in 1979 with policies that included selling off many of its state 'assets'. Some, like the profitable British Telecom, were likely to find an immediate home in the private sector, but others, like British Leyland, would be more difficult.

The sell-off, therefore, went ahead piece-meal, with Jaguar, Leyland Vehicles and Unipart all

I always felt sorry for brand new Land Rovers – this was a late-1980s Ninety pick-up – which looked so polished, and so smart, for there were never likely to look so smart, ever again!

being privatized. Finally, early in 1988, the loss-making Austin Rover Group (which included Land Rover Ltd) was sold off to British Aerospace for the knockdown price of only £150 million. That price, on its own, was attractive enough, but as the old company's accumulated debt (of £350 million) was written off at the same time, and British Aerospace found itself inheriting a great deal of potentially valuable real estate, which might eventually be sold off, it seemed like an incredible bargain.

As part of the deal, BAe had to agree that it would not attempt to sell off any of the companies for at least five years, but this did not

This particular Ninety County Station Wagon actually has V8 power, which made it a very lively cross-country machine.

Just so long as the engine could breathe air (instead of water!) the Ninety model could cope with almost any type of going. This shallow ford would be shrugged off as insignificant, and traction would not be affected.

seem like too much of a hardship. As we now know, BAe honoured that pledge, but only just, as the Rover Group would once again change hands in 1994.

British Aerospace immediately began to make their presence felt, with management teams surging through every factory like a tidal wave. As far as Land Rover was concerned, there was one immediate casualty, as managing director Tony Gilroy soon quarrelled with BAe 'top brass' and resigned, moving off to run the Perkins diesel engine operation instead.

Maturity

Apart from changes to badging, and to minor updates of trim and equipment options, no further changes were made to the Ninety/One-Ten sisters. Although no major technical changes were intended for the moment, it would not be long before these models were replaced by a 'new' type – called the Defender – although the Ninety and One-Ten badges would be retained too.

This, as we shall see in the next Chapter, was little more than a name change at first, and it brought the long-established Solihull 4×4 into line with other types in the line-up.

5 Defender – and Still They Come

The marketing upheaval, which changed Land Rover from a rather traditional 4×4 manufacturer into one that catered more for the trendy 'lifestyle' customers, began in 1989 with the launch of the Discovery – and I cover the launch of this important model fully in Chapter 6.

It also marked the point at which the company made another big change – by dumping long-established and world-famous names like 'Ninety' and 'One-Ten' – and introducing 'Defender' instead. Even so, this was a slightly messy process. Although other Land Rover authorities insist that the first 'Defender' badged 4×4 was not revealed until the autumn of 1990, the 'Defender' name was first used – persistently, and definitely – at the various Discovery press conferences in September 1989! I noted this at the time, for I attended those conferences. So, was the Land Rover a 'Defender' in 1989–90, or was it not? Some say no, but at the time company spokesmen say that it was!

Not that this renaming policy got much publicity at first – whether in 1989 or 1990. When the Discovery was launched, the arrival of the Defender went almost unnoticed (for, in truth, the model was not changed). The Discovery, after all, was a new concept, and looked it, whereas the Defender was – well, it looked just the same as before.

Which it was, really, but only for a year, until the next wave of product improvements came along. There was nothing sinister in this –for the classic and original style of Land Rover was not about to be dropped. Land Rover, however, had taken a long look at its marketing stance, decided that numbers no longer meant as much as names – and started again.

The change was really made because of the proliferation in Land Rover types. In the beginning, of course, there had only been one Land Rover – *the* Land Rover – which was a perfect title. For many years afterwards, this was all well and good – until the Range Rover came along in 1970, which was not really a Land Rover, but built in the same factory.

Then, in 1989, there was to be another new-generation car called the Land Rover Discovery. In which case, the marketing gurus concluded, each and every type of 4×4 built at Solihull should have a name and not a number – hence the introduction of 'Defender' for the 1990s. And where did the name come from? One legend has it that it was first mentioned by a Solihull staffer relaxing with a glass of beer in a bar in North America. Maybe – but the fact that Land Rovers had been connected with military forces throughout the world for more than 50 years must surely have been another factor.

Sensibly, and to provide continuity (for the style looked similar, so surely some aspect of the names should continue?), the old model-name numbers were retained. Therefore, a Ninety became a 'Defender 90', while a One-Ten became a 'Defender 110' – and for the sake of tidiness I will take up this story with the launch of the 1991 models.

New Engineering

Although the general layout of the Defender's chassis and running gear was exactly like that of the older Ninety/One-Ten types – same sturdy box-section frame, same axles, same coil spring and radius arm suspension, same optional power-

Above *The first of many! This is Land Rover's famous 'Old No. 1' pre-production 80in model, which took to the roads in 1948.*

Below *They come in all shapes and sizes – this 109in chassis obviously being a blood-relative of the 'bomb disposal' models used by the British Army.*

Above *The lightweight 'Half Ton' Land Rover became a firm favourite with Britain's Armed Forces.*

Below *The One-Ten Station Wagon, in County trim, has always been a very popular version of the original coil spring suspension type.*

Above Land Rovers have always seemed able to climb anything, anywhere. In a County version, it would do it in reasonable comfort too.

Inset, centre right This Defender 90 hardtop, was typical of so many tens of thousands of working Land Rovers.

Right Seven-seater station wagons on the short '90' chassis were always very popular machines.

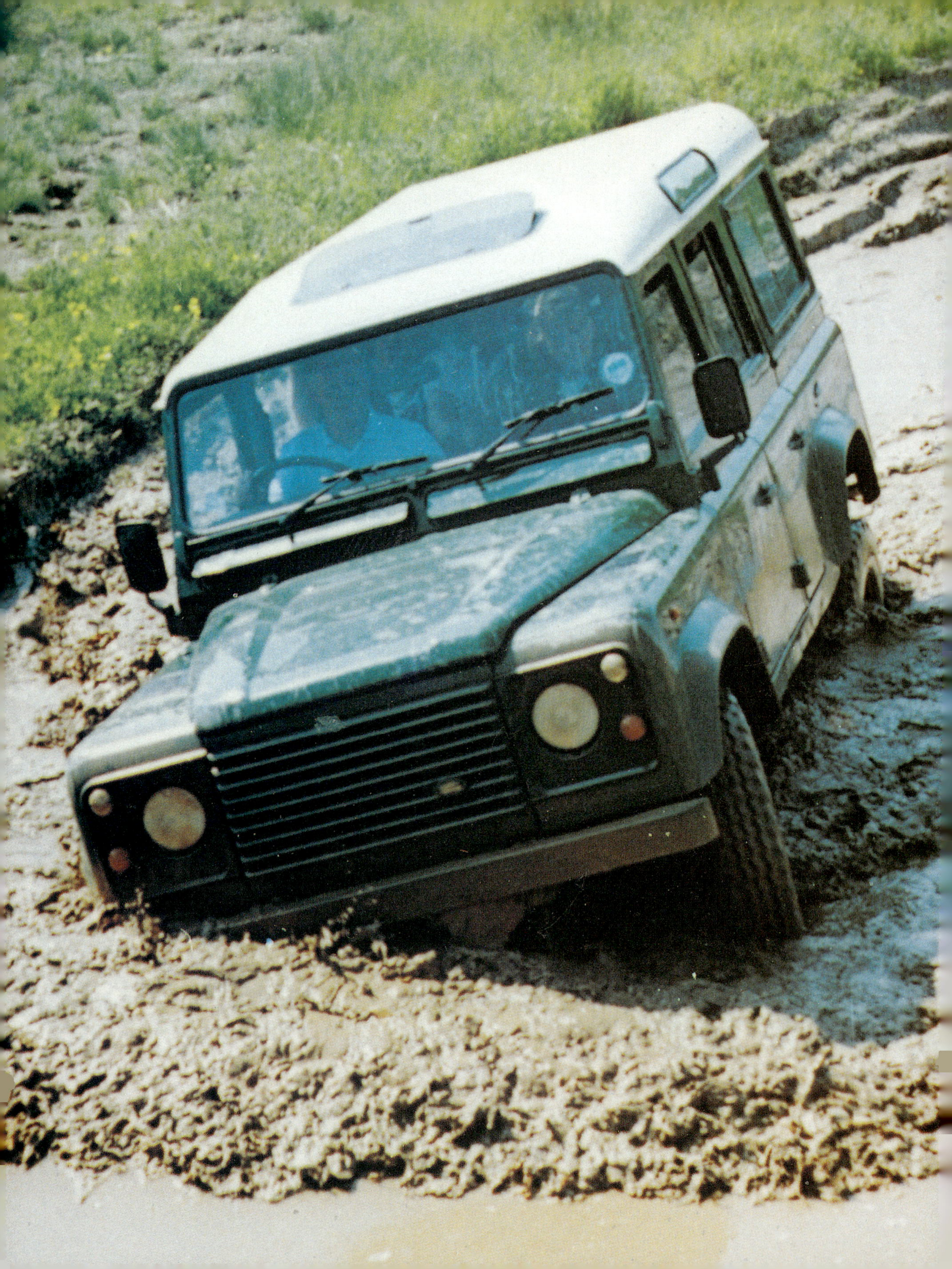

Opposite *'Nothing quite like it for cooling the blood …' – a Defender 110 on a demonstration course at the Gaydon museum in Warwickshire.*

Right *It is in the proportions, somehow – even though the Discovery had a unique body style, the stance and the general chassis attitude spelt out a close relationship to the Range Rover.*

Below *First-generation Discoveries were available in three-door or (this example) five-door varieties. The Tdi decal on the tailgate tells us that this one has a turbo-diesel fitted.*

Above *One picture tells a complete story – the fleet of Discovery turbo-diesels leaving the Solihull factory in May 1995, on their way to compete in the Camel Trophy endurance trial.*

Below *By the late 1990s Land Rover's Solihull body plant was the home to hundreds of spot welding robots. This is the very start of the production assembly process.*

Above You have to look carefully to see how Land Rover up-dated the Discovery into Discovery II. This is a II, complete with a body-colour pressing wrapping around the front grille, and with extra driving lamps let in to the front bumper moulding.

Left The fuel-injected V8 fitted to Discoveries from 1990 onwards. Although the basic engine dated from the 1960s, it became more and more formidable as the years passed.

Below Land Rover interiors grew glossier as the years rolled by. This was the Discovery facia of the 1994–8 period.

Top right One version of the Freelander – that with just two passenger doors, and a tail that could be wide-open to the weather, was always known as the 'softback'; many, in fact, were supplied with a bolt-on glazed moulding and rear door which turned this into a compact estate car.

Bottom right Although the Freelander of 1997 clearly came from Solihull's extended family, it had its own unique unit-construction body style. Note the built-in sump shield under the engine.

Below Although Freelanders always seemed to be ready for anything, even they could not drive across that causeway when the tide came in. Even so, wherever there was traction, and whenever the V6 engine in this type could breath air instead of water, it would keep going.

Above *When the Ninety became the Defender 90, the only significant visual change was to the badging.*

Right *Even into the new twenty-first century, the Defender (this is a 90), was recognizably developed from the original coil spring 4×4s of the mid-1980s. Technically, and in equipment, though, there was change and improvement with every passing season.*

Land Rover Defender 90 and 110 (1989–90)

Layout
Ladder-style chassis frame, with choice of mainly-aluminium body styles. Front engine/four-wheel-drive, sold as pick-up, van, estate and various special types.

Engines

1990–91 (petrol)
Capacity	2,495cc
Bore and stroke	90.47 × 88.9mm
Valves	Overhead valves
Compression ratio	8.0:1
Carburettor	Weber
Max power	83bhp @ 4,000rpm
Max torque	133lb ft @ 2,000rpm

1990–91 (diesel)
Capacity	2,495cc
Bore and stroke	90.47 × 97mm
Valves	Overhead valves
Compression ratio	21.0:1
Fuel injection	DPS
Max power	67bhp @ 4,000rpm
Max torque	114lb ft @ 1,800rpm

1990–94 (200Tdi, diesel)
Capacity	2,495cc
Bore and stroke	90.47 × 97mm
Valves	Overhead valves
Compression ratio	19.5:1
Fuel injection	Bosch plus turbocharger
Max power	107bhp @ 3,800rpm
Max torque	188lb ft @ 1,800rpm

From 1994 (300Tdi, diesel)
Capacity	2,495cc
Bore and stroke	90.47 × 97mm
Valves	Overhead valves
Compression ratio	19.5:1
Fuel injection	Bosch plus turbocharger
Max power	111bhp @ 4,000rpm
Max torque	195lb ft @ 1,800rpm

From 1998 (five-cylinder, diesel)
Capacity	2,495cc
Bore and stroke	84.5 × 89mm
Valves	Single overhead camshaft
Compression ratio	19.5:1
Fuel injection	Lucas plus turbocharger
Max power	122bhp @ 4,200rpm
Max torque	221lb ft @ 1,950rpm

1980–95 (V8-cylinder, petrol)
Capacity	3,528cc
Bore and stroke	88.9 × 71.1mm
Valves	Overhead valves
Compression ratio	8.13:1
Carburettor	Two SU
Max power	134bhp @ 5,000rpm
Max torque	187lb ft @ 2,500rpm

From 1992 (V8-cylinder, petrol)
Capacity	3,947cc
Bore and stroke	94 × 71.1mm
Valves	Overhead valves
Compression ratio	9.35:1
Fuel injection	Lucas
Max power	182bhp @ 4,750rpm
Max torque	231lb ft @ 3,100rpm

Transmission
Type	Four-wheel-drive, with choice of high or low range
Gearbox	Five-speed manual gearbox, synchromesh on all forward gears
Clutch	Single dry plate, diaphragm spring
Final drive ratio (all types)	3.54:1
Ratios	Four-cylinder, high range
Top	4.90
4th	5.89
3rd	8.89
2nd	13.57
1st	21.14
Reverse	21.82

High range step-down ratio
1.41:1 (on 90), 1.66:1 (on 110)
Low-range step-down ratio
3.31:1

Ratios	V8-cylinder, five-speed, high range
Top	3.97
4th	4.99
3rd	7.165
2nd	10.88
1st	18.22
Reverse	19.085

High-range step-down ratio 1.222:1
Low-range step-down ratio 3.32:1

Suspension and steering
- Front: Live axle, by coil springs, radius arms, Panhard rod, telescopic dampers
- Rear: Live axle, by coil springs, radius arms, A-bracket, optional self-levelling, telescopic dampers
- Steering: Worm type, with power assistance
- Tyres: 7.50-6in
- Wheels: Steel disc, five-bolt-on fixing

Brakes
- Type: Disc brakes at front, drums at the rear, hydraulically operated
- Size: 11.8in front discs, 11.0in rear drums (with vacuum servo assistance); rear discs from June 1993

Dimensions (in/mm)
- Track: Front and rear 58.5/1,486
- Wheelbase: (90) 92.9/2,360
- (110) 110/2,794
- Overall length: (90) 146.5/3,721
- (110) 175/4,445
- Overall width: 70.5/1791
- Overall height: From 80.1/2035
- Unladen weight: (90) From 3,737lb/1,695kg
- (110) From 4,156lb/1,885kg

assisted steering (which would be standardized for 1992) – the renamed cars would receive a steady stream of new mechanical features as the 1990s progressed. There would be new engines, new transmissions, and a whole host of cosmetic and equipment updates.

From the autumn of 1990, there was to be a new engine line-up, where the thirsty but charismatic 134bhp/$3\frac{1}{2}$ltr V8 featured as the most powerful type of all. Normally aspirated petrol and diesel engines, though retained for a time, became 'special order' items (and were not actually pushed very hard by the sales force).

The novelty was in the launch of a new generation of turbo-diesel engines – this being the first Land Rover type to use direct (as opposed to indirect) fuel injection. This four-cylinder, 2,495cc direct-injection turbo-diesel 200Tdi power unit, which had an aluminium cylinder head instead of the old cast-iron type, effectively became the 'standard' engine in this range, was a real advance and moved the Defender's performance up a great deal. This was the engine that had already been seen in 1989, in the first of the Discovery models (see Chapter 6 for full details) and had evolved in response to the increasing demands of the European market. For the Defender, it was rated at 107bhp at 3,800rpm – slightly less than that fitted to the Discovery and (from 1992) to the Range Rover.

If we disregard the normally aspirated 'fours' (and almost everyone did, to be fair), this meant that the new Defenders were offered with 107bhp (diesel) or 134bhp (V8 petrol) engines, which was a considerable advance on the general level with which Land Rover customers had been content only a few years earlier. Diesel engine performance, in particular, had rocketed in a very short time.

Compared with the earlier, identical capacity, turbo-diesel, Land Rover made much of the fact that there had been a 26 per cent improvement in peak power, a 25 per cent improvement in peak torque – and they also claimed an improvement of 25 per cent in operating fuel economy.

When it was introduced in 1983, the One-Ten's 2¼ltr diesel engine had produced 60bhp, the original turbo-diesel of 1986 was rated at 85bhp, while in 1990 the 200TDi produced 107bhp. At the same time, the power unit's fuel efficiency, which could be translated directly into on-the-road fuel-consumption achievements, had improved significantly. The power boost itself represented a 78 per cent increase in just seven years, which quite transformed the classic Land Rover's appeal.

To match this improved line-up of engines, the Defender was available with five-speed transmissions throughout – the four-cylinder types retaining the LT77 five-speed transmission of the now-obsolete Ninety/One-Ten types, and the V8 having a new derivative of the same LT77 – which consigned the ex-Santana LT85 back to the parts bin. Indeed, at Solihull there was now a great deal of commonization in the manual transmission department, for the same basic LT77 five-speeder was also being used in the new Discovery, and in the latest Range Rover too. This situation would persist until the mid-1990s, when further improvements would be phased in to all models.

Body Choices

As in previous models, the Defender was to be available in many different guises. First, there was the choice of wheelbase lengths – 92.9in for the '90', 110in for the '110' and, rarely, but still useful, 127in for the Defender 130 – and the different engines.

As to bodywork, soft top, hardtop, pick-up and Station Wagon types were available on both conventional wheelbases, though for the time being the seven-seater '90' Station Wagon was dropped, so that customers for the new Discovery would not become confused! There was also an HCPU (High Capacity Pick Up) style on the ultra-long '130' chassis.

Defenders and Discoveries have always been popular 'chase'; and recovery vehicles behind major inter-continental marathon rallies. This purposeful trio were due to support the Paris–Moscow–Beijing Marathon Raid in the 1990s – left to right: Defender 110, Defender 130 and Discovery.

The Defender 110 County Station Wagon of the early 1990s was a solid and successful all-purpose people carrier – just as successful as its ancestors had always been in the past.

At the same time, and gradually – oh, so gradually – the interior of the Defender was beginning to look more like a car than an agricultural tool that just happened to have some trim and some fittings. It was years, of course, since Land Rovers had used two-piece windscreen glass and sliding windows, and now the interior was beginning to catch up too.

For the first time there was to be a choice of trim colour, above that of utilitarian grey, for the customer could also choose a brown Moorland dog-tooth cloth trim. The actual positioning of the front seats was reshuffled, so that the driver and outer passenger no longer felt as if they were being pushed up against the door trim panels.

Then, of course, there were the details that a Series I or II owner would simply never have considered necessary. Interior courtesy lights (door-operated, as on a conventional car) were a novelty, while for the very first time on these cars there was a cubby box between the seats, which incorporated a lockable compartment.

All this, allied to the definitive 'Defender' badging, and a new layout of side-striping (it did not cost much money to change these), meant that there was real novelty at the utilitarian end of a Land Rover showroom for 1991.

This, though, was only a start, for the Defender specification was to change significantly, and always for the better, throughout the 1990s, for example, the 1991 models had 107bhp (turbo-diesel) and 134bhp (V8) engines, while the 2001 models had 122bhp (turbo-diesel) and 182bhp (V8).

Since there were no exterior facelifts in the 1990s, I will now describe the changes, and improvements, as they arrived.

1992 Model

This was the point at which the choice of power units was simplified. At the start of the Defender's life, the old Ninety/One-Ten four-cylinder petrol, and normally aspirated diesel engines, had been listed as 'special order' options, but these had not attracted much business, and were therefore dropped completely at the beginning of the year.

For 1992, therefore, the Defender was only to be available with the 107bhp four-cylinder turbo-diesel, and the thirsty 134bhp $3\frac{1}{2}$ltr V8. This, though, was not a settled story, as Land Rover archivists were soon to find out.

Power-assisted steering (previously optional) became standard, while the more refined LT77S transmission (same ratios, but more refined in its

In the 1990s, as in every previous decade, a combination of short-wheelbase, diesel-engine and a hard-top body style was one of the most popular of all Land Rovers. This was an early example of the Tdi-engined Defender 90.

action, and with improved synchromesh) took over from the LT77. Yet another type of steering wheel style was standardised, and there were further trim changes.

NAS Defender 110

What looked like a very important marketing change then followed in August 1992, when the company made its first tentative steps towards re-introducing the Defender to the vast North American market. The classic Land Rover, in fact, had been absent since 1974 – eighteen long years – so the NAS (North American Specification) 110 model reappeared as a limited-edition machine.

As you might expect, a combination of American legislation and marketing imperatives meant that the new type was very different from what can be called a 'Rest of the World' Defender. There were two important marketing influences. One was that the Range Rover (introduced into the USA in 1987) had now made its own reputation among well-to-do 4×4 owners in North America, which meant that the NAS Defender had to match up to 'Big Brother'. Another (and this almost goes without saying) was that a new-type NAS Defender would have to fight tooth and nail against the firmly-established Jeep Wrangler: this was a model which, of course, had been North America's favourite 4×4 for a very long time.

Although there were obvious visual styling changes – inside and out – for this new type, the most significant technical advance was under the skin. In order to meet the very latest in North American exhaust emissions regulations, and to provide an appropriate level of performance, the NAS 110 was only to be sold with one version – a 182bhp, fuel-injected, 3.9ltr V8.

Although this was already a familiar engine package at Solihull (it was already found in the latest-model Range Rover), it signalled the very first time that a fuel-injected petrol engine had been used in the classic Land Rover chassis. It was not, of course, a peaky, sporty, engine tune, which therefore meant that the NAS 110 was an extremely capable machine in all conditions Even so, because the aerodynamic qualities of this body style were so awful, the top speed was still limited to 90mph or so.

All the limited-edition NAS 110s (only 510 were apparently built – all of them in 1992–3) were based on the specification of the County Station Wagon, all were painted in white (with black flexible wheelarches) and all of them had what was effectively an external roll cage, which was tightly wrapped around the outside of the estate car shell. The cage was needed so that the NAS 110 could meet North American roll-over legislation, so naturally Land Rover turned to the experts in this field – which was Safety Devices of Cambridgeshire. 'The difference,' Safety

When Land Rover re-introduced the Defender to the North American market, it started with this limited-edition 110 station wagon. For sale only in north America, this type was equipped with an all-embracing exterior roll cage.

Devices' proprietor Tony Fall once told me,' was that our normal cages for competition cars were normally fitted inside a body shell. But we were used to working to very tight tolerances, and the cages looked good.'

Helped along by the presence of this cage, a massive 'roo bar' at the front, and a tubular roof rack on top, the NAS 110 was a 4×4 with real presence. Inside the cabin, the seating was as plushy as any ever before found in a Defender, air-conditioning was standard, there was a specially-fitted-out facia/instrument panel, and there was also a radio/cassette unit in the centre console.

June 1993

In mid-season, it was time for two more Defender novelties and one re-introduction – the first being the standardization of rear-wheel disc brakes on all models, another being the re-introduction of the short-wheelbase seven-seater Station Wagon, the third being the launch of the 90SV 'fun' Land Rover.

The facia/instrument panel of the original North American Defender 110 Station Wagon was very different from that of other contemporary 110s. It included a radio/cassette unit, and addition instruments were standard.

The braking system, in fact, was thoroughly revised, for to match the arrival of rear discs, the front discs became the ventilated type on 110s and 'High Load Suspension' 90s too. Not only was the introduction of four-wheel discs a good selling point, but it also brought the Defender's chassis more in line with the increased performance and extra weight that had crept into the range in recent seasons. Land Rover also had an eye to its future, and the fact that performance was likely to improve even more in the later 1990s.

Apart from the better braking performance, and better resistance to fade, there was another, and perfectly practical, reason why rear disc brakes were an advance on drums. After a Defender had forded its way through deep water, the brakes became thoroughly soaked, and it always took time for the full braking performance to be restored. Drying out the braking surfaces and the friction materials was much swifter with discs and pads, than it ever was with drums and shoes.

The introduction of the 90SV (SV = special vehicles) was something of a surprise, as this was the very first occasion on which the company had begun to market the Land Rover as a 'fun' or 'life-style' vehicle. Because the typical target market was the younger 'let's have fun at the weekend' clientele in Britain, the 90SV was only sold in right-hand-drive form, and was never exported.

Developed from the 'Cariba' concept vehicle, which had originally been shown in 1987, the 90SV was based on the shorter-wheelbase Defender-type chassis (which meant that it had the latest, four-wheel disc-brake installation), with an open pick-up body style and was only supplied with the 200Tdi turbo-diesel engine. County-style front seats, a front bull bar and a different type of soft-top (with roll-up side and rear windows) were all in the standard specification.

Because it was supplied with a full roll cage (Safety Devices built these too), and was often sold with Discovery-type five-spoke alloy wheels as optional equipment, the 90SV was visually distinctive – yet it sold only slowly. The problem (and one that Land Rover found increasingly difficult to beat) was that it cost much more than smaller, less-capable, 4×4s like the Suzuki 4×4s of the day, and by 1995 it had almost ceased to exist.

NAS Defender 90

Only months after the arrival of the 90SV, the car that Land Rover engineers dubbed NAS90', but whose official title in North America was merely 'Defender 90', also made its bow. Originally

Although this Cariba concept on the Defender 90 chassis did not go into production in the same precise form, it was an inspiration for the 'life-style' image, which Land Rover sought for its products in the North American market of the 1990s.

This was a mid-1990s interpretation on a familiar Defender 90 theme, this type having the County Station Wagon specification, along with the 'Freestyle' alloy wheels which were optional extras. The wheels, of course, resembled those used on certain Discoveries of the period.

intended to be another limited-edition model, it went on to figure more strongly in the North American price lists until 1999.

Unlike the NAS Defender 110, however, the short wheelbase machine was an open-top pick-up, and was directly intended to attack the Jeep Wrangler on its own doorstep. A limited-edition, 500-off, Station Wagon type would be sold in 1995. It was logical that this new shorter-wheelbase type intended for sale in North America should have something in common with the limited-edition NAS Defender 110 and with the 90SV.

In what amounted to a 'mix-and-match' engineering exercise, the team put all the best technical features of the NAS Defender 110 into the shorter chassis, and standardized the 182bhp/3.9ltr V8 engine. A four-wheel disc-brake installation, five-spoke alloy wheels (and vast 265/75-16 BF Goodrich tyres), and (depending on the type of hood and weather equipment chosen) two different types of Safety Devices roll cages, were complemented by the use of anti-roll bars at front and rear. The list of optional extras was colossal (and included air-conditioning), and there was a new and striking list of body colours and trim options.

Sales in North America peaked at 2,501 in 1998 but, unhappily for Land Rover, Defender sales in the USA then had to cease in 1999: unhappily, the design came face to face with new legislation that required air bags to be fitted ahead of the driver and passenger. Getting the drivers' side air-bag installation through the legislation was straightforward enough (it had to be mounted in the hub of the steering wheel, which was a technique well-known to the engineers from earlier experience with Range Rovers and Discoveries), but it proved impractical to engineer a unique-to-this-market installation on the passenger's side.

Between 1994 and 1999, a total of 6,585 Defender 90s were sold in the USA.

BAe Out, BMW In

The next big change to affect the Defender was not technical, but financial. By the end of 1993 British Aerospace had tired of its stewardship of the Rover Group. On the one hand, its property-developing subsidiary, Arlington Securities, had made much money by demolishing worn-out old factory sites (such as the various Triumph complexes in Coventry, and the old 'Morris

Motors' factories at Cowley, near Oxford). On the other, BAe had never made much sense out of the sprawling problem represented by the car-building side of the Rover Group. Once its five-year ownership pledge to the British Government had been honoured, it was ready to sell up. On hearing this, BMW of Germany immediately expressed interest, while Rover's technical partner, Honda, suggested that it might increase its minority financial stake.

BMW, which had come to admire Solihull's 4×4s (it had no suitable 4×4 model of its own, and wanted to take the short-cut of buying expertise, rather than developing it), originally offered to buy Land Rover, thus leaving BAe with the private-car business on its own. However, because Land Rover was still making good profits (which were estimated at £100 million a year, at this time) and effectively propping up the private cars side, Rover chairman George Simpson found little attraction in that.

After several weeks of bluff-calling, and what a financial journalist once described as 'playing poker for multi-million stakes', BAe eventually secured a dream deal from the ambitious German concern. Not only was there to be a cash payment of £700 million, but BMW also took on board Rover's debt, and £700 million of off-balance sheet commitments.

In total, say financial journalists Chris Brady and Andrew Lorenz (their book about Rover, *End of the Road* is a real financial detective story), the offer was worth no less than £1.7 billion. At that moment, BMW thought it had secured a bargain, though as far as BAe was concerned, they had made good money out of a less than six-year control of the Rover Group.

The deal was done, and went public, in February 1994, but was not finally formalized until mid-March. And by then yet another series of major changes had been introduced for the seemingly ageless Defender.

March 1994

By this time, Land Rover was actively trying to build up the use of common 'building blocks' – in particular, engines and transmission – in all its models. This was never more dramatically illustrated than in 1994, when at one and the same time the Discovery, the Defender and the Range Rover were equipped with a revamped turbo-diesel engine (300Tdi) and a revised five-speed gearbox titled R380. The fact that this advance

---

BMW – the Predator

When BMW took control of the entire Rover Group in 1994, it was generally agreed that they found Land Rover the most attractive part of the business they had purchased. Not only was it the most profitable (or potentially so) segment, but it was also the activity from which they thought they could learn the most.

It now seems, in fact, that they always considered the Rover car business to be a problem, and that Land Rover was the jewel in the crown. In the six years that followed, BMW pumped huge amounts of investment capital into both sides of the business, but made sure that it was Land Rover that introduced three important new model ranges in four years: the second-generation Range Rover, the second-generation Discovery and the new Freelander. Before the sale (to Ford – see page 164) was agreed in 2000, BMW had also committed huge sums to the development of an all-new third-generation Range Rover, a car that would include much modern BMW technology.

BMW was so enthused by Land Rover that it made Solihull an important, high-tech centre, not only for producing more and more 4×4s, but also for producing steel pressings for the whole Group. At the same time, BMW had great ambitions for their own new 4×4 models (the X5 of 1999 being the first), and made sure that all available Solihull knowledge made the one-way journey to Munich.

While BMW was selling Land Rover to Ford in 2000, much project work that was already under way at Gaydon was swiftly removed (old hands talk about a 'five truck dawn raid'), so that Ford could not know anything that BMW did not want them to know!

Another season, another special edition – this being the Defender X-tech of 2000, with yet another style of special alloy wheels.

came immediately after BMW had taken control was purely coincidental. Major design/manufacturing projects like this take years, rather than weeks, to conclude – and both the new 300Tdi and R380 projects had been brewing for years under BAe control.

In summary, out went the 200Tdi turbo-diesel engine, to be replaced by the 300Tdi, and out went the LT77S five-speed gearbox, to be replaced by the R380 five-speeder.

This was not as dramatic a shake-up as it might first have appeared, for the new four-cylinder engine was the same size as before – 2,495cc – while the new transmission had all the same internal ratios, and step-down ratios, as before!

300Tdi Engine

According to the statistics of the new and old 2,495cc turbo-diesels – the new engine had extra four horsepower, and seven more lb. ft of torque – there was little to choose between the two power units. However, Land Rover pointed out that there were 208 new components – including a new cylinder head, pistons, con-rods, turbocharger, exhaust manifold and fuel injectors. This new package – it was coded 'Gemini 3' at the development stage – had evolved to provide much lower noise levels, to provide better diesel exhaust emissions performance, to make the units easier to manufacture and easier to service. Lower noise, perhaps, was not vital for the Defender, but it was most certainly important for use in the Discovery and Range Rover models of the period. Even so, this multi-million development programme was only destined to have a short life, for yet another turbo-diesel engine – the five-cylinder in-line unit fitted from late 1988 – would eventually replace it.

R380 Transmission

At the same time as the 300Tdi engine appeared, Land Rover also put a new five-speed transmission – coded R380 – into production. Once again, the specification sheets showed no obvious differences, for all the improvement came in the operation, the feel and the effectiveness of the new type.

In particular, this was a new, all-can-do, manual transmission intended to suit every existing (and immediately planned) 4×4 in Solihull's range. With a 4.6ltr/225bhp V8 engine already signed off for the new-generation Range Rover (which would appear later in 1994), the company needed a more robust five-speeder than the LT77S, which had served until then. Accordingly, an all-new all-synchromesh transmission, with a much increased maximum torque capacity of 278lb ft/380Nm, was designed. Not only was this stronger, but it had a much slicker and more precise shift action than before.

At the same time, synchromesh was added to reverse gear (this was a 'first' as far as Land Rover was concerned), and the 'gate' pattern was rearranged, the pattern on the gear-lever knob showing that it had a double-H layout, with reverse opposite fifth gear.

Thus rejuvenated, and with military sales continuing to prosper, Defender sales finally turned upwards again. Having slipped alarmingly to only 16,474 in 1992 (when the British home market was badly hit by a recession), with the aid of these new technical features, they rose to 21,091 in 1994 and rushed up to no fewer than 29,858 in 1996. The happiest times of the 1970s, perhaps, would never return (customers now had three different Solihull-built models from which to choose – and a fourth was on the way in 1997), but that near-30,000 figure was the best seen by any classic Land Rover for over a decade.

Td5 – a New Five-Cylinder Diesel

At the end of 1998, the arrival of yet another engine for the Defender – an all-new five-cylinder diesel – came as a surprise. Although this had the same cubic capacity as the older 300Tdi (2,495cc), it was different in every way. Related rather closely to the Rover four-cylinder L-Series diesel of the new Freelander, and also used in the new-generation Discovery II, it represented another real advance for the defender. No sooner had the new Td5 been launched in the Defender, than the four-cylinder 300Tdi was dropped from European-specification cars, though it remained available for other, non-USA, markets.

Because this engine was specifically developed for use in the second-generation Discovery, it is described more fully in the analysis of that model in Chapter 7 . At this stage, it only needs to be emphasized that the new engine was a snug, but still comfortable, fit into the Defender's engine bay, that it was smoother and more fuel-efficient than the older 300Tdi variety (road tests proved this) and that it became the cornerstone of the early twenty-first century Defender product line (see table p109 for comparison).

Defender for the 2000s

By the dawn of the new century, the Defender was looking distinctly venerable, yet demand was

The 127in. chassis was so much longer that it offered many new opportunities for special bodies to be added. This example was equipped with a 'truckman top'.

By the early 2000s, the Defender's facia/instrument display was looking very different from that first seen in the Ninety and One-Ten type of the mid-1980s. Air conditioning, no less, features in this 2002 display.

Comparison Between the New Td5 and the Older 300Tdi Engines

	New Td5	300Tdi
	Five-cylinder	Four-cylinder
	Turbo-diesel	Turbo-diesel
	2,495cc	2,495cc
Peak power (bhp/rpm)	122/4200	111/4000
Peak torque (lb ft/rpm)	221/1950	122/4200

still robust. The latest model, of course, was already very different from the original of 1989–90, and much more advanced than the original Ninety/One-Ten types of the mid-1980s, yet its character, and certainly its heritage, could still be related, directly, to the first-ever Land Rovers of the late-1940s.

Changes, though, continued to come through. Even while this book was being written, the latest Land Rover Defender novelties included central door-locking (standard on County types, optional on others), electric front-window lifts and the option of four-channel ABS braking, along with new colour/trim specifications. Assembly in the famous old South Works at Solihull went ahead, as for so many years, on a line alongside that of the latest Discovery and – from 2001–2 – that of the brand-new third-generation Range Rover.

Even so, the layout of that assembly line, and the way that this 4×4 came together, was in great contrast to its neighbours. Whereas Discovery and Range Rover bodies arrived, complete and ready painted, from the vast paint-shop in the middle of the complex, painted Defender shells still arrived as a series of sub-assemblies, supported on rather basic-looking transfer pallets, to be bolted together by the workforce at this point. The difference of assembly line pace, too, was remarkable: up to 2,000 Freelanders were being hustled through, every week, compared with about 600 Defenders.

Even so, neither BMW (which controlled Land Rover up to early 2000) nor Ford (which took over at that point) seemed to be in any hurry to produce another brand-new model. Early in 2002 – and immediately after the new-type Range Rover had gone into production – chairman Bob Dover announced that a new-generation Discovery would be next in line at Solihull. Certainly, on my most recent visit to Solihull, major construction was going ahead to prepare for this.

Then there were rumours of a 'baby-Land Rover' to follow, while all manner of 'sneak-preview' drawings kept on turning up in the motoring magazines.

Not that anyone had doubts about the future of the classic Land Rover. A new type, for sure, would follow, one day, and I only have to remember what the company stated, many years ago, before the Series II was introduced: 'When better Land Rovers are made, the Rover company will make them.'

6 Discovery – With Thanks to the Range Rover

So far in this book, the emphasis has been on the ever-evolving 4×4s, which started Land Rover on its way to fame in the late 1940s, and which still took up most of the space, and much of the limelight, at Solihull in the 1980s. The Range Rover, an entirely different type of 4×4, was launched in 1970 and was always a much larger, more costly and more up-market machine than the Series III or Ninety/One-Ten models. Not only that – the Range Rover was only being built as a fully-trimmed estate car.

The very first Range Rover prototype took to the road in 1967. More than twenty years later, the same 4×4 would be the inspiration behind the Discovery.

Then, quite suddenly, it seems, the company decided to evolve a third range of 4×4s – the Discovery. Designed at high speed, it developed very rapidly indeed and was on sale from the end of 1989. It instantly provided a suitable mid-range model in Land Rover's range.

This was not a project that had been brewing at Solihull for many patient years, for new models do not always appear as a result of years of patient market research. The launch of the Discovery is a classic case. If the Range Rover had not already existed, the Discovery might never have been developed. Further, if the Range Rover had not moved steadily up market

Road Rover

Before the Range Rover, there was Road Rover, this really being a logical 1950s development of the Land Rover theme, though originally conceived around the Rover P4 private car chassis. It must be mentioned here as one of a series of might-have-beens. First formally noted in company records in 1952, a car called 'Road Rover' might have gone on sale from time to time during that decade but, somehow, the sales staff could never warm to it. One reason, no doubt, was that it was difficult to categorize such cars. The Road Rover, in effect, was always intended to be a large estate car built on an existing private-car chassis frame. In modern terms, therefore, it would have been ideal for the school run, but virtually useless for off-road motoring. The last of several prototypes used the latest in 2,286cc Land Rover engines, with rear wheel drive (not four-wheel-drive) and with a large three-door estate car style.

In the 1950s, the Road Rover was one of the company's rather half-hearted projects. Does it count, today, as an ancestor of the Discovery?

during the 1980s, there would probably not have been a sizeable marketing slot for the Discovery to occupy.

Earlier chapters have already described how the original Land Rover pedigree was developed towards maturity, and how management had gradually closed down all the ancient fabric of its satellite factories, henceforth concentrating almost every Land Rover activity into the Solihull site. During the 1980s, not only were twelve old West Midlands factories closed down, but huge investment (by British Leyland standards) was being poured into Solihull.

By the early 1980s, and deliberately planned that way, a larger and larger marketing gap opened up between the 'classic' Land Rovers – the Ninety and One-Ten types – and the Range Rovers, and the chance eventually came to plug that gap. Central to the specification of a new model was that it should be an estate car (like the Range Rover), rather than an all-can-do range like the Ninety/One-Ten, which was being assembled in a multitude of styles.

Above *When the Range Rover arrived in 1970, it was a completely new type of 4×4 from Rover. The Discovery which followed in 1989 was really the same successful mixture of running gear, and driving character, hidden under a new body shell.*

Below *This was the chassis layout of the original Range Rover of 1970. The same chassis, suspension, 3.5ltr V8 engine, and four-wheel-drive transmission would be used under the original Discovery of 1989.*

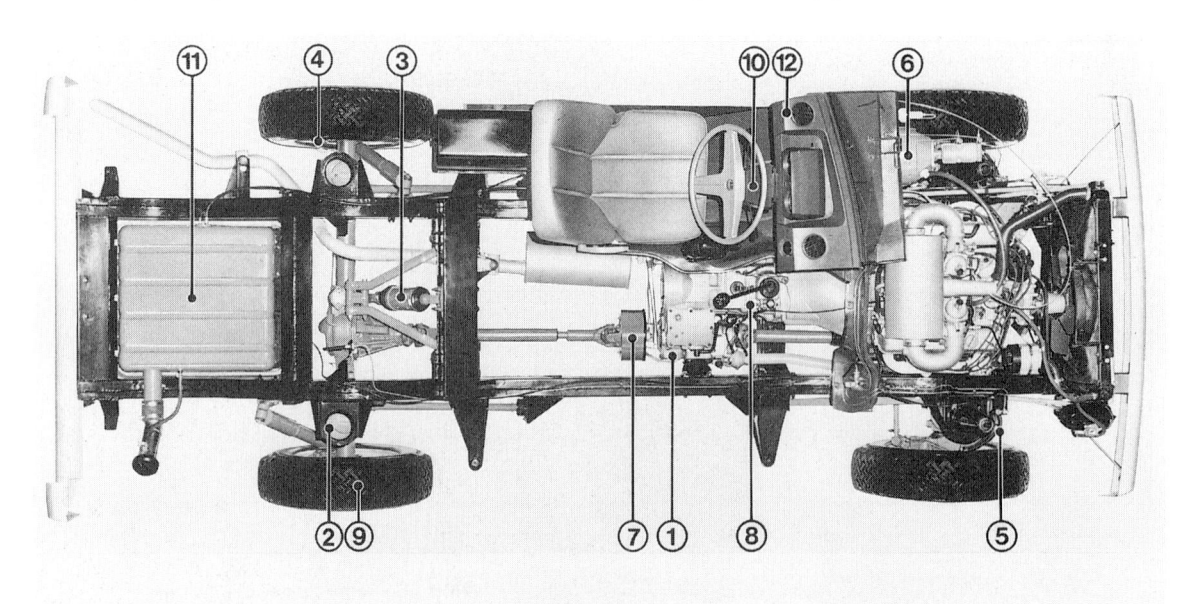

RANGE ROVER

1. Third differential unit
2. Coil springs with beam axles
3. Self levelling unit
4. Disc brakes all round
5. Tandem brake pipes
6. Brake servo
7. Transmission parking brake
8. Four speed all synchro. gearbox
9. Radial ply tyres
10. Collapsible steering column
11. 19 gallon fuel tank
12. Impact absorbing fascia

Discovery – With Thanks to the Range Rover

Maybe the time to actually make the effort was not ripe in the early 1980s, but the intention was always, eventually, to take the opportunity. Paper studies ('Paper is cheap, metal-cutting is expensive' is one famous, eternally true, motor industry saying) began in 1985, resulting in what became known as the 'Gilroy Review' (Tony Gilroy was Land Rover's managing director at this time). This paper covered an 'interim model strategy', and surveyed ways of producing a gap-filling 4×4, which would connect the Ninety/One-Ten and Range Rover ranges, yet which could save a fair fortune on investment by picking up major mechanical parts from one or other of those ranges. One impetus came from the success of cars like the new Mitsubishi Pajero/Shogun and the Isuzu Trooper.

In 1986, though, the brutal fact was that Land Rover was not profitable enough to invest in a totally new model range, so anything chosen as an 'interim model' would have to cut corners, to mix-and-match, in many ways. Maybe this was not the ideal way to tackle the burgeoning Japanese competition, but there was no obvious alternative.

Even before serious engineering and styling work got under way in 1986–7, the company had to make a choice. As a basis for the new model, three existing chassis frame designs were already available. All of them sharing the same type of beam axle and coil spring suspension at front and rear: the Ninety (with its wheelbase of 92.9in/2,360mm, the One-Ten (110in/2,794mm) or the rather different Range Rover (100in/2,540mm). In the end it was the need for a suitable wheelbase (and, therefore, suitable cabin package) that made the choice of the Range Rover's frame inevitable. Worries about the unit cost of chassis frame were soon allayed when it became clear that a spread of fixed cost/overhead expenses over many more units every year would reduce those considerably.

The 'Jay' project (which would, eventually, come to market as the original Discovery) was set up at the end of 1986, though the first full-size clay models had already been completed in the

During 1986 several full-size clay models were made of the 'Jay' project. This particular offering was differently shaped on each side – note the stepped roof panel on the left side, the sloping roof on the right. This sort of 'either or' process is normal in the evolution of modern automotive shapes.

Styling Department before then. No matter what the choice of engines would be, or what would be decided for the cabin specification, the basic mechanical layout was already set in stone – and it would revolve around the existing box-section 100in/2,540mm wheelbase frame of the Range Rover. This meant that much of the company's existing running gear, with a great deal of juggling of 'building blocks' from the Solihull 'parts bin', could be used underneath the skin. It also meant that most of the capital expenditure could be confined to a new body shell, and the furnishing of the cabin.

Marketing Opportunity

But if 'Jay' was to use a Range Rover frame and suspension components, industry cynics suggested that surely this meant that it would never be other than a cheaper and rather down-market Range Rover? Land Rover's marketing team was adamant that it should not, and made every effort to distance one type from the other. When the Discovery was launched in 1989, commercial director Chris Woodwark reinforced the point in this way:

> Discovery is the most important launch for Land Rover since 1970, when we introduced the Range Rover. It sits squarely between Land Rover and Range Rover, and is aimed directly at certain competitors. For the first time, it gives us an opportunity to compete with Japan.
>
> It is a leisure vehicle, not aimed at the luxury sector at all. Discovery, if you like, is for Yuppies, and Range Rover is for people who've already made it.
>
> The first thing that will sell Discovery is the Land Rover badge. Secondly, it rides and handles just like a Range Rover – I don't expect Discovery owners to do much off-roading, but the capability is there.

That, in fact, was only part of the truth, for once launched, the Discovery eroded the Range Rover market significantly. The fact that Range Rover production fell from 28,513 in 1989 (pre-Discovery) to just 16,408 in 1991 tells its own story.

However, by the time that serious work began, Land Rover's management had already decided on the sort of 4×4 they wanted to develop. Not only was 'Jay' to be an archetypal Isuzu Trooper/Mitsubishi Shogun competitor, but it also had to fit into a very specific band of prices.

At the time the 'Jay' project got under way, there was a considerable, and ever-widening, gap between the 'classic' Land Rover, and the range Rover types. The existing range of UK retail prices at Solihull by the time the basic specification of 'Jay' was settled, in mid-1987 is shown in the table.

The Range of UK Retail Prices at Solihull	
Model Range	UK Retail Prices (£)
Ninety	11,361–11,764
One-Ten	12,337–12,741
Range Rover	18,253–20,183

This left an enticing gap of £5,512 between the top-of-the-range One-Ten station wagon, and the 'entry level' Range Rover, one that was ripe to be filled by a new 'interim model'. To give an idea of current price levels at this time: for £5,512 one could buy a Rover Metro.

Even so, for the next two years, at least, Land Rover's marketing department had to grit their teeth and wait – for there is nothing more frustrating than a gap that cannot be filled with a suitable model, and would take that long to get the new project ready for sale.

Style and Layout

At this point, I feel that I should now abandon further references to the 'Jay' project, and start calling this car by its proper name – Discovery. The name, like all those applied to modern motor vehicles, had taken some time to choose. Land Rover apparently started with a massive list of no fewer than 842 titles, rapidly whittled these down to a mere 15, checked out the trade mark

Above *Between 1986 and 1989, when most of the original design and development took place, the Discovery was always known as 'Project Jay'. Here is the team which was mainly responsible for that successful work.*

Below *The first Discovery models, announced in 1989, were only available in this three-door body style, though a five-door style was already on the way.*

> **Discovery – the Marketplace**
>
> Land Rover were very clever in developing the Discovery, a 4×4 based on Range Rover running gear, but with a different body shell, and much cheaper prices. Comparative prices when it went on sale at the end of 1989, are:
>
> | | |
> |---|---|
> | Isuzu Trooper | From £11,999 |
> | Land Rover Discovery | From £15,750 |
> | Mitsubishi Shogun | From £15,469 |
> | Nissan Patrol | From £13,590 |
> | Toyota Landcruiser | From £16,521 |
>
> The Shogun and the Landcruiser were the most significant rivals.

situation (if a name has already been registered by a rival, it cannot be used without a lot of legal huffing and puffing), and finally settled on the name of 'Discovery'.

Interestingly enough, I have searched my memory banks, and dug back into my library, and I do not recall finding this model name ever having being previously used on any type of motor vehicle. Presumably by chance, therefore, Land Rover found themselves acting as world pioneers yet again.

The Discovery set out to be completely different from the classic Land Rover (soon to be re-labelled 'Defender', of course), for it shared few important components with that machine and would have a totally different style. On the other hand, although it was based on the Range Rover's architecture in so many ways – the chassis frame, the suspension, front and rear axle and four-wheel disc brakes were all instantly recognizable – the team made every effort to spell out the differences, functionally and decoratively.

The original Discovery had an all-new body shell, with some aluminium panels, but a mainly steel inner structure. Although the basic proportions were rather like those of the Range Rover, this was a unique machine, for a special purpose.

Above *On the original-specification Discovery, the facia/instrument layout was noticeably rounded and somehow more 'car-like' than expected. Wall-to-wall fresh air vents are obvious – Land Rover clearly wanted its Discovery customers to stay cool.*

Right *This was the interior/driving position/instrument package layout of the original Discovery, showing the well-padded interior, and colour co-ordination inspired by Conran Design.*

And what no-one was willing to spell at out, at that time, was that these differences were about to widen still more, as the Range Rover was about to pushed further up-market in the early 1990s, not only with a longer wheelbase, but with air suspension, and many other technically advances.

Although it retained the same general proportions as the existing Range Rover – because of the use of the same rolling chassis, and the same type of seating package, this was inevitable – the Discovery's body style itself was fresh, in an altogether more rounded style, though with rectangular headlamps and a different style of road wheels. To reduce costs as far as possible, the design of the headlamps was lifted from that of the Freight Rover Sherpa van, and the tail lamp clusters from the Austin Maestro van.

Although it was only to be offered as a three-door type at first (two passenger doors, and the rear, side-opening, door), a five-door style would follow just one year into the life of the new model. This was done without altering the length, or even the proportion, of the car's original body outline. The interior style, choice of furnishing fabrics and colours, was completed with the aid of Conran Design, and featured some rather chi-chi pastel shades with easy-to-clean surfaces. All this was much less utilitarian than that of a One-Ten (soon: Defender), and rather less plushy than the 'gentleman's-club' ambience of the Range Rover.

Except that some inner panels were shared with the Range Rover, the Discovery's body shell was totally new. Although the roof panel itself was in pressed steel, much of the shell was in pressed aluminium. The style itself featured a raised rear-roof panel with extra glass – the Discovery being nearly six inches taller than the Range Rover, which made it just that important bit less convenient for parking in enclosed spaces or (for instance) for loading on to Channel Tunnel trains! Right from the start there was to be a long and impressive list of more than fifty 'lifestyle'

This was the original Discovery centre console/radio installation/transmission lever layout.

Land Rover Discovery (1989–98)

Layout
Ladder-style chassis frame, with steel/aluminium estate car body style. Three-doors or five-doors, or two-door 'commercial' style. Front engine/four-wheel-drive.

Engines
1993–98 (four-cylinder, petrol)
Capacity   1,994cc
Bore and stroke   84.45 × 88.9mm
Valves   Twin overhead camshafts
Compression ratio   10.0:1
Fuel injection   Lucas
Max power   134bhp @ 6,000rpm
Max torque   137lb ft @ 2,500rpm

Four-cylinder, diesel
Capacity   2,495cc
Bore and stroke   90.47 × 97mm
Valves   Overhead valves
Compression ratio   19.5:1
Fuel injection   Bosch and turbocharger
Max power   111bhp @ 4,000rpm (120bhp with automatic transmission)
Max torque   195lb ft @ 1,800rpm (221lb ft at 2,000rpm with automatic transmission)

1989–90 (V8-cylinder, petrol)
Capacity   3,528cc
Bore and stroke   88.9 × 71.1mm
Valves   Overhead valves
Compression ratio   8.1:1
Carburettor   Two SU
Max power   145bhp @ 5,200rpm
Max torque   192lb ft @ 2,800rpm

1990–93 (V8-cylinder, petrol)
Capacity   3,528cc
Bore and stroke   88.9 × 71.1mm
Valves   Overhead valves
Compression ratio   9.4:1
Fuel injection   Lucas
Max power   164bhp @ 4,750rpm
Max torque   212lb ft @ 2,600rpm

1993–98 (V8-cylinder, petrol)
Capacity   3,947cc
Bore and stroke   94 × 71.1mm
Valves   Overhead valves
Compression ratio   9.35:1
Fuel injection   Lucas
Max power   182bhp @ 4,750rpm
Max torque   230lb ft @ 3,100rpm

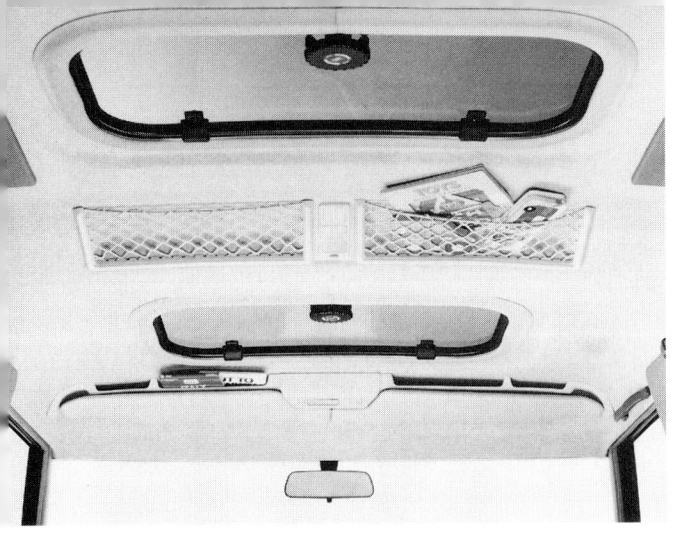

Above *Land Rover immediately developed many optional extras and accessories for the Discovery. Twin removable glass sun-roof panels were optional extras on the original Discovery, though nets for holding maps were standard.*

Right *With a fishing rod and net artistically laid out on the rear load floor, the option of a dog guard, and the option of extra, inward-facing, sixth and seventh seats are both clear.*

Transmission

Type	Permanent four-wheel-drive, with choice of high or low range
Gearbox	Five-speed manual gearbox, synchromesh on all forward gears
Clutch	Single dry plate, diaphragm spring
Ratios	(High range)
	Top 3.33
	4th 4.32
	3rd 6.04
	2nd 9.22
	1st 14.36
	Reverse 14.82
	High range step-down ratio 1.222:1 (1.41:1 with four-cylinder 1,994cc)
	Low-range step-down ratio 3.321:1 (3.76:1 with four-cylinder 1,994cc)
Final drive ratio	3.538:1

From 1992, V8s; from 1993, turbo-diesels ZF four-speed automatic transmission available as an option, with same final drive ratios

Suspension and steering

Front	Live axle, coil springs, radius arms, Panhard rod, telescopic dampers; anti-roll bar from March 1994
Rear	Live axle, coil springs, self-levelling strut, radius arms, A-bracket, telescopic dampers; anti-roll bar from March 1994
Steering	Recirculating ball (power assisted)
Tyres	205R-16 radial-ply
Wheels	Steel disc, five-bolt-on fixing

Brakes

Type	Disc brakes at front, disc brakes at rear, hydraulically operated with vacuum servo assistance; ABS anti-lock from March 1994
Size	11.8in. front discs, 11.4in. rear discs

Dimensions (in/mm)

Track	Front and rear 51.5/1,486
Wheelbase	100/2,540
Overall length	178/4,521
Overall width	70.6/1793
Overall height	75.6/1920
Unladen weight	From 4,551lb/2,064kg

accessories — these included air-conditioning (V8-engined cars only, at first), luxury trim/electric window lift packs, bull bars, ski racks and winches.

Chassis and Driveline

The use of a lightly-modified Range Rover rolling chassis, complete with its axles, its 16in wheels and its long-travel coil-spring suspension, has already been mentioned. Almost automatically, this ensured that the Discovery would have the same lolloping, high-roll on-road handling characteristics, and the same high-clearance, go-anywhere capability on loose, rough or other low-grip surfaces.

To bridge the gap between One-Ten/Defender and Range Rover, the company decided to equip the new Discovery with a choice of petrol and diesel engines, the petrol option being yet another version of the ubiquitous light-alloy V8, while the diesel alternative was a brand-new 200Tdi (turbo-charged, direct-injection, intercooled) four-cylinder design:

Because of the Discovery's considerable weight and bulk, the company needed a more capable diesel power unit than ever before. The 200Tdi was a new-generation 2,495cc compression ignition engine, and although I have already mentioned it in Chapter 5 (in connection with the development of the Defender types), it made its world debut in the Discovery in September 1989.

Although it retained the same four-cylinder layout, bore, stroke and general architecture of the earlier Land Rover's turbo-diesel, the 'Gemini' project was quite fresh. Not only did it have a new aluminium cylinder head and a belt-driven

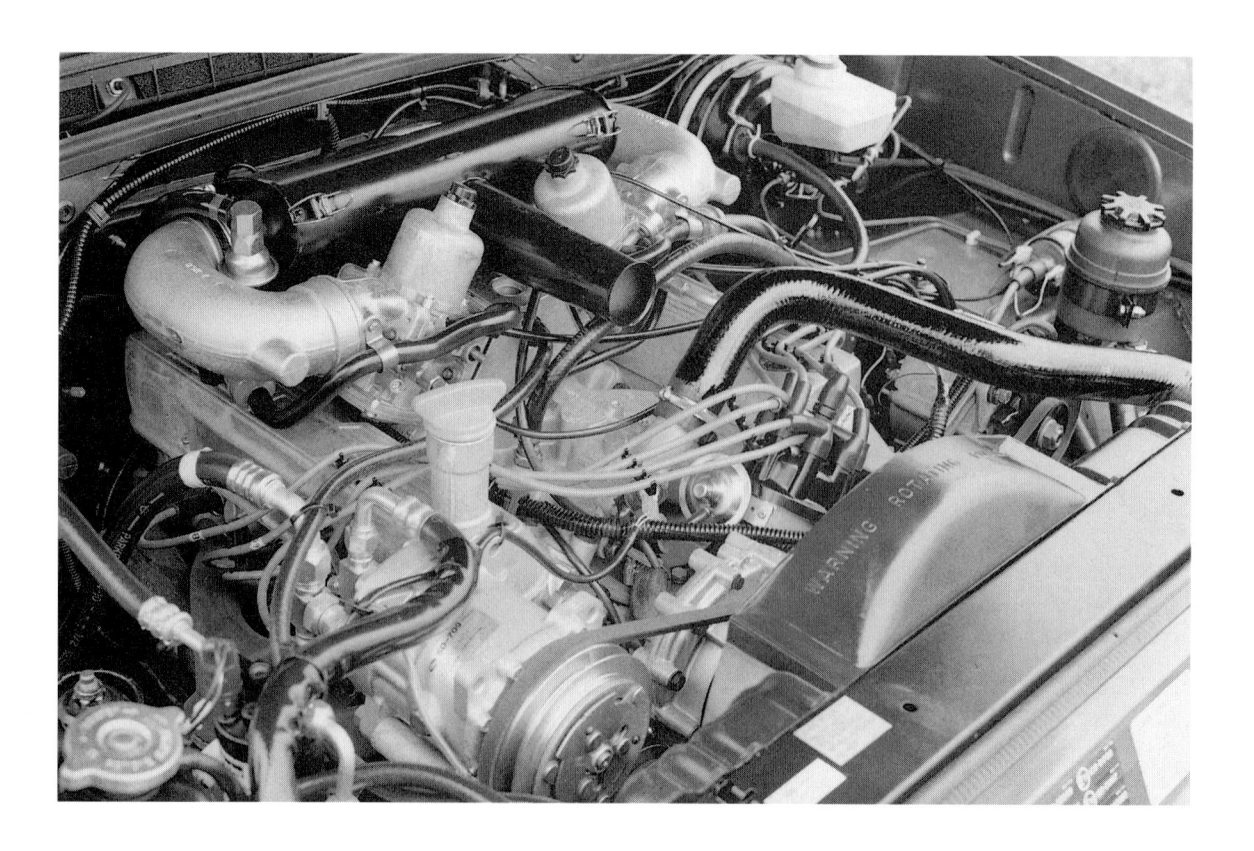

The Discovery has always been available with petrol and diesel engines. The first types had this twin-SU carburettor V8 power unit.

Diesel power for the original Discovery was provided by the newly-developed 'Gemini' power unit, which was officially called the 200Tdi engine. Because of its excellent torque, its 111bhp power output, and is well-proven fuel economy, it soon became the best-selling Discovery engine.

camshaft, but it also featured direct (i.e. straight into the combustion chamber, rather than into an ante-chamber) fuel injection by AVL/Bosch.

With the additional feature of an air-air intercooler (an air-cooled radiator that would lower the temperature of the pressurised air as it made its way from the turbo-charger to the inlet manifold), the designers not only aimed for more than 100bhp, but they also looked for a 15 per cent improvement in fuel consumption too.

With much development carried out at AVL in Graz, Austria, and with the clock always ticking ahead of an ambitious timetable, the 'Gemini' programme involved much liaison between companies and countries, but the result was a triumph. As released for use in the Discovery, the new turbo-diesel was no less than 26 per cent more powerful than its predecessor, and had 25 per more torque – but was exactly the same size – 2½ltr (see table).

Although the press and the pundits (none of whom, one presumes, had to pay for their own fuel!) were more impressed by the V8 petrol engine, there was no doubt that this was an extremely significant power unit, and one that had a considerable future at Solihull.

The V8 originally fitted to the Discovery, on the other hand, was positively familiar, for it was an evolution of the two-SU-carburettor 3,528cc power unit, which had powered the Range

Comparison Between the Gemini and Original Turbo-Diesel Engines

Feature	Discovery 'Gemini' turbo-diesel (2,495cc)	Original Turbo-diesel (2,495cc)
Peak power (bhp/rpm)	111/4,000	85/4,000
Peak torque (lb ft/rpm)	195/1,800	150/1,800

Rover for so many years (though the up-market Range Rover had featured a fuel-injected derivative since 1985, and a 3,947cc size since 1988 – these being two ways of further differentiating the two big 4×4 ranges). For the Discovery, it was still a low compression (8.1:1) type, which developed 145bhp at 5,200rpm.

Discovery on Sale

Although Land Rover needed to set up new, and separate, assembly facilities for the Discovery within the South Block, the job was complete by the time the new model was launched. Assembly built up rapidly during the winter of 1989–90, with an initial target of 300 vehicles a week soon being exceeded. After 3,296 cars had been produced in the last months of 1989, no fewer than 23,067 flowed out of Solihull in 1990. After a slight dip in 1991 (this was due to a fall in demand due to the British economic slowdown), production then soared to new heights, and would breach the 50,000/year barrier in 1994.

One reason for this, undoubtedly, was because of the Discovery's very keen pricing. Here was a massively built, serene-riding, 4×4 with all the technical capability of the Range Rover, and very similar performance, but available at much lower prices. In the autumn of 1989, there was a very telling comparison. Whereas Range Rover prices started at £23,784, the entry level Discovery sold for only £15,750. That difference (£8,034) effectively meant that a Discovery was available at a 33 per cent discount on the Range Rover. By any standards, this was astonishing, and it surely explains why demand for the Discovery took off at such a rate.

It was a very capable machine too. Soon after its launch, *Autocar & Motor* compared a diesel-engined Discovery Tdi against its obvious rivals, the Isuzu Trooper and the Mitsubishi Shogun, and concluded that:

> Faster, more economical, better-riding and with the extra traction and balance of permanent 4WD, Discovery has the measure of its rivals. The cleverly designed and well-executed interior is way ahead of the opposition and it has a clear advantage should anyone actually venture off-road.
>
> It has been a long time coming but, with the Discovery, Land Rover shows just how good a 'recreational' off-roader can be. With the right build quality, this new champion of Britain's motor industry is good enough to send the Japanese back to the drawing board.

All this for a machine whose new-generation Tdi engine offered 24mpg (try achieving that from a Range Rover of the period), and which was equally as rapid as all its rivals.

The same test also fell heavily for the capability, handling and packaging, of the the Discovery too:

> Off-road, the pedigree of the Discovery's chassis and drive-train outclasses the Japanese by a large margin. The ride is superb – long travel, supple and well-controlled wheel movement with fine articulation keeping all four wheels on the ground for more of the time, providing usefully superior grip. A lower ratio transfer box allows better engine braking down steep descents .... All in all, a convincing win, on or off the road, for the British newcomer.
>
> Despite its size, the [Isuzu] trooper has only just enough rearward seat travel for 6-foot-plus drivers, while the Discovery has room to spare .... For interior stowage, the Discovery wins hands down. As well as bins in all three doors, dash, either side of the rear seat and between the front seats, there are pockets for maps above the sun vizor, stowage nets in the stepped roof section at the rear and pouches on the back of the front seats.

The most chilling remark, however, came a little later:

> With alloy panels, the Discovery still has the generous panel gaps that characterise the Range Rover, and its paint finish is not as smooth as the Shogun's. How the test car's light blue interior will stand up to muddy wellies has yet to be seen, though rubber mats and waterproof seat covers are available.

It was in this rather nebulous area, of what the marketing gurus might call 'perceived quality', that the original Discovery always found itself with a problem. This was, in fact, one of the first areas addressed by BMW in the mid-1990s, for by this time there was a very well-known, and oft-quoted quip in the motor trade:

> Question: What are the two man-made structures visible from outer space?
> Answer: The Great Wall of China, and the shut lines on the Discovery.

That irreverent motoring writer, Jeremy Clarkson, once wrote that it was so kind of Land Rover designers, to arrange for Discovery panel gaps to be so wide that one could get in and out of the cabin without opening the doors.

Land Rover bosses got used to such quips, learned to smile through gritted teeth and carried on making as many Discoveries as possible. In the early days, of course, they knew, even if we did not, that a whole raft of improvements, additions and modifications were planned for this model.

The first Discoveries, after all, had been specifically equipped to be as different as possible from the Range Rover — three-door instead of five-door, carburetted V8 engine instead of fuel injection and no automatic transmission option — and it was only in future years that the differences could be eroded. Management all hoped — and experience tells us that they were right — that this was the correct strategy to unfold. Now let's consider how the Discovery changed during the 1990s.

September 1990

Only a year after the new model had gone on sale, there were two major improvements. The five-door model, which Land Rover staff had steadfastly refused even to discuss when the original three-door had been launched, duly appeared (henceforth, three-door and five door types were available), while the original carburettor-equipped V8 was cast into the spare parts bin in favour of a 164bhp fuel-injected type.

Anyone with experience of styling, product planning and body pressing technology (and there were many of those in the media) had taken one look at the panel layout of the original three-door Discovery, and realized that a five-door type could, and would, be added in due course. And so it was, for with no change to the general proportions, to the front doors, or even to the rear quarter windows, the extra pair of doors slotted smoothly into their destined place.

Adding a fuel-injection installation to the V8 engine was also an inevitable change, for by this time the same basic type of Lucas injection had been added to the Range Rover model, and to V8 engines supplied to companies like Morgan and TVR. At a stroke, the Discovery moved up

The five-door Discovery appeared in 1990, just a year after the original three-door types had been launched.

Above *The first fuel-injected V8 for the Discovery was introduced at the start of the 1991 model year: in many ways this was same as a more powerful V8 being fitted to contemporary Range Rovers.*

Below *The fuel-injected V8 fitted to Discovery models from late 1990 was a big, yet surprisingly light, piece of machinery. The aluminium inlet manifold above the engine hid a series of individual inlet trumpets, one to each cylinder. The fuel injectors were positioned in the manifold, immediately upstream of the inlet valves.*

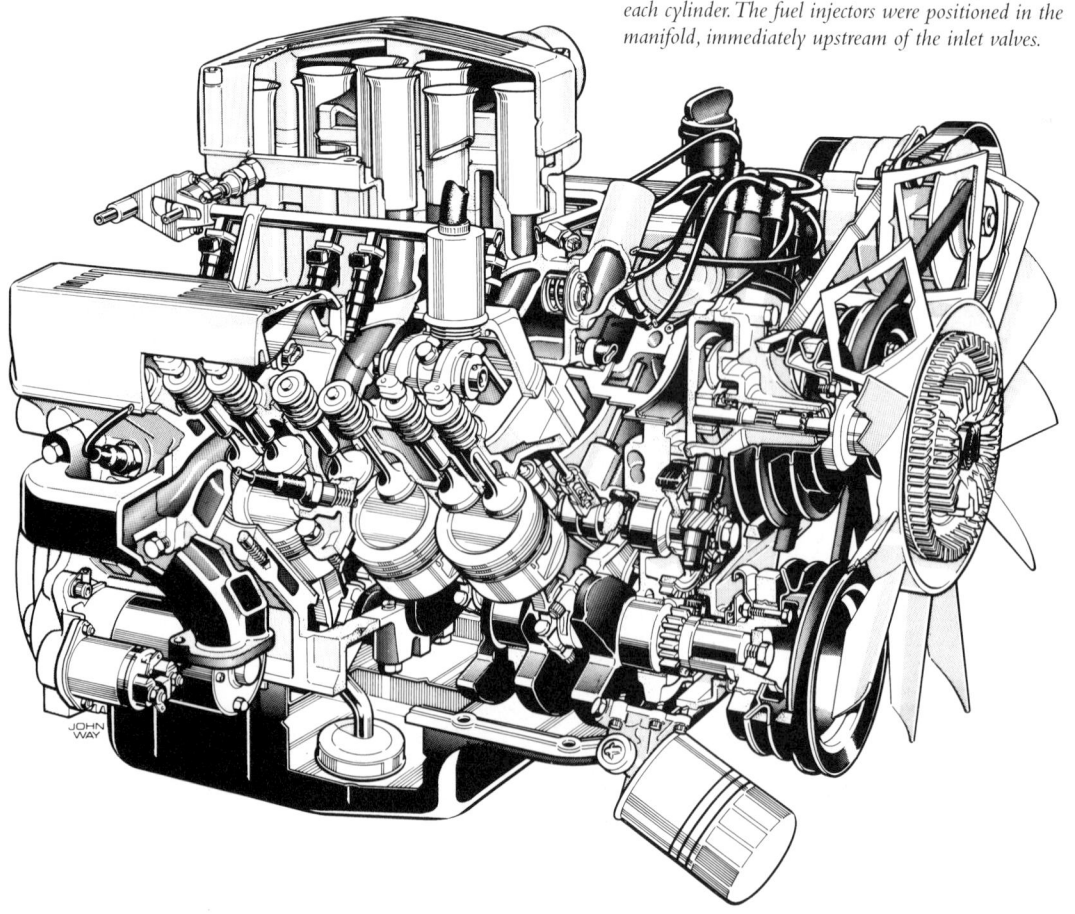

from a 145bhp to a 164bhp machine – and its top speed moved up from the original 97mph to a more publicity-worthy 105mph. The bad news, though, was the price also rushed up – to no less than £20,750.

The product planners, incidentally, had made sure that the Range Rover was still one jump ahead, for at this time it was already equipped with a 185bhp/3,947cc version of the same power unit. In due course, the policy appeared to be that the Range Rover would be the first Solihull 4×4 to gain any technology advancing novelties, and that the Discovery would eventually follow suit.

At this time, incidentally, a catalytic converter became available as an optional fitment for V8-engined cars, though demand was low at first.

Alloy wheels were added to the list of line-fitted options, and power-sapping air conditioning also became optional on diesel-engined types.

Demand rose further, production soon passed 500 vehicles a week, and by the end of 1992 it would sometimes reach 700 a week. Within three years, in other words, the Discovery had become Solihull's most popular 4×4, easily outstripping the combined production of Defender and Range Rover types. More than seven out of ten Discoveries were being sent overseas.

For many years, Land Rover supported the running the extremely demanding Camel Trophy. In 1991 this fleet of thirty-six vehicles, most of them Discovery Tdis, took part in the event, which was held in East Africa.

Because it was so much faster, and more capacious, than the Defender, the Discovery was ideal for use by the world's security forces.

September 1992

At the start-up of the 1993 model year, Land Rover then made automatic transmission available on the Discovery. This was the well-known and well-liked four-speeder from ZF of Germany, a transmission that had already been optional in the Range Rover since the end of 1985.

By almost any standards, of course, the ZF four-speeder was the standard-setter for all other automatic transmission manufacturers to match, this being a transmission family that was suitable for use in many vehicles. In due course, the four-speeder would give way to an even more capable five-speeder. Once again, there seemed to be an element of careful 'product planning' in this introduction, for whereas the ZF automatic was linked to a modern chain-driven transfer box in the Range Rover, in the Discovery it was still linked to the older, and less sophisticated, gear-driven LT230 type.

As an aside, when BMW arrived in control of Solihull in 1994, the fact that Land Rover had settled on the use of the ZF automatic was a source of great joy, as ZF and BMW had been seemingly 'joined at the hip' for many years. As far as Solihull was concerned, this was a very successful piece of kit, which sold very well in the company's modern 4×4s.

April 1993

Only a few months later, there was a surprise announcement, when the Discovery was suddenly made available with a third engine choice – the high-revving 134bhp/2.0ltr Rover T16 four-cylinder power unit, known in this application as the Mpi.

At first it was difficult to see how, and why, this engine was added to the range, for its character was totally different from that of the other engines in the line-up. The V8 and turbo-diesel power units were both tuned and presented as high-torque, low-revving sluggers, but here was an engine more often found in Rover saloons, such as the 220GTi coupe and the 820i saloon.

Land Rover, in fact, had found that they needed a 'tax-break' engine for use in certain markets where the tax laws favoured engines of less than 2,000cc: Italy, an important market for Land Rover, was a prime example. The choice of engine virtually made itself – Land Rover was a part of the Rover Group, and it needed at least 130bhp for such an engine to provide the Discovery with competitive performance. Here was such an engine, which was already in use in Rover products and manufactured at Rover's vast Longbridge factory: The T16 facility was not then working at full capacity, and any engines supplied to Land Rover would provide a real financial bonus.

The T16 was normally an 'east–west' engine (in other words, transversely mounted, for use in front-wheel-drive cars), which would have to be slightly-re-engineered for fitment in the Discovery's in-line installation. This was a straightforward conversion job, though even a re-tune could do little about the engine's disappointing low-speed torque delivery characteristics.

Although this 2ltr petrol-engined Discovery was significantly more powerful than the turbo-diesel – 134bhp compared with 111bhp – it had much less torque. Perhaps this explains why the maximum speed was higher – 98mph instead of 91mph – and that when revved hard it accelerated slightly faster through the gears; yet it was never a good low-speed lugger, and usually felt sluggish when left in a particular gear ratio.

Predictably enough, it always sold well enough in the markets for which it was intended, but not on the home market. Land Rover expert James Taylor has pointed out that it was 'disappointing off-road, or as a tow car, but its top speed of 98mph helped it to appeal to a certain type of buyer'.

October 1993

The next up-date came only months later, when the V8 was further up-graded, and when automatic transmission became available with the turbo-diesel engine.

In marketing terms, this was a seemingly important change of policy for Land Rover. For the very first time, the Discovery was to share exactly the size of V8, in the same tune, as that of the current Range Rover. This situation, however, did not last for long – as a new-generation Range Rover, with a further-up-rated V8, would appear just one year later.

In essence, the V8 engine was as previously used, in that it was the famous light-alloy power unit, fitted with Lucas fuel injection. However, by using a larger cylinder bore – 94mm instead of 88.9mm – this pushed up the capacity from 3,528cc to 3,947cc. This, as we would soon find out, was by no means the limit to the possible

In the early 1990s, the Discovery was taken into service as part of the Queens' Flight. Behimd is a Wessex helicopter of the Flight.

enlargement of this V8. Land Rover would eventually introduce its own 4,552cc version for a Range Rover model, and very special versions developed by TVR for its own use would measure no less than 4,997cc.

As always, this change – from 3.5ltr to 3.9ltr, along with the fitting of a catalytic converter in the exhaust system as standard – had been done for a long-term purpose. Land Rover would shortly introduce the Discovery into the highly competitive North American market – which meant the USA and Canada. For all the usual financial and legislative reasons (for having a new engine certified for use in that market was a lengthy and costly business), it made sense to use the same V8 as was already on sale there – in the Range Rover.

At the same time, Land Rover made a unique move – of putting the five-door V8I version of the Discovery on sale in Japan, as the 'Honda Crossroad'. At this time Honda, of course, was a close technical and business associate of Rover (several Rover passenger cars were really re-worked Hondas), and it was the Japanese who initiated this 'badge-engineering' approach.

This, however, was not a successful venture. Because Land Rover was already selling the Discovery in Japan behind its own badge, the fact that a so-called 'Honda' version suddenly appeared alongside it merely confused the clientele. Sales targets of 1,200 a year were never achieved, and the project fizzled out by 1996.

March 1994

This, though, was only a temporary set-back, for a face-lifted and much improved version of the Discovery was already on the way. In what was usually known in the industry as a 'mid-term makeover', this fast-selling 4×4 not only got a cosmetic up-date, but benefited from a new type

Although the Defender was always seen as a genuine off-roader, usually in countryside settings, the Discovery always seemed to be a more urban-based 4×4. This is an early-1990s V8I, with automatic transmission, pictured in a Warwickshire town.

of turbo-diesel engine and a new type of main gearbox.

Not only that, but this was also the time when the Discovery was introduced to the North American market. Rest-of-the-World launch was timed for the Geneva Motor Show in March 1994, while the Discovery went on sale in the USA in April. Right from the start, incidentally, these cars were always known as 1995 models – and 6,495 of them would be sold there before the 1996 models took over, when sales would double.

Although little change would be made to the very accomplished chassis and general suspension/braking installations, this was the moment at which ABS anti-lock braking became standard, and when front-and-rear anti-roll bars (previously optional) were also standardized.

Mechanically, therefore, the two principal innovations were the introduction of the latest (300Tdi) turbo-diesel engine, and the new R380 five-speed gearbox. Because Land Rover was

The chassis frame shared between the Discovery and the Range Rover was an extremely solid, and rigid, box-section structure. Mountings for the coil spring suspension are just visible in this Solihull shot.

busily rationalizing as much of its engineering as possible, the new engine and new gearbox types were also introduced into the Defender chassis at the same time. Accordingly, these important 'building blocks' have already been described in detail in Chapter 5.

Although the design and engineering team had been working on this, the 'Romulus' project, for some time, they had not been allowed to make many visual changes, so it needed more than a casual glance to pick the new from the old.

The most noticeable style changes were at the front and the rear (both of these with USA-market requirements in mind). At the front there were larger headlamps, different turn-indicator shapes and a modified bonnet pressing to suit, while at the rear, the turn indicators were now

The T16 engine – a 134bhp/2ltr petrol-fuelled unit, which was made available in the Discovery in 1993, was very different from the usual type of Land Rover engine. Originally evolved at Longbridge for use in transverse-engined front-wheel-drive cars, it was a 16-valve unit with twin overhead camshafts.

separate from stop/tail lamps and recessed into the bumper moulding itself.

Inside there was a new-style facia, which not only included changes to incorporate drivers' (steering wheel – actually it was that of the existing Rover 800 saloon) and passenger's side airbags, it also had an altogether more curvaceous style and a more integrated layout of heater, sound system and fresh-air central controls.

Along with a strengthened body shell (which included anti-intrusion door beams), a series of new fabrics and new colour schemes, and an even wider list of options, this was exactly the type of enhanced specification to take the Discovery up-market, and on to higher sales. In the UK, prices spanned £17,640 to £25,765 – whereas the even more glossy Range Rover spanned £28,895 to £40,899. And so it proved, for no fewer than 69,919 such vehicles would be produced in 1995, and 65,039 in 1996 – this being a period when more Discoveries were being made than the combined total of Defenders and Range Rovers. Extra production from existing plant, however, sometimes caused some corners to be cut, and details to be neglected, so this was not a time of top-quality assembly at Solihull.

Maturity

For the next four years, the only important mechanical change made to home-market models was that the 300Tdi engine was re-tuned (actually made more powerful) for use with automatic transmission, this being done to close the

Motorsport entrepreneur Nick Brittan used this three-door Discovery Tdi as a pre-event route survey vehicle for Middle East and Asian sections of the 1993 London – Sydney Marathon.

otherwise inevitable performance gap caused by power losses in the transmission itself.

It is always a sign that a model is reaching the end of its mechanical development life when a variety of 'special editions' or 'limited editions' is progressively put on sale, for this happened more and more frequently with mid- and late-1990s Discoveries. Most extrovert of all was probably the 'Camel Trophy' version (150 of those in mid-1995), but more costly (and looking it) was the 500-off 'Goodwood' at the end of 1996. The Horse and Hound (only twenty produced) was even more exclusive still. There were several more to follow, especially once the clientele got wind of a forthcoming (but still not available) new-generation type.

One of the final special editions, which celebrated fifty years of the Land Rover marque, was the 'Anniversary 50'. Special editions, with special names, proliferated, and it would be a brave author who attempted to list them all – especially as some dealers got together with the factory to obtain their own, strictly limited-region models, too!

The original Discovery received a facelift in 1994, at the same time as deliveries began to North American markets. This five-door ES model shows the enlarged headlamps and the different grille/front bumper combination adopted at this time.

North American Discovery

Once launched in the USA, the Discovery soon established itself as the slightly cheaper but still highly desirable relative of the Range Rover, and the first deliveries north of the Mason–Dixon line – to Canada – followed early in the 1995 calendar year. After the longer, higher and distinctly top-of-the-market Range Rover II had appeared for 1995, the Discovery found itself with a definite and important market slot to fill – and has done so remarkably well ever since. In the latter part of the 1990s, average annual North American sales of about 15,000 Discoveries were recorded every year (though less than 1,000 of these would be registered in Canada), and in the 2000s these figures moved up yet more. This was remarkable, for in that marketplace the rather similar Jeep Cherokee had already established itself as the all-American hero, and was not about to give it up without a fight.

All North American Specification Discoveries of this period had the same 3.9ltr V8 engine, which, with its 182bhp output, ensured a top speed of at least 105mph. In a country where open-highway speed limits rarely exceeded 65mph, this was ample to keep such a big (and expensive) machine competitive. By this time, too, and more than thirty years after General Motors had unwisely cast it aside, it was highly unlikely that many American customers even realized that their Discovery had ancestry in Detroit.

That engine, in fact, came in for a major redesign in 1996. Although the swept volume and nominal power output did not change, the basic architecture was brought in line with that of the latest Range Rover, most noticeably by the introduction of a new cylinder block that incorporated cross-bolted main bearing caps and a complete

Early in the 1990s, Land Rover introduced a commercial version of the Discovery, which came with a Tdi diesel engine, and had no passenger fittings, or windows aft of the doors.

Facelift Discoveries – those built as a result of the 'Romulus' project - had this new and altogether better-equipped facia layout. One of the most important up-grades was the addition of airbags – that for the driver being in the centre of the steering, that for the passenger being behind the padded trim panel above the glovebox lid.

re-jig of the front end, so that the engine's length was reduced, and with all accessories now to be driven by a single multi-vee belt.

The most significant mechanical change was the adoption of the latest GEMS (Generic Engine Management System), which was a project that had been evolved jointly by Land Rover and Segam Lucas, and which took over from the familiar Bosch-Lucas system of earlier types.

This, now, was the high-point of mechanical evolution of this original-generation Discovery. Although trim and paint choices, special editions and other equipment changes continued to proliferate in 1997 and 1998, the end for this model was in sight.

BMW, in the meantime, had been leaning hard on the design team, with their thoughts on the future. With nearly 400,000 of the original Discovery already built, and sold, now it was time to make way for the second-generation model.

7 Discovery II: The Second Generation

Nine years after the original Discovery had appeared, and had caused such a huge expansion in Land Rover's fortunes, it was time for the second-generation machine to take over. Although there was technical innovation in every corner of the new-generation machine, the most interesting novelty of all was – that it looked almost the same; BMW, the world's greatest proponents of gradualism in styling, had made sure of that.

It was BMW of Germany, vast, profitable, ambitious, and with a burning desire to embrace the 4×4 market sector, that had done so much to prepare Land Rover for expansion in the late 1990s. Without the truck-loads of capital that arrived from Germany after 1994, it was never likely that the Land Rover business could have been modernized or given such a range of new models. The Freelander (described in Chapter 8) had been the first of the German-financed 4×4s, and now it was the turn of the Discovery.

Early in the 1990s, Land Rover's existing owners, British Aerospace, were still struggling to make sense of the Rover Group. Not even the 20 per cent shareholding, which had been taken by Honda, nor the massive technical support offered by the Japanese concern, could make the business stable. The realities were stark – that while Land Rover itself was profitable, the larger part of the Group's empire – Rover, based at Longbridge and Cowley – rarely looked like making money.

Enter BMW

Even before BAe had taken control of Land Rover in 1988, the business was an attractive target, and no sooner had the original Discovery gone on sale than that attraction redoubled. Way back in 1986, when the British Government seemed to be ready to sell off its still-nationalized British Leyland business, Ford and General Motors had both tried to purchase Land Rover, but had been warned off on political grounds. Then, in 1988, BAe's agreement to buy what had become the Austin–Rover Group included an assurance that they would never split up the assets, nor sell any off, for at least five years.

From mid-1993, therefore, and with Austin–Rover still losing a lot of money, Land Rover was theoretically in play once again. BMW looked over the business, decided that Land Rover was the jewel in its crown, and made an offer for the Solihull business. This was refused. The rest is history. BMW's Bernd Pischetsrieder returned to Munich. BMW's board brooded for a time, then came back early in 1994, with an offer to buy the entire Rover business. This was accepted and was formalized in March 1994. Within hours, it seemed, BMW directors swept into the factories and began their appraisal of what should (and could) be done to rejuvenate, and expand, the product range.

At Land Rover, their first major new-product decision was to confirm the introduction of a second-generation Range Rover – they already knew all about the new model, for it was to include a BMW turbo-diesel among its line of engine options. The new model was almost at the pre-production/pilot-build stage, and would make its public debut in September 1994.

BMW's second move was to approve a start on the CB40 Freelander project, and this all-new product would be ready for launch in the autumn of 1997.

When Land Rover introduced the Series II Discovery in 1998, it looked very similar to the original type, though most exterior panels had been modified. From the front end the recognition points included the grille surround panels, and the low-mounted driving lamps.

The third major decision was to decided on a strategy for updating, improving, and perhaps even completely renewing the Discovery range. More than ever before, this was likely to be a 'lifestyle', rather than a purely functional, model, with several different trim packs and many options. Four trim levels were available at once and by the early 2000s this had risen to five – from 'E', through S, GS, XS and ES.

When the original Discovery had been announced in 1989, no-one dared to hope that a second-generation car would follow so quickly – quickly, that is, by previous Land Rover standards, where the life of models had previously been measured in decades, rather than in years. When first discussions were held in 1994, the current Discovery model had not yet been established in production for five years, which by Land Rover traditions meant that it was only just getting into its stride. In the normal scheme of things, all manner of engine, transmission and detail updates could be expected in the future – and the engineers at Solihull had already prepared a 'why don't we?' folder of good ideas.

There was, however, a total difference between the attitude of previous managements, and that of the new masters from Germany. In the past, Land Rover had become used to struggling on, with innovation sometimes stifled by a lack of investment capital, and with its own profits often siphoned off to help prop up less successful parts of the group. BMW, however, looked at things from a different aspect. Not since 1959 had their profitability ever been in question, and never in all that time had they had to consider serious retrenchment. For Land Rover, in fact, whatever they planned could surely be achieved.

BMW, in fact, not only wanted to deal with all those obvious and well-documented Discovery product shortcomings – not only those notorious panel gaps, but a new type of diesel engine was needed – but they wanted to make a new machine, bigger and more versatile than before. Although they were still happy with the proportions of the existing Discovery, they wanted to provide a lot more stowage space in the rear of the shell.

Not only that, but BMW had great global ambitions for their 4×4s, which included selling a larger number of new type Discovery models in the United States.

The Tempest Project

It was in this bold, confident, forward-looking atmosphere, that a new-generation Discovery gradually began to take shape. The 'Tempest' project, under project leader Nick Fell, was well under way by 1994–5 and the styling was settled at Gaydon by the end of 1995, to a brief that seemed to become more demanding with every passing month.

The marketing team had a difficult task ahead. Although the existing Discovery was immensely successful —approaching 400,000 would have been built by the time the new-generation machine took over – the actual marketing slot in Solihull's 4×4 family of models was about to change radically. We must never forget that a new 'small' Land Rover – the Freelander – would go on sale at least a year before this new Discovery could be ready, and that the second-generation Range Rover, which had gone on sale at the end of 1994, was not only physically larger, but faster and better-equipped, than the car that it had replaced.

Compared with the existing machinery, a new Discovery would therefore have a somewhat different gap to fill. The Freelander, in fact, was not only a welcome addition to the line-up at Solihull, but it would definitely have an effect on Discovery sales.

Not only that, but because of resource priorities, for some time the new-type Discovery would have to take second priority at Solihull, behind the Freelander project. By 1995–6, though, it had gradually built up a momentum of its own, though it was never likely to be ready for launch before 1997–8.

Right from the start there was a lot of internal discussion about the styling of the new model, and particularly its interior 'package'. In marketing terms, because it would have to fit in between the Freelander (which, in fact, would be very little smaller in its cabin, though clever styling made it look smaller), and the Range Rover (whose second-generation shape would be well-known, and which would ride on a magnificent 108in/2745mm wheelbase), there would clearly have to be some type of family resemblance.

But how similar should the new machine be to the original-shape Discovery? And how many derivatives should be planned? Should it be a three-door or a five-door model – or both? Should there be an open-top version? Should there be a commercial type? The rejuvenation, in other words, would not be simple, for like could not replace like.

Style – Similar but Different

Looked at without detailed analysis, the second-generation Discovery appeared to be very similar indeed to the original type. And so it was, yet almost every skin panel had been changed, there was more rear overhang, a bigger cabin and the panel gaps had been reduced to positively quality-car standards. Land Rover eventually announced that the 'Tempest' shell included 200 new body pressings, and that there were 100 carryover or lightly-modified items from the existing Discovery. The new type, incidentally, was only to be available as a five-door version

Comprehensive and carefully-targeted surveys of the opinion of original-style Discovery owners had shown that, while they seemed to be totally happy with the looks, they were not all happy with the perceived product quality. There was certainly a demand to make a new model even more versatile, and to be even more of a 'road', rather than an 'off-road' machine – and the handling needed to be tightened up without destroying the ride.

BMW and Land Rover management were delighted to note these conclusions, for by the mid-1990s they had come to a similar conclusion. Top management all liked what they saw on the original Discovery, and they resolved merely to make the new type better, but not sensationally different. A new model would take shape around the same basic 100in wheelbase chassis and chunky 16in tyres (though with 2in wider wheel tracks), but could perhaps be allowed to grow – to be longer, a touch wider, and to have more powerful engines and more performance.

In a process that took months to evolve, the design engineers worked away at improving every aspect of the Discovery style. Although the existing proportions were all retained – not least the commandingly high driving position, the step-profile roof and the relatively flat sides – the sides could be re-profiled, and more pronounced wheelarch 'eyebrows' added to take account of the wider wheel tracks. The tail behind the line of the rear axle was lengthened by a full 5in, and the tail lamps were raised considerably on the rear quarter pillars.

At the end of this process, every outer panel, except the rear door, had been substantially revised. Even so, it was not easy to pick one from the other. Both types had the characteristic rectangular headlamps at the front and both had the same type of stepped roof profile with high corner windows at the tail. Both had twin, parallel, feature lines along the flanks, and both shared the same stance of the D/E post pillar behind the rear-seat passenger doors. Even so, a size comparison is interesting (see table).

Because Land Rover measured the car's width across the door mirrors, there had been no increase in overall width to report, but this hid a slightly wider and more spacious cabin.

For the Series II Discovery, Land Rover lengthened the tail of the body shell by 5in, which increased stowage and carrying capacity. At the same time tail lamp clusters were relocated to a position much higher on the rear quarter pillars. This, in fact, is the slightly facelifted model which was introduced early in 2002.

| Size Comparison Between Discovery I and Discovery II ||||
Dimension (in/mm)	Discovery I (1989)	Discovery II (1998)	Increase
Length	178/4521	185.2/4705	7.2/184
Width	86.2/2190	86.2/2190	Nil
Height	75.6/1920	78.0/1980	2.4/60

This Land Rover publicity shot of a Series II Discovery makes much of the machines higher performance image. Even though it was a bulky machine, its sophisticated control of the suspension made it a much quicker car on the open road than the earlier types.

Recognition points? At the front, there was a U-shaped pressed surround to a bolder, three-bar, grille, along with a pair of low-mounted driving lamps let in to low body panels at each side of the black-painted front over-riders. From the side, there was the black edging to the wheel arches, along with new style five-spoke alloy wheels (several different styles, in fact, depending on the specification/trim package chosen). Then, from the rear, there was the repositioning of the stop/tail/indicator lamp clusters, which were placed alongside the rear windows – and on the roof there were two longitudinal luggage bars.

The new structure was claimed to be much stronger than the original type, this thanks to the greater accuracy of the new jigging assemblies, and the use of many robots in the welding fixtures. The door skins were in pressed steel (not aluminium, as in the past – this being done because of their greater resistance to minor dents) and the windscreen itself had been enlarged.

Inside the cabin, the extra length allowed for the fitting of a third row of seats in the extreme tail – these being standard in top-of-the-range S, XS and ES types at first, and in one version of the GS derivative when that arrived. As before, these hinged out from the sides of the loading bay, but they could be stored away when not required, this reinstating the luggage space. These seats, incidentally, had hi-fi jacks and controls so that the occupants (often, but not always, these would be children) could listen to different music or audio entertainment from the rest of the occupants. When the third row of two seats was in use, of course, this meant that the luggage space was completely occupied by seating (and people!), but nevertheless there seemed to be a demand for this feature. In any case, as Land Rover pointed out, they had provided for the fitment of roof racks.

Wherever one looked at the interior, there were new materials and fabrics, all of them further up-market than on the original type: leather or cloth seats, for instance, depending on the model and the application. Even on the 'entry level' model, the seating package was as plush as expected, the fifth passenger being provided with a shaped central rear seat, which was slightly narrow but no less padded than its neighbours. The facia layout was all new, though it bore a family

Land Rover Discovery II (from 1998)

Layout
Ladder-style chassis frame, with steel/aluminium estate car body style. Front engine/four-wheel-drive.

Engines
Five-cylinder, diesel
Capacity	2,495cc
Bore and stroke	84.45 × 89mm
Valves	Single overhead camshaft
Compression ratio	19.5:1
Fuel injection	Lucas and turbocharger
Max power	136bhp @ 4,200rpm
Max torque	221lb ft @ 1,950rpm

V8-cylinder, petrol
Capacity	3,947cc
Bore and stroke	94 × 71.1mm
Valves	Overhead valves
Compression ratio	9.35:1
Fuel injection	Bosch
Max power	182bhp @ 4,750rpm
Max torque	250lb ft @ 2,600rpm

Transmission
Type	Permanent four-wheel-drive, with choice of high or low range
Gearbox	Four-speed manual gearbox, synchromesh on top and third gears
Clutch	Single dry plate, diaphragm spring
Ratios	(High range)
Top	3.15
4th	4.32
3rd	6.04
2nd	9.22
1st	14.36
Reverse	15.31
High range step-down ratio	1.222:1
Low-range step-down ratio	3.321:1
Final drive ratio	3.538:1

ZF four-speed automatic transmission available as an option, with same final drive ratios

Suspension and steering
Front	Live axle, coil springs, radius arms, Panhard rod, anti-roll bar, telescopic dampers
Rear	Live axle, coil/air springs, radius arms, Watts linkage, anti-roll bar, telescopic dampers
Steering	Recirculating ball (power assisted)
Tyres	225/65-16 radial-ply
Wheels	Cast alloy disc, five-bolt-on fixing

Brakes
Type	Disc brakes at front, disc brakes at rear, hydraulically operated, with anti-lock
Size	11.8in front discs, 11.8in rear discs.

Dimensions (in/mm)
Track	Front and rear 60.6/1,540
Wheelbase	100/2,540
Overall length	185.2/4,705
Overall width	(over mirrors) 86.2/2,190
Overall height	78.0/1,980
Unladen weight	From 4,641lb/2,105kg

---

resemblance to the dashboards already in use in current Freelanders and Range Rovers. The steering wheel was a big, and massively padded affair (to accommodate the air bag), while in the centre of the panel there was a complex layout including heater/air conditioning, and radio/cassette installations.

Even so, although 'Tempest' was even more of a 'junior Range Rover' than the first Discovery had been, it was still meant to provide superlative off-road performance in the most atrocious conditions. Accordingly, the new and very well-equipped body shell was still laid out with ground clearance, durability and agility in mind. The approach angle (of a ramp that could be cleared as the Discovery II drove up and over it) was a very creditable 31 degrees (on-road), while in spite of the greater rear over-

The Series II Discovery facia was different from that of the previous model, but not fundamentally so. Complete with special colour scheme and trim details, this was the 'Autobiography' special edition.

hand, the departure angle was still a completely competitive 21 degrees (on road) or 25 degrees (off-road).

Confident about the prospects for its new model, Land Rover coined a new catch-phrase, which might have been considered arrogant in some competitors' programmes: 'Every Vehicle You Need'. If that is, your needs, encompassed a massive, rock-solid, estate car weighing a minimum of 4,641lb/2,105kg.

Improved Chassis, New Hardware

There was never any argument about the basis of Discovery II. Like the original, it was always intended to be built up around a separate chassis, with a mixture of steel structure and some aluminium skin panels in the body shell. Once Land Rover had decided to continue to 'position' the Discovery II squarely in the gap between the Freelander and the Range Rover, the use of a very similar seating package to the original almost sold itself.

Accordingly, it was soon agreed that the new Discovery did not need any overwhelming chassis or suspension changes, and that the new model should be based around an improved and lengthened version of the existing Discovery/Range Rover 100in chassis frame. All the project studies were agreed on this.

The 'Tempest' frame, therefore, was recognizably developed from the original, though it now had an extra (sixth) cross-member to add torsional stiffness (and was, of course, longer behind the line of the rear axle, to support the lengthened body shell), while the mounts linking body to chassis frame had been completely redesigned: there were now to be no fewer than fourteen mounting points. Although the suspension, steering and braking installations were all based on those of the earlier Discovery, this was the time to make improvements on all sides:

Although the front and rear suspension was still basically by beam axles and coil springs, spring and damper rates had been redeveloped. Front and rear wheel tracks were 2.0in/50mm wider than before, there was a different type of

Panhard rod location of the front end and at the rear, the original A-bracket was abandoned in favour of Watts linkage, which had the effect of raising the height of the roll centre. Different steering geometry (this work was inspired by work already done for the second-generation Range Rover) allowed power-assisted steering efforts to be reduced, and the steering itself to feel more precise.

In addition, to look after the fact that the new model had to cope with heavier loads, further overhung, at the rear (extra passengers sometimes, extra baggage sometimes), there were self-levelling air springs at the rear too. This was called SLS, for BMW was very fond of using mysterious acronyms.

The big story, though, was that a new feature called Active Cornering Enhancement (ACE) was now provided – as standard on the two top-of-the-range models, and optional on the others. This was Land Rover's cost-effective method of improving on-road handling and response without destroying off-road comfort and capability.

Basically, when the new-generation Discovery was pushed briskly along a winding road, the ACE system, which was electronically and hydraulically sensed, detected the onset of cornering forces, detected the tendency for the body to roll on its suspension, and reacted against it.

This was done by providing what looked like massive chassis-mounted anti-roll bars at each end of the vehicle, each of these units being connected to the nearby axles by an arm on the right (offside in the UK) of the bar, via a hydraulic actuator. When cornering forces caused the Discovery to begin to roll, a series of sensors (which monitored speed, forces and body shell attitude) combined to detect this, and applied counter-acting forces through the bars themselves.

Up to 0.5g cornering – equivalent to the Discovery being pushed quickly, but not insanely so, through tarmac-surface corners – ACE almost eliminated roll completely, which initially felt strange, though drivers rapidly got used to it. As cornering loads built up still further, the system then allowed some roll to develop, but neither as much, nor as uncontrolled, as in the past.

Off-road driving, however, was unaffected, for at low speeds the hydraulic actuators freed off completely, which left the axles without anti-roll bars and did not affect their actuation. Incidentally, driver control over the air spring even allowed the driver to jack up the rear end by an extra couple of inches in extra-rough going – or to lower it to allow a towing hitch to be attached.

The new car's braking system was also improved – not merely by providing larger discs (ventilated at the front), but by using the same electronic wheel sensors to control the transmission characteristics too.

All in all, the second-generation Discovery's chassis was engineered, operated and felt completely different from the original model of

For the Series II Discovery, the ACE hydraulic suspension system brought real complication to the otherwise simple coil spring layout. Roll-Control in on-road conditions was very impressive.

1989–98. The difference was stark and compelling. In mechanical terms, original-type Discovery models were downmarket Range Rovers, and handled accordingly. The new model, however, was meant to have its own character, and its own engineering capabilities. Not only in the study of its engineering, but in the driving experience, it succeeded on all counts.

Engines and Transmissions

History shows us that the original Discovery had bemused everyone by a near-constant change in its engines line up – for the original choice of two types in 1989 had eventually been modified and extended, reaching a lifetime total of five by 1998. For 'Tempest', the project team settled on a simple choice of two initial power units – one petrol, and one diesel – and even four years after the car had been launched this policy had never changed, nor had the engines been up-graded. In due course, though, the latest 'common rail' injection technology would have to be applied to the diesel engine, to keep it abreast of the competition.

One engine – the most glamorous but not the most commercially significant – was an updated version of the famous V8, while the other was an all-new straight-*five*-cylinder $2\frac{1}{2}$ltr turbo-diesel, which had always been coded 'Storm' during its lengthy development period. As already noted in Chapter 5, this new five-cylinder diesel was also about to find a home in the Defender range.

But why five cylinders and not four, or six? And why is it that no related four-cylinder or six-cylinder types were ever offered? The solution to this conundrum, financially reasonable or not, dates from the mid-1990s, and well before any such engine was ready to be launched. The fact is that an entire family of four-, five- and six-cylinder diesel engines were designed, but that Land Rover's new owners, BMW, cancelled two out of the three.

Land Rover had wanted to develop new four, five and six-cylinder diesel engines, all in the same family, but only the five-cylinder Td5 actually went into production. It was taken up by the Defender at the same time.

Details of the cancelled 'four' and 'six' types have never been released. Though it must surely be reasonable to infer that these might have been 2ltr and 3ltr types, respectively. Solihull's designers and planners, presumably, were looking forward to making a closely integrated family out of these units, and had certainly considered the installation of flexible machining facilities, which could deal with all three types.

Certainly there was a slot for a 2ltr 'four' – in the forthcoming Freelander (which ended up with a Rover L-Series diesel instead),- and for a 3ltr 'six' (in the Range Rover). But neither engine made it beyond the project stage. And for why? Jealousy, it would seem, from BMW. Once the German company had taken control of Land Rover in 1994 (which, no question, it considered to be the most desirable of all marques acquired in the Rover Group purchase from British Aerospace), it surveyed the project work being done at Solihull. Informed that a new turbo-diesel engine family was being developed, it soon directed that the 'four' and 'six' cylinder types be abandoned.

Since this was a period when BMW was actively evolving its own new-generation 'common-rail' diesels – and that these just happened to be closely-related four-cylinder/2ltr and six-cylinder 3ltr types, which would have many more applications than Land Rover could possibly cover, it seemed reasonable to cancel the Land Rover equivalents. But why leave a five-cylinder project intact? Why could not BMW produce a straight-five instead?

The new five-cylinder 'Storm', officially to be called the Td5 engine, was a big advance on the older four-cylinder turbo-diesel that had been used in the earlier Discovery. However, although it shared exactly the same swept volume with the old engine (2,495cc), it was different in every detail, much more powerful and (this was immensely important) it was dramatically more refined than before.

Conventional in many ways – the Td5 featured a cast iron block, a cast aluminium cylinder head, and single-overhead-camshaft valve gear – in some ways it was related to Rover's four-cylinder L-Series diesel: the bore and stroke dimensions were the same, the connecting rods and pistons were common, and some other components were shared.

Fuelled by Lucas Electronic Unit injectors, which worked at more than twice the fuel pressure of the old 300Tdi and which had already been well-proven in other truck engine applications, there was ultra-precise electronic control of the injection period, and of its timing. This was claimed to be so accurate that no catalytic converter was needed to meet all current or forecast diesel exhaust emissions requirements.

Drive by wire throttle control, and a new electronic control module (ECM), which was linked to every other ECU throughout the vehicle, meant that this was by far the most advanced diesel engine yet put on sale by Land Rover. It was much more powerful than the old 300Tdi unit, as the table shows.

Comparison Between New and Old Engines		
Feature	New Td5 Five-cylinder 2,495cc Diesel	Old 300Tdi Four-cylinder 2,495cc Diesel
Peak power (bhp/rpm)	136/4200	111/4000
Peak torque (lb ft/rpm)	221/1950	195/1800

Compared with the earlier type, the 22 per cent increase in peak torque, and the 13 per cent in peak torque meant that the latest diesel-engined Discovery would not only be significantly faster than before, but might also be suitably more fuel-efficient when driven in a relaxed manner.

By comparison with this innovation, the improvements to the venerable petrol-injected alloy 3,947cc V8 were evolutionary, rather than completely fresh. For use in the Discovery II, this V8 picked up the improvements already made for the latest-generation Range Rover, which included a modified and stiffer cylinder block, a new crankshaft and cross-bolted main bearing caps. In addition, there was a new cast alloy sump, and a new-generation Bosch Motronic 5.2.1 engine management system (of the type that BMW already employed in their own 7-Series saloons and 8-Series coupes).

Improvements to the top end included the use of a new curved-plenum inlet manifold, a distributor-less ignition system and maintenance-free (72,000 miles before one had to look at them) spark plugs. Once again there had been improvement, though this time it was minor (see table) – the distinct impression being that, as far as Rover (and, at the time, BMW), was concerned, the V8 was coming gracefully towards the end of its development life.

Comparison Between Old and New V8 Versions		
Feature	New	Old
	3,947cc	3,947cc
	V8	V8
	Discovery II	Discovery I
Peak power (bhp/rpm)	180/4750	182/4750
Peak torque (lb ft/rpm)	230/3100	250/2600

Transmissions

Compared with the final, outgoing, Discovery I model, there was only one major change to the transmissions, which, as before, offered a choice between a Type R380 five-speed manual and a ZF four-speed automatic transmission. None of the ratios in the transmissions, nor the final drives themselves, were changed, and although the front and rear axles were wider-tracked than before, they were technically little changed.

The big innovation came inside the familiar dual-range transfer gearbox (which was mounted immediately behind the main gearbox, whether manual or automatic). In the past this had always included a centre locking or viscous control of differential – but in Discovery II it had been eliminated completely.

Instead, there was one of the most advanced of all electronic traction control systems, in a system that used the same wheel sensors as the ABS (anti-lock braking) installation, which constantly monitored wheel rotating speeds, from side to side and from front to rear. What was called ETC (electronic traction control – another BMW-favoured acronym!), a system that had already been proven on the latest Range Rover, used sensors on all four wheels. If a wheel began to lose traction, the ABS wheel sensor electronically informed the central control unit, which lightly braked that wheel and thus transferred all the remaining drive to the opposite wheel, through the action of the axle's differential.

Although this sounded like space-vehicle technology, it was perfectly practical and viable for motor car use, and demonstrated just how far electronic controls had advanced in less than twenty years. Its action, of course, completely duplicated the action of a locking centre differential, for if only one wheel was capable of providing traction, the electronics would safely channel driving torque in that direction.

The system, incidentally, was developed and programmed so that it could control wheel traction all the way up to 62mph/100km/h, and had different operating strategies for High Range and Low Range: brake intervention and operation in Low Range was stated to be more vigorous than in High Range.

There was still one further traction feature (and a BMW-inspired acronym) in the standard specification. As in the Freelander (see Chapter 8, where this is more fully described) the hill descent control feature (HDC) was also standard. Selected by the driver by operating a dashboard switch, HDC also used the ABS sensors to monitor and limit the speed of the Discovery II when it descended a steep hill. This was done by an

The Discovery Autobiography was a special-edition model announced at the NEC Motor Show of 2000. Because of the different paint treatment, the ultra-solid front bumper mouldings were even more obvious than usual.

electronic installation using the ABS system and brakes in conjunction with engine braking and fuel supplies – and in this mode the Discovery could not possibly exceed 8.8mph/14km/h.

Discovery II on Sale

The new-generation Discovery met its public for the first time in September 1998, with deliveries beginning immediately, and with Discovery I assembly ending at once. Although a casual glance suggested that this was no more than a facelift of the earlier type, serious observers soon discovered that this was a considerably better, more advanced and more capable, all-purpose, go-anywhere, estate car than its predecessor.

Not only was Discovery II faster and more fuel-efficient than its ancestor, but it handled better. Not only was there a bigger and more versatile accommodation package, but a more versatile towing capability. Not only was there hill descent control but there was also electronic traction control too. All this, along with a higher level of trim and equipment (Land Rover PR staff made sure we did not miss the 'curry hook' and the cup-holders in the cabin!) meant that a formidably new package was on offer.

At its height (in 1995), the original Discovery had sold nearly 70,000 examples in a year – and that was before sales to the USA market had matured. Now, BMW concluded, it was time to make a further assault on that vast market, which explained why a higher standard of equipment and capability was essential.

In the British market, it is interesting to note the difference in the range of Discovery I prices (autumn 1998) and those of the Discovery II (early 1999), for these indicate how the new model had been pushed deliberately up-market. For information, the other model price ranges at the beginning of 1999 are included (see table):

Model Price Ranges at the Beginning of 1999	
	UK Price Range (£) January 1999
Defender station wagons	19,920 – 23,560
Freelander	16,570 – 21,420
Old-type Discovery (1998)	21,270 – 31,490
Discovery II	25,520 – 35,070
Range Rover II	39,640 – 51,165

So, what would the public think of the new model? Would they be impressed by the new turbo-diesel engine? And, more important, maybe, would they be impressed by what BMW was certain was a better-specified and better-engineered machine?

One of the marque's greatest media supporters, *Autocar* magazine, soon put everyone's mind at rest with a glowing report of the new Td5. Testing it in XS form, they summarized as follows:

> The new Discovery makes its rivals look backward and seriously under-developed. What's more, it makes you wonder whether paying extra for the cachet of owning a Range Rover is really worth it....
>
> Existing Discovery owners will not believe how much better the new car is. And those who had always discounted the car because of its poor on-road dynamics and build quality should have another look. It's a different animal today.

For those, and many other, reasons, they bottom-lined their piece: 'The best Land Rover on sale'.

First of all, it was interesting to see what the Td5 engine had done for the Discovery's performance, and for its refinement. Here was a Disco diesel with a top speed of 96mph, and one that recorded a day-to-day fuel consumption of 26.6mpg (Imperial), all this allied to the comment that the new model had 'decent refinement and a smooth five-cylinder thrum'.

Reaction to the new-fangled ACE (Active Cornering Enhancement) feature was positively ecstatic:

> In practice, ACE does its job incredibly well. In fact we would go so far as to say that it refines the way that a heavy-duty off-roader should handle and ride on the road. A taut, comfortable, ride quality is truly astonishing compared with the previous Discovery. Small ripples almost go undetected and larger potholes are easily dealt with.
>
> Through a series of corners, the Discovery glides from one to the next like no other off-roader this side of a Mercedes M-Class ... The process is seamless, making ACE a resounding success....

That, and similar reaction from other trustworthy sources, meant that the new Discovery got off to a flying start. Deliveries forged ahead in the first few years, which not only convinced management that it had settle on the correct balance of features, and that the new model was right for its major intended market – North America.

At this time, sales of Discovery models (I and II in 1999) in North America told their own story – the figures for recent years are shown in the table on page 147.

A rough analysis would be that the clientele took its time to assess the new-generation Discovery in 1999 (it had gone on sale in North America in the winter of 1998–9), before

In March 2002 Land Rover introduced this front-end facelift for the latest Discovery, the new headlamp treatment following a trend established with the new third-generation Range Rover, which had appeared just months earlier.

What Land Rover called the '2003 Model' Discovery actually appeared as early as March 2002! From the front end, the visual changes were limited to a new front corner/headlamp treatment, and there were modifications to the bumper moulding and the lower driving lamp positions too.

Sales Figures for Discovery in North America	
Calendar Year	Sales
1997	15,491
1998	14,704
1999	14,230
2000	21,931
2001	20,860

surging into the showrooms in the years that followed. The USA, please note, was the home of Jeep, so sales at this level were truly remarkable.

This explains, to some extent, why the technical specification of this second-generation Discovery was remarkable stable for the first three years after launch. It was not because the design team had run out of ideas, but that they were confident in the depth of research which had gone into specifying the new model in the first place.

In any case, there were other pressures: after 1998, Solihull's management team was tied up in preparing to put the Freelander on sale in North America (that event taking place towards the end of 2001) and in evolving a brand-new generation of Range Rover (also launched in 2001–2), so that further changes to the Discovery had to take a back seat.

But not for long. In March 2002 – the company actually calling it their '2003 model', which sounded a bit premature to almost everyone else – a minor facelift for the Discovery was unveiled, this having a new headlamp/driving lamp arrangement that looked much like that which had only just appeared in the third-generation Range Rover. Solihull watchers looked, nodded sagely and knew that for the time being little else could be expected.

And for why? Because in December 2001, chairman Bob Dover had already announced that the company's next new model, a further new-generation Discovery, would be launched in the middle of the coming decade, and would be produced at Solihull:

> We concluded that Solihull provided the best business case to justify the level of investment and expected returns. It is also a tribute to the dedication and commitment of our Solihull workforce, and recognition of the improvements that have been achieved in the last 17 months, since Land Rover became part of Ford Motor Company's Premier Automotive Group.

For the time being, however, Land Rover sales in general continued to rise, more than 1,000 Discoveries were being completed every week and, in particular, deliveries to the USA were on the increase. If an existing Discovery was this successful, what would be the prospects for a new model?

8 Freelander: New Structure, New Engines, New Thinking

While Land Rover was busily expanding its range of Defenders, Discoveries and Range Rovers in the 1980s and 1990s, its rivals in the marketplace were pushing ahead with smaller 4×4 models. While a series of bigger and better Land Rovers streamed out of Solihull, the opposition began unveiling a series of smaller, less capable but well-marketed 4×4s. Land Rover, it seems, had confirmed the traditions – yet everyone else was moving in another direction.

Yet Land Rover was not blind. It realized, all too well, what was going on, and could recognize the same new markets and new opportunities. But it was all a matter of priorities. While Land Rover developed rugged 4×4s, which could conquer almost any condition except a vertical sheet of wet ice, the opposition produced rivals that looked the part, but could sometimes struggle to cope with the wet grass of a point-to-point car park. The opposition, in other words, were producing what the Americans called SUVs (sport utility vehicles), where style triumphed over function, whereas Land Rover was still producing genuine off-road vehicles.

For Land Rover, where sufficient investment capital was always the limiting factor, there was always a matter of priorities to be met. Until BMW took control of the Rover Group in 1994, this was one inescapable fact of financial life. To move out of the range of machines for which it was famous, Land Rover would have to make a step change – not only in engineering, but in the

Freelander – the new face of Land Rover. Launched in 1997, this was a smaller, lighter and altogether less expensive 4×4 than the Discovery. This was the five-door Station Wagon version, a surprisingly roomy machine.

size of the factories needed to accommodate new types, and in the capital needed to back it all.

Developing and marketing a smaller, prettier, type of 4×4 – the sort of machine that some observers sneeringly dubbed a 'Sainsbury's car park special' – was going to cost a fair fortune – far more than Land Rover's current owners could ever afford. The paradox, though, was that all manner of larger, more profitable, and very determined industrial predators kept circling the business, anxious to take it on, and willing to make such moves.

Enter BMW

As already made clear, it was BMW of Germany who eventually bought the entire Rover Group in March 1994. Soon it was what seemed like unlimited German capital that finally made it possible for Land Rover to put a new, smaller, type of model on sale.

Which explains why the CB40 project, which had existed as a 'paper' model for some years, did not finally get official approval until 1994. For months it was suggested that the new product would be called Highlander (though Volvo actually held that name as a trade mark), yet it was actually as the Freelander that it finally went on sale late in 1997.

Even before buying Rover (which, of course, included the profitable Land Rover business) BMW had had their eyes on Land Rover for some time. Then, as later, BMW was totally committed to its worship of famous brands: it saw Land Rover as an icon among 4×4s, and coveted it for years. The immediate consequence of the takeover was that BMW confirmed that the imminent launch of the second-generation Range Rover would go ahead while, behind closed doors, they also agreed a serious start on a new 'baby Land Rover' project.

Under the guidance of project director Dick Elsy, Land Rover had already started work on a 'Cyclone' project in 1993:

> When we stood back and looked at our medium-term strategy, it became more and more obvious that

For the first time, it seemed, Land Rover had developed a 4×4 for the 'lifestyle' market, for the new Freelander was more glamorous than its bigger relatives. Not as up-market as the Range Rover, of course, but much smaller and much more affordable!

> there was a blank space in the Land Rover product plan about three years ahead. So we set ourselves the rather ambitious target of plugging it with the definitive leisure 4WD vehicle.
>
> We concluded that there was room for a cheaper model aimed at younger buyers and the leisure market. So we built a little prototype and presented it to the [BAe] board, just to juice them up a bit.
>
> We called it Cyclone, and it was a bit smaller than Freelander is now, but looked a lot like it.

Six months later, with all the basic design and engineering work complete, the CB40 project was shown to Bernd Pischetsrieder and Wolfgang Reitzle of BMW, when it received almost immediate approval: 'Pischetsrieder called for a roll of black tape, to suggest a small shape modification to a rear window,' Elsy recalls. 'When he did that, I knew we were "cooking with gas".'

It is not generally known that before BMW arrived, to save on working capital, Land Rover was proposing to go ahead in the manufacture of the CB40 in a 50–50 per cent joint venture with

Right from the start, the Freelander was available in two styles on the same platform, this being the three-door version which was available with a bolt on hardtop (this version), or in what Land Rover called 'soft back' guise where the all-weather kit could be removed.

Valmet of Finland (Valmet was, and is, a very experienced builder of other people's products – including the Porsche Boxster). BMW swiftly decided that this was not a way they wanted to do business, and pulled the Rover Group out of this deal.

Development work then went ahead rapidly, and according to the 'leak merchants' who supply rumours to the British motoring magazines, CB40's launch was to be as early as August 1996. They were wrong in this – the project actually occupied a still-remarkably-short 37 months – and they were equally wrong in forecasting that CB40 would take shape around a separate ladder-style chassis frame, complete with beam front and rear axles!

Design Revolution

In all but detail and decoration, the general layout of CB40 was settled by the summer of 1994 – by which time it was clear that this would be a totally new type of Land Rover. Totally new? Well, if you understand that not a single mechanical component, nor body panel, nor design layout was carried over from the existing Defender, Discovery and Range Rover models: yes, of course.

Amazingly, development and testing of the new car went ahead in remarkable secrecy, though one heavily-disguised prototype featured in one episode of that notorious TV series *When Rover Met BMW*, which was transmitted in 1996. That screening was a miscalculation, for it was a series that showed neither BMW nor Rover Group managers in a favourable light. Even so, it was not until the summer of 1996 that the first blurry spy shots of prototypes appeared in the motoring press. This was quite surprising, for the new car should have been easy enough to spot. Comparing the new car with the contemporary Discovery, shows just how different the new car was going to be:

Comparison of the Freelander with the contemporary Discovery

CB40/Freelander	Discovery
Unit construction shell	Separate chassis frame and body shells
Independent front/rear suspension	Beam axles at front/rear
Transversely-mounted engines	In-line/fore-aft engines
1.8ltr petrol/2.0ltr diesel engines	3.9ltr petrol/2.5ltr diesel engines

Land Rover Freelander (Introduced in 1997)

Layout
Unit-construction chassis/body structure, with choice of body styles. Front engine (transversely-mounted)/four-wheel-drive.

Engines

Four-cylinder, K-series petrol
Capacity	1,796cc
Bore and stroke	80.0 × 89.3mm
Valves	Twin overhead camshafts
Compression ratio	10.5:1
Fuel injection	MEMS
Max power	118bhp @ 5,500rpm
Max torque	121lb ft @ 2,750rpm

1997–2000 (four-cylinder, L-series diesel)
Capacity	1,994cc
Bore and stroke	84.5 × 88.9mm
Valves	Single overhead camshaft
Compression ratio	19.5:1
Fuel injection	Bosch and turbocharger
Max power	96bhp @ 4,200rpm
Max torque	155lb ft @ 2,000rpm

From 2000 (four-cylinder, BMW diesel)
Capacity	1,951cc
Bore and stroke	84.0 × 88.0mm
Valves	Twin overhead camshaft
Compression ratio	18.0:1
Fuel injection	Bosch and turbocharger
Max power	110bhp @ 4,000rpm
Max torque	192lb ft @ 1,750rpm

From 2000 (V6-cylinder, KV6 petrol)
Capacity	2,497cc
Bore and stroke	80.0 × 82.8mm
Valves	Twin overhead camshafts
Compression ratio	10.5:1
Fuel injection	Siemens
Max power	177bhp @ 6,250rpm
Max torque	177lb ft @ 4,000rpm

Transmission
Type	Permanent four-wheel-drive; all models except V6-engined versions had:
Gearbox	Five-speed manual gearbox, synchromesh on all forward gears
Clutch	Single dry plate, diaphragm spring
Ratios	Top 3.33
	4th 4.32
	3rd 6.04
	2nd 9.22
	1st 14.36
	Reverse 14.82
	Step-down ratio 1.46:1
Final drive ratio	(1.8ltr petrol) 3.188:1 (front), 3.214 (rear)

From 2000, on 2ltr turbo-diesels, Jatco five-speed automatic transmission available as an option: step-down ratio 1.359:1.
From 2000, on V6 versions, Jatco five-speed automatic transmission: step down ratio 1.359:1; final drive ratio 3.66:1

Suspension and steering
Front	Independent, coil springs, MacPherson struts, anti-roll bar
Rear	Independent, coil springs, MacPherson struts, wishbones and trailing links, anti-roll bar
Steering	Rack and pinion (power assisted)
Tyres	195/80-15 radial-ply
Wheels	Steel disc or cast alloy, five-bolt-on fixing

Brakes
Type	Disc brakes at front, drum brakes at rear, hydraulically operated, with anti-lock
Size	10.3in front discs, 10.0in rear drums; 10.9in front discs from 2000

Dimensions (in/mm)
Track	Front 60.4/1,534
	Rear 60.8/1,545
Wheelbase	100.5/2,555
Overall length	172.5/4,382
Overall width	(over body) 71.0/1,805
	(over mirrors) 81.7/2,074
Overall height	69.2/1,757
Unladen weight	From 3,142lb/1,425kg

Here, in fact, was a car that was to be aimed firmly at the sizeable market sector that had first been dominated by 4×4s like the Toyota RAV4: Even while Land Rover's new product was under development, the Honda CR-V would also join in – these two Japanese cars being serious competition, all round the world.

> **Toyota RAV4 – Starting a New Market**
>
> Although Land Rover was always discussing new models, its marketing staff admit that the arrival of the Toyota RAV4 focused the company's efforts on the opportunity for a smaller model – which led to the development of the Freelander.
>
> The original RAV4 appeared in 1993, originally as a high-ground clearance three-door estate car. The transversely-mounted 16-valve 2ltr engine produced 133bhp, the wheelbase was a mere 86.6in, and with all four seats occupied there was previous little room for luggage. This was not thought to be a very serious 4×4 – but more of a 'leisure' machine.
>
> Two years later, however, Toyota wiped the scornful smile of their rivals' face, with the launch of the longer-wheelbase five-door version. Here was a genuine five-seater with a lot of stowage space. Riding on a body that was a massive 16in/41cm longer, it had an 8.3in/21cm longer wheelbase and was a much more serious proposition.
>
> The second-generation RAV4 appeared in 2000, but by this time the Freelander was well established.

To get down to the planned weight and fuel consumption targets, it was decided to give the new CB40 a choice of smaller-displacement, four-cylinder, petrol and diesel engines at first. All the initial paper studies suggested that a power output of about 120bhp (petrol) and 100bhp (diesel) would be appropriate. For all the obvious timing and financial reasons, there was never any likelihood of having new engines designed – so existing Rover Group power units would be employed.

To follow this up, the choice of an ultra-compact transversely-mounted engine/primary transmission layout influenced almost every other aspect of CB40's packaging. As with most private cars of the period, this was done for practical and economically-efficient reasons. A look at the Rover Group's line-up of engines and transmissions provided the perfect power trains.

Not only was a torquey, 118bhp/1.8ltr version of the celebrated 16-valve twin-cam K-Series Rover engine about to be introduced for the still-secret MGF sports car, but the latest version of the single-overhead-cam, turbo-charged, 2.0ltr Rover L-Series diesel was also available. Both engines were already configured for transverse engine/front-wheel-drive installation (the

Amazingly, the Freelander shared its 1.8ltr petrol engine, in the same tune, with the MGF sports car. Land Rover motoring, for sure, had come a long way since the 1940s!

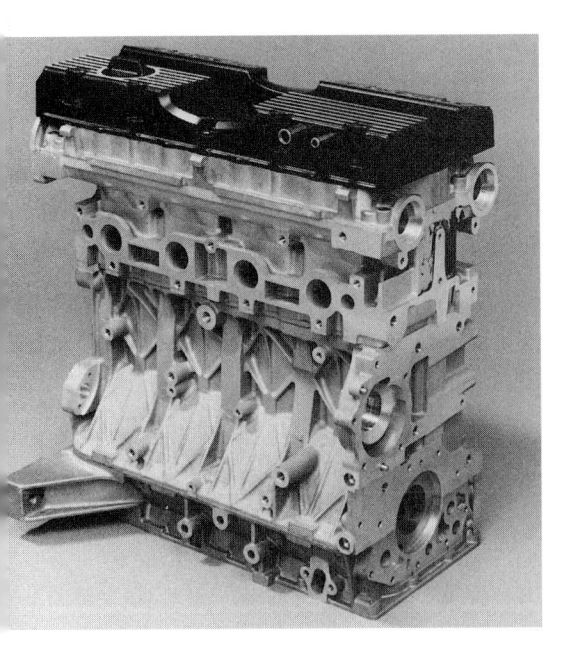

Above Rover's fine, modern, high-tech K-Series twin-cam engine was central to the design of the Freelander, and was a dedicated transverse-engine design. With four-valves per cylinder, alloy block and cylinder head, and sandwich style construction, it was a high-tech. solution to a new traction problem.

Above right This K-Series display engine/ transmission (this being a front-drive application from a Rover car) shows how the cylinder block was clamped between the head and the sump by a series of extraordinarily long bolts.

Right The Freelander's K-Series engine featured twin overhead camshafts, four valves per cylinder, and was not only a lightweight but rigid and versatile power unit.

154 Freelander: New Structure, New Engines, New Thinking

Initially, diesel power for the Freelander came from Rover's corporate L-Series diesel, a 2ltr power unit that was already used in several of the corporation's passenger cars too. Right from the outset, it had been designed for transverse installation.

L-Series diesel was being used in cars like the Rover 400, 600 and 800 saloons) as was the robust PG1 type of five-speed manual transmission, which bolted on to them. Thus configured, and with normal front-drive type drive shafts leading to the front wheels, it would be a straightforward engineering job to 'grow' the 4×4 layout out of this transmission, and arrange to drive the rear wheels.

The centre differential, neatly placed behind the engine/gearbox assembly, featured a viscous coupling – when one axle speed rose, relative to the other, the VC stiffened up in that characteristic manner, locking front and rear diffs to each other. This, however, would be the very first Land Rover model not to have a choice of high (normal) or low ('crawler') gear trains.

For Land Rover, however, the biggest and (in investment terms) the most costly decision was to choose a unit-construction type of structure. After nearly half a century, this would be the very first Land Rover to use this type of base (the third-generation Range Rover, launched in 2001, would be the second). Almost by definition, this meant that almost every body/structural panel would have to be a steel pressing. Theoretically this made the new car more prone to rusting than the original Defender, but corrosion-proofing had come a long way in recent years; BMW was determined that it should be effective, and there were no qualms on that score.

This decision was not made without a great deal of discussion. On the one hand, the use of a unit-body would impose extra expense in press tooling, robotization, and manufacturing facilities. To get a return on financial investment, it would also limit the number and frequency of changes that could be made to the style in future years. On the other hand, however, the use of modern computer-aided stress analysis techniques would keep it light, and endow the CB40 with a super-rigid type of structure.

It was typical of the Land Rover engineers' experience and attention to detail, that they provided the unit-shell with a static ground clearance of 7.9in/200mm (slightly less than that of the Discovery, but totally competitive in its class). In addition, there was a sturdy, bolt-on, aluminium/composite undershield fitted up front, as standard, under the radiator/engine position. It looked so 'right' and was so obviously functional, that Gerry McGovern's visual design team made a feature out of it.

Having settled on a wheelbase of 100.5in/2555mm (which was actually slightly longer than the classic 100in/2540mm dimension of the Discovery/original Range Rover type), McGovern's team set about shaping a versatile body and seating package. It is a measure of their artistic genius that although the new car looked significantly smaller than, say the Discovery, it was larger in some respects (see table).

Size Comparison of Freelander and Discovery

Feature	CB40/Freelander	Discovery
Wheelbase (mm)	2,555	2,540
Overall length (mm)	4,382	4,521
Overall height (mm)	1,757	1,920
Overall width (mm)	1,805	1,793
Front wheel track (mm)	1,534	1,486

As ever, Land Rover designed the Freelander to live in the 'school of hard knocks', making the vulnerable headlamp corners as robust as possible.

Although the new CB40/Freelander would be 139mm/5.5in shorter overall, it would actually be slightly wider than the Discovery, and only slightly less lofty (this being due to the Discovery's unique, stepped, high-roof profile). Space inside the vehicle – the 'interior package' as provided to the customer – would be equally as roomy as before. More than that, the use of the weight-saving unit-construction body shell, the smaller engines and the new chassis components meant that the new car was likely to be up to 1,000lb/454kg lighter than the Discovery – a remarkable gain.

McGovern's team took their time, then produced an attractive choice of styles. These were completely different from the other 4×4s in Solihull's stable. The Discovery was relatively angular, the Defender almost perversely so, whereas CB40 would have a much more shapely, more 'viewer-friendly' style. There did not seem to be a straight line on any of the panels or at the joints. The new car, in fact, looked curvaceous from all angles, and had what I will call a 'soft' nose, which gave it a far less aggressive stance than any of its larger relations.

Not only that, but right from the start, Land Rover decided to provide a choice of styles on the same wheelbase/platform/front end structure, claiming twelve derivatives at the time of launch. Not only would there be body options but carefully graded levels of standard equipment too.

Although it was certainly possible to order an entry-level three-door type, this version would lack HDC (hill descent control), passenger airbags, five-spoke alloy wheels and other useful (some would say vital) features; although all of these, of course, would be available as optional extras.

Having studied their rivals, Land Rover made sure that they would cater exactly for the SUV or 'fun' market and for the purely-practical sector too. Accordingly, there was to be a five-door estate car type of style – the more conventional of the two, and called 'Station Wagon' – and a three-door type, which could be supplied either with a softback or hardback rear door, depending on what kind of rear roof and tailgate cover was chosen.

Five-door Station Wagons had seating for five, with a rear bench seat whose back-rest split 60/40, but with rear safety belts for three people. The three-door type was configured for a maximum of four people, with two individually shaped rear seats and a tray between them. Not only that, but the three-door type, which had a steeply-sloping D-post, could either be supplied as 'softback' with a detachable soft top and sidescreens at the rear, whereas the alternative 'hardback' version had a removable bolt-on hardtop behind those steeply sloping rear quarters. 'Hardback three-doors and all five-door Station Wagons had electric glass tailgate drop windows.

There was no trace of the utilitarian inside the cabin, which was trimmed and equipped as carefully as any car – two-wheel-drive or four-wheel-drive – in this price class. Reclinable front

Above *Unmistakeable rear quarter view- more than quarter of million such rumps had already been made by the early 2000s.*

Below *Had you forgotten what the name was? Land Rover was, and is, mighty proud of its modern' small' 4×4.*

Freelander: New Structure, New Engines, New Thinking 157

Compared with earlier Solihull 4×4s, the facia/instrument panel of the Freelander was from a totally different world. Modern steering wheels, of course, were bulky because they had to accommodate an inflatable safety air bag. Only one gear lever? That's because there was no HiLo change speed facility on this model.

seats, with sporty and figure-hugging 'wings' at each side of the passenger's body over any type of going, and by any standard there was a nicely-detailed and well-equipped facia. Features like a driver's airbag (a bag for the front passenger featured on some derivatives), a rev-counter, electric front window lifts, electrically-controlled mirrors and remote central locking were all included.

New Chassis Engineering

Under the skin, here was a completely new type of Land Rover. Not only did the new model have a choice of transversely-mounted engines, but it

Freelander and its Competitors

When the Freelander went on sale at the end of 1997, its marketing sector was already well populated. Here, with early 1998 UK-market prices, is the line-up:

Daihatsu Fourtrak	From	£15,000
Daihatsu Sportrak	From	£10,750
Honda CR-V	From	£17,020
Isuzu Trooper	From	£20,360
Kia Sportage	From	£14,429
Land Rover Freelander	From	£15,995
Nissan Terrano	From	£16,295
Toyota RAV4	From	£14,441
Vauxhall Frontera	From	£15,725

Of these, the Honda, Toyota and Vauxhall were much the most significant rivals.

When the V6-engined Freelander came along in 2000, the front end needed little change to accommodate a remarkably compact power unit. Three-door and five-door types rode on the same wheelbase/platform.

had all-independent suspension along with power-assisted rack-and-pinion steering. Suspension would be by MacPherson struts but, unlike the Discovery, there would be no provision for self-levelling. This, allied to the somewhat limited ground clearance (especially when the independent suspension went in to its full bump state) showed how the design team was tailoring this car to the 'leisure' rather than to the out-and-out 'off-road' market sector.

Brakes – disc front, drum rear – looked conventional enough, but in addition there was a sophisticated ABS anti-lock installation, along with two other related features (not standard on all models) – ETC and HDC.

My apologies for the acronyms, but they seem to be everywhere in automotive circles in this electronic-age: ETC stands for electronic traction control, a piece of electronic trickery donated to Land Rover from BMW (for I had the same feature on my BMW 3-Series cars at the same time). In effect, this used ABS wheel sensors, and the logic in reverse, for under certain circumstances it can apply a gentle braking force to the wheel, which loses torque, thus feeding torque to the wheel on the opposite side of the car. Over slippery ground it really does work.

HDC (hill descent control) is an even cleverer spin-off from the ABS mechanism, and works like this. In first or reverse gear (and available by engaging a yellow collar on the gear lever), and with the throttle pedal released, HDC automatically limited the Freelander's hill descent speed to 5.6mph/9km/h, while also avoiding any wheel lock-up or skidding. Very reassuring, especially to less-experienced drivers faced (perhaps for the very first time) with crawling down a hill with only limited wheel grip.

Apart from the sturdy, but otherwise conventional, all-steel combined chassis/body construction, there was detail innovation on all sides.

Although the MacPherson struts looked conventional enough, by comparison with private cars they were much more sturdy in detail – including larger ball joints, larger bushes and larger mountings. Links that might otherwise be damaged by hitting huge rocks were engineered to break rather than to distort the suspension subframes or the body shell itself. The rack-and-pinion steering (itself a novelty for Land Rover) was mounted high up on a very rigid area of the chassis, to keep it out of harm's way.

CB40, in other words, might have been designed for what some observers call the 'light-duty' 4×4 market sector, but it was not about to let itself down by being fragile. Solid like every Land Rover should be, but much lighter and therefore more fuel-efficient than before, it must surely be a winner?

New Solihull Facilities

Even before the Freelander's engineering was settled, it was clear that Solihull's existing factory facilities could not cope. For one thing, the existing buildings were already bursting with assembly of the other three ranges – Defender, Discovery and Range Rover – and for another the use of a unit construction structure would impose an entirely different final assembly sequence.

When 4×4s take shape around a separate steel chassis frame, much of the mechanical assembly takes place at floor level, without restriction from body panels, and with the painted and near complete body shell being lowered into place well down the assembly lines. With a unit-construction shell, that is not possible. Work has to begin on a painted and only partly-completed shell, which sometimes has to be tipped on to its side on a carefully-aligned 'spit', while the engine/transmission and suspension assemblies do not meet the vehicle until a later stage in the process.

But that was not all. Although Solihull's Range Rover assembly, and the factory paint shop facilities were still quite modern (they had originally been set up to cater for Rover SD1 private-car assembly in the 1970s), those occupied by the

This absolutely side view study of the five-door Freelander hides the fact that its cabin was almost as roomy as that of the original Range Rover.

Defender and Discovery lines were frankly antiquated. Further, by the mid-1990s, all of them were working to capacity.

Land Rover's solution (which, naturally, had to be financed by BMW, and not entirely from internal cash flow) was to re-jig the Solihull factory in a radical manner. Before preparation for CB40 began in 1995 (backed by BMW money, of course), Solihull was at once busy and profitable, yet in need of modernization. If BMW's long-term plans for Land Rover, and the Rover Group in general, were to come to fruition, there was simply no space, on existing assembly lines, for CB40 to be built there.

The solution – a medium-term, total rearrangement, was to erect a brand-new paint shop, and a brand-new assembly hall. Fortunately, the centre of the complex – between what had become known as 'North Works' (where Range Rover was assembled) and 'South Works' (where Defenders and Discovery types took shape) – was still largely undeveloped so, to serve the entire complex, a vast and brand-new paint shop was built there. Then, alongside 'North Works' (actually in the north-eastern sector of the factory grounds, and linked to North Works) another new building, dedicated for CB40/Freelander assembly, was also built.

Except for in-filling, and total reconstructional activities, effectively this meant that the Solihull complex, which had been occupied by Rover for more than more than fifty years, was

---

Solihull Then, Solihull Now

Anyone connected with Solihull when the original Land Rover was launched in 1948 would scarcely recognize the early twenty-first century layout. Although the factory entrance, from Lode Lane, is still in the same place, and the factory boundaries remain, most of the site is now built over, with further expansion and alterations always seeming to take place. Here is a summary of what has already happened in half a century, and the situation in 2002.

In the beginning, Land Rovers (the ancestors of the Defenders) and Rover passenger cars were assembled in the original aero-engine buildings, and there was much surrounding space – enough, in fact, to build a useful test track, and an off-road demonstration facility. Those buildings, much modernized, now embrace final assembly of Defenders, Discoveries and third-generation Range Rovers operating in parallel. By comparison with the state-of-the-art range Rover facilities, those allocated to Defender assembly looked positively 'cottage industry'.

In the early-1960s, a new complex known as 'North Block' or 'North Works' was set up to accommodate the brand-new Rover 2000 (P6) passenger car. In the 1970s/1980s, after the P6 was discontinued, this block was re-equipped for the assembly of Range Rovers, and then second-generation Range Rovers. In addition, much of it was given over to Rover engine and transmission manufacture. When the second-generation Range Rover was discontinued in 2002, the assembly area was mothballed, before being re-equipped for the next new-model range being developed – thought to be a third-generation Discovery.

In the mid-1970s, a new 'East Works', also known as the 'SD1 block', was erected, originally as a completely integrated paint/trim/assembly facility for the Rover SD1 passenger car. After production of this model was moved out in 1982, it was swept into the integration of Land Rover facilities. By the early 2000s, it had became a colossal body-in-white assembly block for all the company's 4×4 models. At the eastern extremity, too, an extension housed a massive multi-function press shop, which was busily stamping out skin panels for Range Rover, and for the new Mini (which was manufactured by BMW at Oxford).

In 1997, a large extension, which doubled the size of North Works, appeared and was given over to assembly of the Freelander. At the same time, a huge new paint-shop was built in the centre of the complex, from which completed painted shells could be fed to the three different assembly halls. This, though, is not the end. While I was preparing the first edition of this book, I made yet another visit to Solihull. Seeing yet more digging, ground clearing and the erection of further steel work on the south side of the site, I innocently asked what it was for. All I got from my guide was a charming smile, and the remark: 'We are expanding even further, and this will allow us to put in yet more body and final assembly lines'.

So now we must wait and see …

now nearly full, though on recent visits in the early 2000s I saw evidence of further expansion, in search for yet more capacity.

As far as the Freelander was concerned, of course, there was one major difference – that the engines and main transmissions were to be built off-site – actually at the Rover Group (ex-Austin/ex-BMC) factories at Longbridge, which was about ten miles away, on the southern edge of Birmingham.

As a result, in the early-2000s, this meant that there were three main final assembly areas at Solihull. Much expanded, and heavily modernized, the original, historic, Land Rover assembly buildings now looked after the assembly of Defenders, Discovery types and new-generation Range Rover model lines, each of them having dedicated flow lines, roughly parallel to each other. The Freelander had its own dedicated facility in the expanded North Works.

The third area, once given over to Range Rover assembly, was mothballed when second-generation (1994–2001) assembly came to an end. Land Rover make no secret of their plans to bring it back into use when the next new 4×4 models were ready.

What had once been known as the SD1 block, where Rover private cars had been assembled from 1976 to 1982, had been the centre of Land Rover body shell assembly since the mid-1980s. By the early 2000s, much-modernized and completely stuffed full of modern machinery, it was split into three dedicated areas – one for Discovery body assembly, one for Range Rover assembly, and one for the completion of Freelander monocoques. At the far south eastern end of this building, a new extension housed a colossal 'multi-strike' Muller Weingarten press tool, which was used for shaping huge outer skin panels (including those for the BMW-manufactured Mini too!).

But that was not the end of the story. In 2002, while researching this book, I visited Solihull to see that the body shop was already being extended, so that the last vestiges of undeveloped factory land were to be covered over – for chairman Bob Dover had announced that preparations

Rocks like that are just child's play for any Land Rover product!

were going ahead to launch a new (third-generation) Discovery at Solihull, and because completed cars seemed to be stored, temporarily, in many corners, it was clear that more space was always needed.

Freelander on the Market

When CB40 became Freelander, and was officially unveiled in September 1997, Land Rover suggested that they might make 60,000 Freelanders a year, and that the new model might add 40 per cent to Land Rover's annual vehicle sales. More than 125,000 Defenders, Discoveries and Range Rovers had been built in 1996, still more were currently being assembled, and BMW hoped that up to 190,000 could now follow. After that, a further doubling of production was already being talked about.

Land Rover's pricing policy with the

162 Freelander: New Structure, New Engines, New Thinking

The Freelander looked fresh when launched in 1997 – there being little family resemblance to other Land Rovers, and even at four years old (this was an original V6-engined type) it had not become over familiar.

Freelander was certainly right. As ever, there was a big pricing spread between 'entry-level', and 'full-bells-and whistles' types in each range. The table below shows how the new car lined up with the other models at Solihull at the start of the 1998 calendar year (by which time volume production was well under way).

Price Comparison of Freelander with other Models at Solihull at the start of 1998	
Freelander	£15,995 – £20,995
Defender	£16,354 – £22,164
Discovery	£19,765 – £30,220
Range Rover	£35,130 – £47,765

For the first time, therefore, Land Rover now had a full range of 4×4s to sell – different not only in sizes, and prices, but different too in their approach to marketing. There could be nothing so diverse, after all, as a three-door Freelander with a turbo-diesel engine, and a sumptuously-equipped Range Rover with a 4.6ltrV8.

As usual in the UK, it was *Autocar* that was the first of the motoring magazines to get its hands on a test car. The first of several types tried was a five-door 1.8i Station Wagon, complete with the high-reving 118bhp/1,796cc K-Series petrol engine, which the testers described as: 'A totally convincing new baby Land Rover'.

Autocar observed, probably correctly, that:

> It is probably true to say that, had Toyota not created the RAV4 at the beginning of the decade, Land Rover might not have bothered with the Freelander. But such was the runaway success of the RAV4, and the sport utility market it tapped in to, that Land Rover could no longer just observe ….

It is probably true to say that BMW's marketing

experts, who rarely missed a trick at this time, were quick to spot the trends.

The testers also concluded, rightly, that here was a Land Rover whose chassis was aimed in a different direction. Here, for the first time, was a chassis meant to handle very well on sealed surfaces (the use of a high-feedback, hydraulically-assisted, rack-and-pinion steering system was a pointer), yet be competitive off-road. By Land Rover standards, the grip and the agility was seemingly as good as ever, yet one big off-road compromise had had to be made – that there was no low range that might otherwise equip the Freelander for clawing its way up otherwise impossible gradients.

'It seems faintly ludicrous that we've reached a stage where an engine can be shared by a mid-engined sports car and a vehicle like this' the testers noted, before going on to record a top speed of 108mph, with 0-60mph acceleration (on a sealed surface) in 10.5 seconds. It is worth remembering, surely, that no Range Rover had ever achieved such figures until the fuel-injected 3.9ltr V8 type came along at the end of the 1980s. The Freelander's overall fuel consumption – of 24.6mpg (Imperial) – was also well up to expectations.

The testers seemed to be quite overwhelmed by the new car's agility:

> It is true that the Freelander lacks the ultimate on-road chassis response of the [Honda] CR-V in particular; it always feels bigger and heavier when it's hustling along narrow B-roads. But the upshot is a ride which knocks that of the RAV4 and CR-V for six, and a steering system that is as precise as it is well damped against intrusion. The fact that the Freelander isn't quite as sharp as the opposition on twisty roads pales into insignificance. [It provides] … a degree of handling fluency and composure that you'd just not credit from a vehicle that looks so rugged.

However, the lack of a crawler-gear set-up provided the down-side:

> Which leaves only the question of its off-road capability unanswered. We tried to climb several hills in the Freelander, and it only managed some of them. It wasn't the lack of articulation that thwarted us, but the severe clutch smell that soon appeared due to the lack of a low ratio. Don't expect to go serious mountain-climbing in this car, even though it is far better equipped to tackle the rough stuff than any rival.

However, the way that the car leaned towards the 'fun', 'leisure' and sheer 'car-orientated' market was also made clear:

> The passenger car genes run thick and fast in the Freelander's cabin. You could almost be fooled into thinking you've just climbed aboard a Rover 600 by the Land Rover's conventional car-like driving position. Which is precisely the impression Land Rover's interior designers were attempting to create here….

Because this was the 'basic' 1.8I version, the fitment of anti-lock brakes and hill descent control, plus a passenger's airbag, alloy wheels, a six-speaker stereo and mud flaps pushed up the total price to £20,134, yet no-one was complaining:

> As it is, the Freelander represents a refreshing departure for Land Rover … What truly distinguishes the Freelander from most of its opposition is its exterior, and its unmatched feeling of solid quality. It looks like a class act. And from the moment you climb aboard, it feels like a class act. There's only one logical conclusion to be drawn from that….

That was the sort of verdict welcomed by Land Rover, especially when a straight comparison with the rivals from Honda and Toyota provided the remark that:

> But there's something more to the Freelander than pure ability. It also has that crucial gene of desirability running through it that makes BMWs and Mercedes somehow more distinguished than Volvos and Saabs. Be in no doubt: it's a class act, the Freelander. And no one will be more aware of this, right now, than Honda and Toyota.

A good start, then, and one that was noted in the marketplace. Demand for the Freelander took off like a rocket, and even before export deliveries began, the company (and BMW, the cash-rich parent) could see that this gamble was going to pay off.

The same magazine, however, was less complimentary about the softback version, which it tried a few weeks later, and this confirms what other, private, observers later concluded. Although the softback looked trendy enough, especially when the roof was furled, and it might even be mistaken for a semi-sporting off-road machine, the inescapable conclusion was that the softback hood was awkward, both to put up and take down, but in its operation:

> Land Rover is having problems with the softback roof. Not only is this one complicated, but you also need to be strong to muscle each section into place.

Each side window is secured by a zip on two sides, and is fed in like a caravan awning along the C-pillar. It opens from the outside, meaning the car is badly exposed to break-ins.

The rest of the roof is similarly difficult to operate …and requires the combined efforts of at least two people….

Pointing out that this was 'the ultimate lifestyle Landie', *Autocar* also noted that the loss of two passenger doors reduced comparative prices by £2,000 – or £1,000-per-door – while pointing out that the optional bolt-on hardtop cost £500 and that you would have to arrange for storage, in your garage, when it was not fitted.

No matter. Quite clearly, the Freelander was exactly what the Land Rover market had been waiting for, sales surged ever upwards, and it was

---

Ford Takes the Prize

In the winter of 1999–2000, when BMW decided to rid itself of the Rover Group, the fate of Land Rover was initially not certain. BMW's favoured buyer for the Rover Group was Alchemy Partners (a British company that was widely seen as a potential asset-stripper), but that concern had no interest in taking on Land Rover, and neither was BMW yet convinced that it should sell it off. At least three BMW main board members (including Wolfgang Reitzle, who would re-enter the story only months later) had already resigned because they could not agree to that sale.

Shortly, however, Alchemy Partners convinced BMW that the way to 'balance the books' of taking a huge loss on Rover was to sell off Land Rover for close to £2 billion, and this was done very rapidly indeed. Ford, which had previously tried to purchase Land Rover in the 1980s, was already sniffing around the margins, and speedily agreed to buy the Land Rover business complete.

Although Land Rover was only marginally profitable at the time, it had buoyant sales, an extremely good marketing image, and (except for the Defender) an up-to-date product range. Not only that, but as part of the deal Ford also purchased the ultra-modern R & D headquarters at Gaydon, which included a state-of-the-art design/styling studio, along with massive and still developing complex of test tracks and other facilities.

Ford was delighted with its new purchase, while BMW seemed to be delighted to have rid itself of such a turbulent, on-going, British problem. However, before Ford could even inspect the Gaydon HQ, BMW's planners swept through it, not only getting rid of any evidence of the Rover business, and extracting the remains of the Mini project (which they were to keep), but making sure that any evidence of BMW four-wheel-drive technology was also removed.

Ford, however, seemed to be content with its purchase, and immediately installed a new team of top managers. Gaydon became the new corporate Head Quarters of Land Rover while, fresh from his triumphs with the Ford-owned Jaguar and Aston Martin businesses, Bob Dover was speedily installed as chairman and chief executive.

The first fruits of the merger – the launch of the third-generation Range Rover (which was already well on the way to completion at the time of the sale) – followed at the end of 2001, by which time Ford had apparently approved the development of new-type Discovery and Defender ranges.

For Land Rover, the early 2000s were going to very exciting.

The 2.5ltr V6 engine fitted to the Freelander was known as the KV6, and came from the same family of Longbridge designed/manufactured engines as the K-Series four-cylinder type.

not long before the new factory block was as busy as it could possibly be. Importantly, exports were booming as never before – with three out of four 4×4s finding a home overseas.

This was only the beginning, for several new, and extra, derivatives were already being planned. Even at this early stage, the pundits noted the promise of new-generation four-cylinder engines, which BMW was about to start producing at the massive new Hams Hall factory (which was a mere seven miles north of Solihull). There was also the compact four-overhead-cam Rover V6, which was a close relative of the Freelander's existing four-cylinder petrol engine.

New Engines for 2001

Although the arrival of a commercial version of the three-door Freelander in mid-1999 went almost unnoticed, in 2000 there was avid interest in the prospects for new-engined models. A V6-engined version was previewed at the Geneva

Motor Show in March 2000, but two new types – one with the V6 petrol engine, the other with BMW's modern common-rail direct-injection Td4 2ltr diesel – were not officially put on sale until September 2000. Both these varieties were a real advance on what had gone before. Even though Ford had bought Land Rover from BMW in March 2000, it went ahead with a long-evolving plan for the twin-overhead-camshaft 1,951cc BMW turbo-diesel to replace the more conventional Rover L-Series with which the Freelander had started its career.

The new BMW diesel was ultra-modern, state-of-the-art in every way and was a corporate unit, built at Steyr in Austria, which had already found a home in the Rover 75, along with the BMW 3-Series and 5-Series types. Not only was the BMW unit lighter than the L-Series, but it was quieter in operation, more powerful, more torquey and (it was claimed) significantly more fuel-efficient too. The figures in the table on page 167 tell their own story.

Land Rover was so content with this new engine that it also made a five-speed Jatco automatic transmission (with fully automatic or Steptronic 'clutchless manual' changes available)

No nonsense from this Freelander, with the spare wheel mounted sturdily on the tailgate.

Comparison of the BMW Td4 Turbo-Diesel and the Rover L-Series Engines		
Feature	Rover L-Series	BMW Td4 Turbo-Diesel
Capacity (cc)	1,994	1,951
Peak power (bhp)/rpm	96/4200	110/4000
Peak torque (lb ft)/rpm	155/2,000	192/1,750

as an option. Except in tune, and in detail, this engine/auto combination was one that already existed in the Rover 75.

Independent road tests proved Land Rover's point (though not the claimed 10mpg economy gain). An automatic-transmission Station Wagon Td4 could almost reach 100mph, could sprint to 60mph in a very creditable 14.6 seconds, and could record at least 33mpg in normal day-to-day motoring.

Installing Rover's high-revving 177bhp KV6 was an even more ambitious project. Although provision had always been made for it at the project 'packaging' stage in 1994–5, this 90-degree V6, complete with twin-overhead-camshaft cylinder heads, was a very snug fit in the engine bay. This V6, however, had always been engineered for transverse installation, so no compromises were needed to slot it into the Freelander. Because it reved so highly – peak was 6,500rpm, while 7,000 was easily possible – Land Rover had to drop its final drive ratio significantly, but the overall on-the-road effect was the same as before.

Here was the flagship that brought a grin to every Freelander follower's face. With a claimed top speed of 113mph, 0–60mph in no more than 10.1 seconds, all delivered in turbine-like smoothness, and with the transmission control that only a BMW-developed Steptronic system seemed able to deliver, this was a totally different 4×4 from the sort of machinery which Land Rover had once produced.

Not that the new cars were cheap. Starting in

BMW Engines – What Might Have Been

When BMW sold off Land Rover to Ford, both companies had to unravel inter-company future projects, which were already in place. Even before BMW purchased the Rover Group, it was clear that they would shortly need to design and develop a modern range of four-cylinder petrol engines.

After a good deal of research into possible locations – not only in Germany, but also in Austria and in the UK – BMW elected to build a brand-new engine manufacturing plant in Britain. At the time, BMW not only intended to use these engines in new BMW models, but in forthcoming Rover and Land Rover models too.

Fortunately for them, a vast and rambling industrial site (which included an obsolete power station) at Hams Hall, just north of Birmingham International airport, became available. Permission was soon gained for the old facilities to be razed, and for a new state-of-the-art factory to be erected.

Started in 1997, meant to be ready in 2000, with serious mass-production starting in 2001, this factory was dedicated to the building of a new generation of four-cylinder petrol engine. Coded NG42 (NG = new generation), with a 16-valve twin-overhead camshaft and technologically advanced valve gear control, these aluminium engines were immediately available in 114bhp/1,796cc and 143bhp/1,995cc form.

Before BMW elected to sell off Land Rover to Ford, the long-term plan was that these engines would eventually find a home in the Freelander, where they were intended to replace the expensive-to-build Rover 1.8ltr K-Series. Because the K-Series developed 118bhp, whereas the larger KV6 2.5 ltr developed 173bhp, the use of these new-type BMW engines would have been ideal gap-fillers for the still evolving range of 'small' Land Rovers.

In the aftermath of the acquisition of Land Rover by Ford, this strategy was immediately made redundant. Although nothing in the latest multi-national business was ever easy to predict, it looked as if future Freelander engine swapping would henceforth be confined to the use of modern Ford units – and there were plenty of those.

When the Freelander was launched to the North American market, the company produced this 'exploded' example of the V6 engine, to show off its construction.

the autumn of 2000, British-market Freelander prices (a 1.8i. softback, for instance) started at £15,995, but Td4 engined cars kicked in at £17,195, while the range of V6-engined types cost between £21,595 and £24,595. Not cheap – but still much lower than those for the current-market Discovery II (£21,995 – £32,940), and no-one was complaining about those either!

Objective USA

The rumours had been around for some time, but it was not until January 2001 that Land Rover confirmed its intention to start selling V6-engined Freelanders in the USA. Starting its career towards the end of 2001, and complete with its Jatco automatic transmission, this splendid machine was out to take on USA 'domestic' competition from Ford's Maverick and the Jeep Cherokee, along with the Japanese Toyota and Nissan 4×4s, in what they had come to treat as their own special sales territory. The company's immediate hope was to sell 20,000 Freelanders a year in the USA.

The North American media was introduced to the new 'Federal' Freelander on an ambitious ride-drive appraisal in Iceland, where the cars appeared in 2002-Model Year guise, along with a promise that sales would begin in December 2001. These cars, therefore, included the more prominent front bumper (which was needed to

Above As re-engineered for the North American market, the Freelander had big crash beams built into the doors, and rear quarters, to made the car totally safe against side intrusion crashes.

Below This display example shows how the transversely-mounted V6 engine slotted easily into the Freelander's engine bay.

cover the extra cooling and air-conditioning installations), along with the new-style five-spoke cast alloy road wheels, more sporty front seats and the latest black trimmed facia/centre console arrangements. Not only were new colours on offer, but satellite navigation had become optional too, while the sound system now had a six-speaker layout, and the interior was liberally equipped with cup holders.

USA buyers, by the way, had to pay considerably less for their Stateside V6-engined Freelanders, for 2002 MY prices started at $26,500 (equivalent to £18,300 and, car for car, perhaps £6,000 cheaper than you could buy it in the UK).

In the meantime, the Freelander carried on selling fast all round the world, and in the early 2000s it was always the best selling of all the 4×4 types being built at Solihull. However, with Ford now in control, and with other corporate 4×4s to be considered in other parts of Ford empire (not least the Freelander-sized Escape, which was called a Maverick in Europe and its very close relative, the Mazda Tribute), it seemed certain that many changes, and improvements, would follow in the next few years.

A new angle on a very popular Land Rover 4×4, this being an overhead view of the Freelander five-door.

Soaring Production

After a fallow period in the 1980s, Land Rover/Range Rover sales and production surged ahead in the 1990s, reached new peaks in the early 2000s, and looked likely to expand even further in the first decade of the twentieth century.

To recall previous glories – annual production first exceeded 20,000 in 1953–4, then nudged ahead of 50,000 for the first time in 1968–9. Helped along by the arrival of the Range Rover, the first peak, of 70,460 vehicles, was achieved in 1975–6. Then, after staying within the range 40,000 – 60,000/year band for a decade (with Range Rover forming a larger and ever larger proportion), the arrival of the Discovery helped push the figure to new heights. By 1996 – the year before the arrival of the Freelander – no fewer than 125,000 4×4s streamed out of the gates at Solihull. Thereafter, the Freelander began to sell at up to 85,000 a year on its own and by 2002, with Freelander deliveries to the USA just getting under way, beating the 200,000/year barrier was in sight.

Ford, having bought Land Rover from BMW in 2000, had even wider ambitions, and early in the 2000s began a major redevelopment at Solihull, which might – one day – produce a plant capable of producing 400,000 4×4s every year. All this, I remind you, from a one-time aero-engine plant, which was thought to be fully occupied in the 1950s.

Solihull in the early 2000s was almost, but not quite, running out of space. This aerial view, taken in 2002, shows just how much more of the site had been developed, or enlarged, since the mid-1960s (see page 44). In this view, the one-time 'shadow factory' building, which houses Defender, Discovery and Range Rover final assembly, is at the bottom left, the Freelander assembly plant is top centre, the huge body assembly plant for all models is bottom right, and the state-of-the-art paint shop is in the centre of the complex. Engine manufacture is top left, while the mothballed ex-Range Rover facility is between that and the Freelander building. As ever, at this time, more development, and more new building, was already under way!

Appendix
Oddities, Militaria and Specials

It was inevitable, of course. No sooner had the world of motoring discovered the Land Rover, than enquiries for special versions began to flood in. It was not just that Solihull's little marvel had four-wheel-drive. It was not that it had a robust separate chassis, and it was not that it had a simple easy-to-assembly body shell – it was the combination of all those factors.

The result, over the years, was a positive explosion of special versions – both for the civilian market and for military services all round the world. As Humpty Dumpty once so famously said of Alice (*Through the Looking Glass*): 'With a name like yours, you might be any shape, almost'.

If I attempted to write a comprehensive survey of Land Rover 'specials', this section would completely overwhelm the book, for the list is almost endless. The obvious and high-profile special types – extra-long-wheelbase models, special conveyances for HM The Queen and other overseas dignitaries, and all-terrain ambulances – seem to be well known. In addition, there are the light armoured cars, vast wheeled models for soggy conditions, amphibians, mobile canteens, cinema-screen supports and bases for extending ladder appliances; there have been many intriguing one-offs, and new applications continue to emerge.

Then, of course, there were the many and varied military vehicles, which found a use on almost every continent, and every military theatre.

Soon after the 80in Land Rover went into production, the company made one of its very first special editions – a Fire Engine derivative. Fortunately, there was never much need of it within the Solihull factory itself.

Above How do you develop a golf ball? By making changes to alter its flight, its tendency to spin, and its speed through the air. World-famous company Penfold needed a specially-portable machine, and a Series I Land Rover to take it all around the country.

Right Tractor wheels and tyres and special body alterations were needed to produce this machine, whose immense ground clearance and traction were considered for forestry commission use.

174 Oddities, Militaria and Specials

Above Because of its sturdy separate chassis frame, and great strength, the Land Rover was almost infinitely variable. This 6×6 conversion of a Series IIA needed a new rear chassis frame, though, to accomplish the impossible!

Below What had started life as a gargantuan 120in forward-control project was finally transformed into a front-wheel-drive one-off with 'kneeling' rear suspension, so that it could be used a transporter for the Rover-BRM Le Mans race car.

Military Applications

I have already mentioned the way in which the original style of Land Rover was first assessed by Britain's armed forces, but it is worth rehearsing the way that it came to take so much business. Most of that business, by the way, has been with 'classic' Land Rovers, for Discoveries and especially Range Rovers have usually been found too glossy and too costly for military use.

During and after World War Two, for so many applications Britain's military transport machine came to rely on the Jeep, which was made in huge numbers in the United States. To succeed it and (the planners hoped) to provide a British-made machine that would be bigger, stronger and even more capable, the Nuffield-designed/Austin-produced FV1800/Champ was developed. In military form, the Champ was powered by the 2.8ltr Rolls-Royce B40 engine, which was a relative of the power unit being used in Bentley Mk VI and Rolls-Royce Silver Dawns of the period.

In the meantime, the Army tried a small batch of B40-engined Land Rover SIs (these needed a wheelbase of 81in, just to accept this engine, which was much more bulky than the existing Rover 1,595cc power unit). These were satisfactory, but no more came of the project for the time being.

Then, in 1950, Land Rover was invited to pit its standard 1.6ltr-engined machine against the FV1800 production machine, in tests at Chobham (in Surrey): to the military establishment's embarrassment, the Land Rover outperformed their baby. Nonetheless, a big batch of FV1800/Champs were built (between 1952 and 1956) and in the meantime batches of Land Rovers began to be supplied.

Once Champ assembly had closed down, however, the Army soon announced that the Land Rover would henceforth become its standard $\frac{1}{4}$-ton payload 'forward area' vehicle, and regular deliveries then began. In the coming years, Solihull usually found itself busy producing large numbers of specially-adapted, specially-equipped, 4×4s – not only for the Army, but for the Navy and the Air Force too. In due course, too, a series of equal special machines would be developed for Britain's special force but – for

An 88in Series II leads a selection of British military vehicles, in Middle Eastern territory in the 1960s. That is a Humber 'Pig' armoured car behind it, followed by two Bedford transport trucks.

Above This extraordinary conversion was evolved for use by the Army's bomb disposal squad, so that it could pick its way across the most impossible terrain without grinding to a halt.

Left The 'bomb disposal' 88in military Land Rover used separate front and rear drive sub-frames, along with eight steel wheels and tracks to spread the load on boggy ground. One example of this type is still to be seen at Gaydon.

obvious security reasons – little was ever said about these.

Once the world's military services had seen how the British were using Land Rovers, and had realized their merits and their amazing versatility, there was a constant stream of orders. By the end of the century, almost every non-Communist bloc nation that did not rely on the USA for its transport supplies, had ordered a fleet of special-purpose Land Rovers. Each order seemed to specify more special features than the last.

The variety was enormous. Complete books have already been written about military Land Rovers, and much information has been published. In some cases, however, because of the sensitive use to which these vehicles were put, and because of the special equipment fitted, not all the information about specifications and equipment has been made public.

By the 1960s, too, military-specification types often had considerable style changes, and many had 24V electrics. An increasing number (though still in a minority) were manufactured with diesel engines, so that they could tap in to the same fuel supplies as the trucks and tanks in the same military 'fleets' – though petrol power was usually confirmed because of the extra performance it offered.

More and more kit – radios, scaling ladders, machine mountings, carrying provision for camouflage nets and mounts for extra fuel cans – all became familiar, as did special bodywork, including Command and Control types and ambulances.

Conversions carried out by specialists included half-track vehicles, and even light armoured cars – but it would be futile of me to try to list everything, as I would be sure to omit something significant. It is enough to point out that such vehicles have already been supplied to no fewer than 140 military or para-military forces, worldwide.

As far as the British Army was concerned, the majority of their orders were for short wheelbase types, because they were more compact and more manoeuvrable, and it was the longer-wheelbase types that were often treated to the more specialized bodywork. These might be for use, for instance, as ambulances, commanders' caravans, communications centres, personnel carriers,

Somewhere under all that special military equipment – including two machine guns, smoke dispensers, camouflage netting, and sand ladders, there is a 109in military Land Rover. This picture summarises just what Solihull's best could achieve, if carefully and professionally, prepared!

The Army found another use for the forward control Land Rover in this fire engine.

equipment-towing vehicles or generator trucks. If Solihull's roomy and versatile go-anywhere 4×4 could be used for any task, the Army soon pressed it into service.

The most bizarre-looking type, I believe, was the matt-pink painted variety used by the special services in desert conditions. Experience has shown that this is the best colour to use for camouflage in desert conditions – people who think that the desert is yellow should go there to see for themselves.

This, of course, was – and is – a non-ending story, for the ubiquitous Land Rover was just as useful for the Armies of the world in the 2000s as it had ever been in the 1950s. Gradually, but definitely, over the years, the world's Governments put more and more demands on to Solihull's best – so perhaps it was as well that the chassis designs, and the engines provided to power those chassis, improved persistently. It was once estimated that at least one-third of all 'classic' Land Rovers ever built had either been used by military or para-military clients, and that many more had been used by Governments on official business closely related to those tasks.

Accordingly, when the leaf-spring chassis gave way to the Ninety/One-Ten types of coil spring chassis in the mid-1980s, Land Rover had already evolved military versions of them. It was at this point, by the way, that diesel-engined machines began to be supplied in larger numbers, as their performance had finally risen to a level acceptable to the military planners. This process, one of gradual change, improvement and evolution, carried on in the years that

This Shorland Armoured Patrol Car was a private-enterprise conversion on the 109in chassis, originally shown in 1965. Some such vehicles were used by the security services in Northern Ireland. Here, Stuart Bladon of Autocar *magazine is enjoying a new experience in Solihull motoring.*

followed. The choice of 'Defender' for the 1990s was doubly appropriate in these cases. Significantly, once the 127in Land Rover appeared, this soon attracted interest from the military men, too.

In certain countries, the authorities required (and took delivery of) special versions for their own use. After the Gulf War of 1991, for instance, the US authorities took delivery of a fleet of 'Special Operations Vehicle' models for their Rangers, these including a permanently-fitted roll cage incorporating the mounting for a machine gun behind the seats. Then, in Australia thousands of much-modified One-Tens were produced with Isuzu diesel engines. Other, smaller and less high-profile, orders, came from all sides.

Development of military-style Land Rovers never stopped, and from the mid-1990s the company had finalized the detail of a series of Defender XDs (where XD stood for eXtra Duty), which were available in 90, 110 or 130 varieties. Visually, and under the skin, these were

180 Oddities, Militaria and Specials

This 'Perentie' One-Ten is seen on test by the Australian Army in the 1980s – the company secured a very large and important contract, for 2,600 vehicles, which were delivered between 1987 and 1994.

very different from civilian Defenders, for they included reinforced chassis frames, more rigid chassis/body mountings and sturdy roll cages, which would often be hidden beneath the canvas tilts.

In the meantime evolution, and improvement, continues non-stop.

Air-Transportable Types

One of the most ambitious of all military-specification types developed in the 1960s was what the British Army came to call 'Rover 1', but which is now equally well-known as the Half-Ton Lightweight. This evolved to satisfy a long-held Army belief that, if only go-anywhere soft-skinned vehicles could be parachuted, or carried, into particular situations, then they might be tactically invaluable.

It took ages for viable vehicles to be made. During World War Two both Standard (with the bug) and SS-Jaguar (with the side-valve Ford-engined VA) had a go, but neither was taken up.

As late as the early 1960s BMC produced the Mini-Moke, whose principal disadvantages included limited ground clearance and front-wheel-drive (though a four-wheel-drive version was proposed).

The problem was, that for this off-road requirement, the Army wanted such vehicles to have four-wheel-drive, Land Rover ground clearance standards and the same sort of rugged reliability. All of which was possible, from a number of sources, but not at the sort of (light) weight that was necessary.

Once the Army had become besotted with the Land Rover in the 1960s, it once again began to hanker for an air-transportable version, though the standard vehicles still seemed to be far too heavy. Helicopters with suitable cables and webbing slings would be needed to carry such vehicles, and the latest Westland Wessex (a modified

Opposite *Land Rover was asked to develop a lightweight air-transportable type in the 1960s, this being the result. The Westland Wessex is lifting a stripped-out half-ton model.*

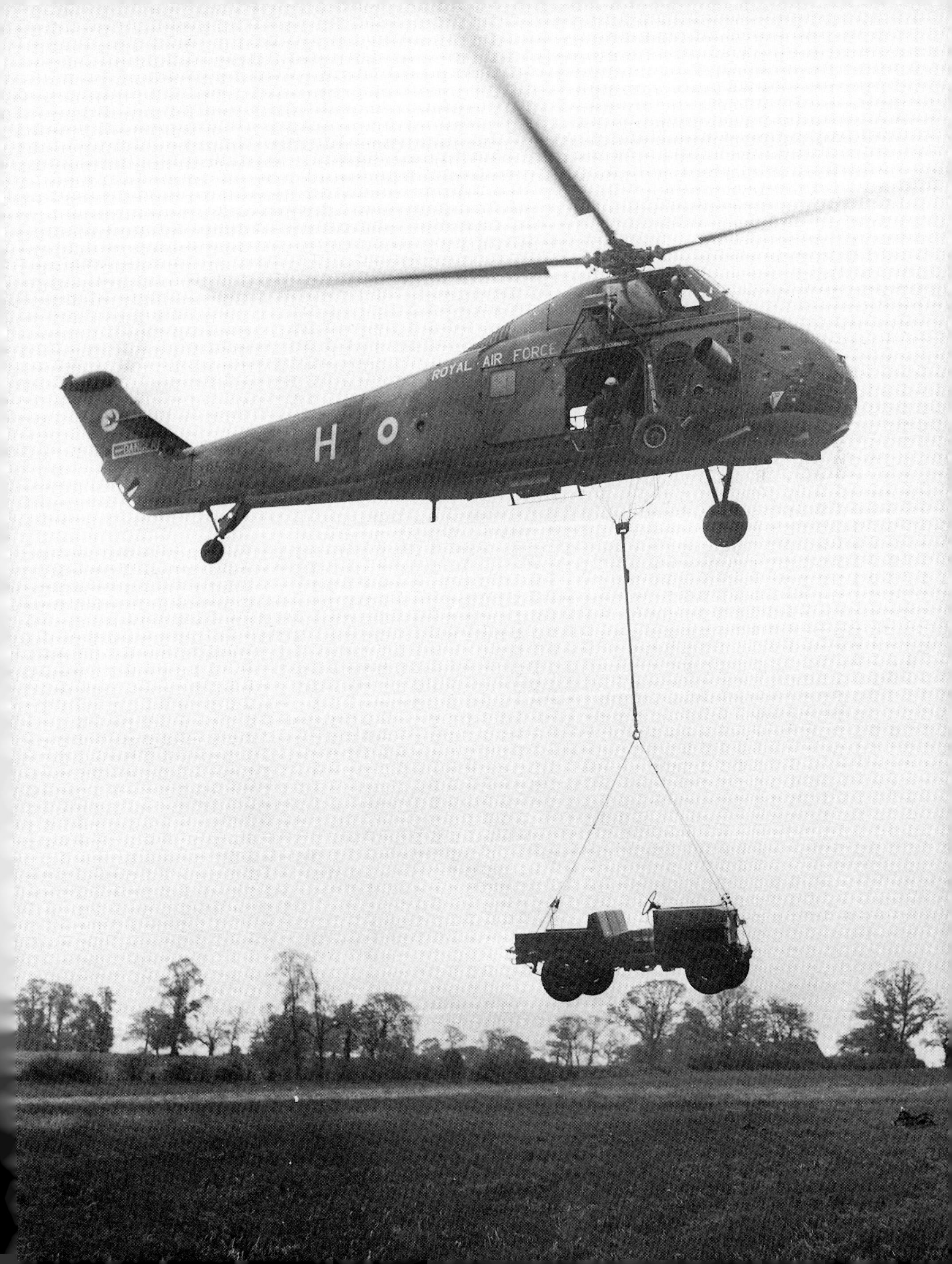
ROYAL AIR FORCE
H

182 Oddities, Militaria and Specials

version of the Sikorsky S58) was only then rated to lift 2,500lb/1.134kg in addition to its normal internal payload. At this time, a conventional 88in Land Rover weighed at least 2,950lb/1,338kg (more with a diesel engine fitted, even more with extra equipment), and the 109in was no less than 3,300lb/1,496kg.

The question was then asked, 'Could a Land Rover be stripped out to weigh less than 2,500lb/1,134kg – or, at least, could it be arranged for much weight to be stripped out for separate carriage, and for speedy assembly on site?'. From Solihull, the answer was encouraging. Although there was no way that a 109in chassis vehicle could be stripped out to approach that idea, with a complete redesign of the bodywork it might be possible to reduce the 88in vehicle's weight to that level.

Sounds easy, right? Well, it was not. The complete redesign produced a starkly styled lightweight (which was only 60in/1,524mm wide), with a 2¼ltr petrol engine, many of whose panels could be stripped off and delivered by another helicopter. When fully assembled, the lightweight was not all that light – it weighed no less than 3,210lb/1,456kg – but when stripped out, the main hull weighed in at only 2,660lb/1,206kg. Land Rover could do no more – so, could the Army compromise?

They could. According to the Army Air Corps, this might still be too much for a Wessex to lift, However, in due course, and to make the entire project viable, the Forces were persuaded to reduce the helicopter's internal payload limits to make the entire lifting package feasible.

In production from 1968 (when, therefore, it was based on the Series IIA civilian chassis), the lightweight remained available until 1984. Though only 2,989 Series IIA types were produced, sales of the later Series III-based machine

The air-transportable lightweight 'half ton' military 88in machine had unmistakable 'styling', and the very minimum of frills.

(with a different headlamp arrangement) carried on steadily throughout the 1970s and early 1980s. Well over 10,000, for example, were produced in the 1970s alone.

Earlier in the 1960s, incidentally, Rover had also dabbled with producing an air-transportable 109in type, though because of its weight and bulk this would have had to be carried in heavy-lift fixed-wing aircraft (latterly, that is, in aircraft like the Lockheed Hercules). Such vehicles had restyled bodywork behind the front seats, which incorporated a long, flat, rear platform, and they could carry a payload of up to 2,205lb/1,000kg in personnel or cargo. Only twenty-eight of these vehicles were ever produced.

The half-ton military Land Rover made no concessions towards comfort, or weather protection – but it got the job done.

Forward Control 101in Model

The first truly-specialized military Land Rover emerged in the 1970s, and was specifically developed for used by the British Army. This was the big, brawny, forward-control machine, which is always known by its wheelbase as the '101'. In production at Solihull between 1975 and 1978, with a total production run of 1,945, it was at once more powerful and with a bigger payload than the normal-control 109in Land Rovers being built at the time.

The need originally arose because the Army saw the need for an artillery tractor – a 4×4 that could not only transport personnel and ammunition, but that could also tow powered trailers, and might also tow the artillery piece itself. The 109in model, however carefully built and serviced,

184 Oddities, Militaria and Specials

could not cope with this requirement.

Before Tom Barton's engineers got down to designing a new model, a modification of the existing 'civilian' 110in forward-control model was considered. In addition, a normal-control 109in chassis, which used one of the most powerful straight six-cylinder engines (a 2,995cc version), and whose transmission was also modified to drive a powered trailer, was also tested.

None of these modifications hit the spot. All fell down on what I might describe as the 'military misuse' factor – the Army always demanded more than they were guaranteed, and all fell down on the payload and towed load requirements.

A new machine, therefore, had to be designed – and as far as I can see, no thought was ever given to evolving a civilian version out of it. In 1970 and 1971 the need to provide a lot more power, and a lot more torque, was central to the whole design. In the mid-1960s, by the way, Land Rover had made one notable false start, by developing a huge all-new chassis. Not only did this have a monstrous wheelbase of 120in, but it was powered by a 5.8ltr Perkins diesel engine, and weighed nearly 7,500lb/3,400kg: This was not a success, and was swiftly discarded.

Fortunately, by the 1970s, the new Range Rover had already gone into production: Although the Range Rover's chassis and long-travel coil-spring suspension was never considered, its V8 engine, all-synchromesh main gearbox, transfer gearbox and centre differential were all considered ideal. To provide the maximum possible payload area and the longest-possible load floor (which, in fact, was 98in/2,489mm), the 101in chassis was provided with a forward-control driving position. As finalized, the 101 was at least 84in/2,134mm tall – its fuel consumption can be imagined!

The Range Rover's power train, therefore, was mated to the latest heavy-duty Salisbury axles (which had 5.57:1 ratios), all being fitted into a rugged new chassis frame, which was finalized with a 101in wheelbase. Simple, half-elliptic leaf spring suspension was chosen, the minimum ground clearance was 10in, and 9.00-16in tyres completed the layout.

Styling? Here was an ultra-simple, bluff-fronted, flat-sided, 4×4 pick-up, where the driving compartment space was shared between crew and V8 engine, and where creature comforts and

The 101in military forward-control Land Rover was not only a good load carrier, with great off-road ability, but it was also used to tow the Army's new-type 105mm 'Light Gun'. It used early-generation Range Rover V8 engine and main transmission components.

The 101in forward-control Land Rover, which was supplied initially to the British Army, and never went on civilian sale, was V8 powered, and could also drive a powered trailer through a rear power take-off.

elegance had simply not been considered. If anyone was ever brave enough to measure the aerodynamic qualities of this model, their findings were never published.

In ready-to-roll condition it weighed a sturdy 4,040lb, but when stripped out it weighed in at only 3,500lb. Because helicopter lifting capabilities had advanced considerably since the original 'Rover I' lightweight had been developed, this meant that it could also be air-transported by the latest Wessex and Puma choppers.

When it was first unveiled in 1972, one of the main attributes of this new '101' was that its transmission could be augmented to incorporate an extra rear-facing propeller shaft, which could then be linked up to powered trailers. The result was an articulated 6×6 combination. This, when linked to the enormous ground clearance of the new 101, and to all the usual Land Rover virtues, meant that it was well-nigh unstoppable wherever there was any grip.

Rubery Owen's single-axle powered trailer was engineered so that the rear-power take-off of the 101 was combined with the towing hook in a very mechanically elegant solution to the complex engineering and geometry problems this caused. However, though this worked very well indeed, it was not actually taken up by the military forces, for to them the 101 was much more useful as a simple towing device for its latest 105mm gun, while carrying the gun crew and the ammunition behind the seats.

The first 101 deliveries were made in 1975 – a dedicated assembly line was set up at Solihull for this purpose – though this was always a low-key project in which never more than twenty vehicles were produced in a week. Almost all these brutal but unlovely 4×4s were delivered to the British Forces, though a few orders also came in – from Australia, Egypt and Luxembourg.

After many of these massive machines had completed their military careers, they were sold off to the general public, and a number became familiar sights at club events in the 1990s.

In the 1980s, Land Rover hoped to sell this new-generation forward-control vehicle to the British Army, but it was never taken up. A prototype of this 'Llama' project survives, and can usually be seen on display at Gaydon.

In the mid-1980s Land Rover proposed a new machine, the forward-control V8-powered 'Llama' project, as a replacement for the forward-control 101s, but although several prototypes were built and tested by the Army, no production contract was ever placed.

Specials – an Endless List

Even before the Land Rover became everyone's favourite 4×4, the demand for special derivatives was evident. If it had such a solid structure, and if it had such amazing 4×4 cross-country ability, some thought, it must be possible to fit ... (whatever – add your own special requirements here!).

Land Rover itself started this off by offering the 'Compressor', the 'Fire Pump' and the 'Welder' varieties (already mentioned in earlier chapters) but that was just the beginning. In the flood that followed in the 1950s, there were mobile service schools, emergency repair units, ambulances, extending ladders for servicing high structures and tall street lamps, caravan conversions, transporters for racing cars,

Yet another useful, indeed, vital, special purpose vehicle – the sort of machine which local authorities might use for inspecting and maintaining high structures, light standards, and gantries or here, perhaps, to trim otherwise inaccessible foliage. The base was a 109in Series III machine.

Above *Located in Middlesex, and later in Berkshire, the Government-owned Road Research Laboratory needed a special chassis for special haulage and lifting jobs. In the early 1960s Land Rover provided the forward-control chassis to do the job.*

Below *By altering the rear of the chassis frame, and providing an all-can-do hitching pivot, the Land Rover chassis could be adapted to towing horse-boxes, or similar specialized trailers.*

Above *Good joke, but not much practical use! Land Rovers with flanged steel wheels for use as railway shunting engines would neither have been powerful, nor have had good enough brakes to be much use. Even so, this made a few headlines when briefly shown off.*

Left *Taxi! In 1995, when the Judge Dredd movie was being made, the producers could think of only one suitable vehicle for providing secure transport in the hostile streets – a much-modified 101in Land Rover. I drove one of these machines once – unforgettable!*

half-track conversions for military use, light armoured cars, and much more.

Then there would be Fire Service 'chase cars', longer-wheelbase 6×6 chassis conversions, snow plough conversions for road clearance in winter conditions, fire tenders for airports (including foam dispensers), tipper trucks, vehicle recovery trucks, hydraulic work platforms, mobile catering units, tracked derivatives (tracks at front and rear, that is), cut-and-shut tow truck versions, mobile cinema screens, and even – as a gimmick – conversions to hovercraft usage.

Like every other Land Rover enthusiast, I was impressed by the way the design was amended to produce smart off-road/parade conversion for use by HM The Queen. I was also startled by the way that I once saw a mobile cinema screen deployed as part of a Range Rover model launch.

And I also hooted with laughter at the idea of a Land Rover being fitted out with flanged

Right *After pop star Bob Geldof started the 'Band Aid' campaign to get massive aid to East African countries, in 1985 this much modified coil spring machine was prepared as a mobile workshop.*

wheels and put to use on a railway as a shunting locomotive. It was not that I thought it could not tow the trucks up and down the tracks, it was stopping everything with one set of drum brakes which caused me to ponder!

It was no wonder that Land Rover set up the Special Projects Department (or 'Technical Sales', as it was originally known) in 1957, with George Mackie at the helm, and before long their reputation was such that they were challenged to tackle, assess, test (or approve) the most amazing and outlandish conversions.

By the time this department was eventually subsumed into another, larger, department, it had made its name, all round the world, in no uncertain manner. The demand for special Land Rovers, however, continues to grow – whether it is for a special purpose machine, a special accessory or merely for a special trim/colour combination.

Not bad, as I have so often said, for a stopgap that was originally supposed to have a five-year life, in the 1950s.

Below *At the time the publicity claim for this monstrous conversion was that it was 'The World's Longest Land Rover' – it being a 6×6 built by the SVO department for Eastern Electricity. It was 21ft long, and weighed 2.8 tonnes unladen.*

Index

Alchemy Partners 164
Alfa Romeo (and models) 34
Allied Motors Ltd 29
Alvis 28, 90
Arlington Securities 105
Aston Martin 24, 35, 90, 164
Austin company 20, 35, 161
Austin models
    Champ/FV1800 35, 175
    Gipsy 356, 56
    Maestro 117
Austin-Morris Division 65
Austin-Rover Group 94, 134
Australian army 180
Autocar 36, 47, 85, 146, 162, 164, 179
Autocar & Motor 122

Bache, David 37, 40, 76
Band Aid 189
Bantam 4x4 12
Barton, Tom 13, 15, 33, 35, 53, 56, 63, 65, 69, 76, 77, 184
Bashford, Gordon 13–14, 16
Bedford (and models) 175
Bentley 175
Birmabright 13
Black, Sir John 10, 29
Bladon, Stuart 47, 179
BMC 35–6, 90, 161, 180
BMW (and models) 7, 90, 105–7, 109, 122, 126, 133–6, 141–6, 148–50, 154, 158, 160, 162–7, 171
Boyle, Robert 9

Brady, Chris 106
British Aerospace (BAe) 89–90, 94–5, 105–7, 134, 143, 149
British Leyland 7, 8, 35, 45, 53, 56, 61, 65, 67, 86, 89, 90, 93, 111, 134
British Motor Holdings (BMH) 90
British Motor Industry Heritage Trust (Gaydon) 21, 176, 186
British Telecom 93
Brittan, Nick 130
Broadhead, Mike 77, 80
Buick (and models) 70

Camel Trophy 125, 131
Centurion tank 28
Churchill, Sir Winston 30
Clarkson, Jeremy 122
Conran Design 117–18
Cowley (also known as Oxford) factory 8, 86, 105–6, 134, 160

Daihatsu (and models) 157
David Brown Industries 35
Dell, Edmund 68
Dick, Alick 29
Dover, Bob 109, 147, 161, 164

Edwardes, Sir Michael 68
Elsy, Dick 149
End of the Road 106

Fairey Winches Ltd 63–4
Fall, Tony 103
Farmer, George 40
Fell, Nick 136
Ferguson, Harry 29
Ferguson, John 20
Ferguson tractor 10, 29, 31, 33
Fiat (and models) 34
Ford (and models) 7, 11, 12, 20, 35, 65, 70, 89–90, 106, 109, 134, 147, 164, 167–71, 180
Freight Rover Sherpa 117

Geldof, Bob 189
General Motors 43, 46, 70, 89, 132, 134
Gilroy, Tony 85–6, 95, 113
Goddard, Lord Chief Justice 28
Gulf War 179

Hillman 9
Hodgkinson, Mike 68, 85
Honda (and models) 106, 128, 134, 152, 157, 163
Honda Crossroad 128
Humber (and models) 175
Hutchings, Tony 23

International Scout 65
Isuzu (and models) 65, 113–14, 116, 122, 157, 179

Jaguar (and models) 24, 82,

Index   *191*

90, 93, 164
Jeep 8, 11–18, 22–3, 29, 34, 37, 41, 65, 76, 102, 105, 132, 168, 175
Jowett (and models) 24
Judge Dredd (movie) 188

Keikhafer, Carl 70
Kia (and models) 157
Kidson case, the 28
King, Spen 67

Lada (and models) 65
Lagonda 35
Land Rover Ltd 68, 69, 85, 86, 89, 94
Land Rover factories
   Acocks Green 8, 9, 10
   Garrison Street 80, 86
   Gaydon 106, 136, 164
   Pengam 55
   Percy Road 86
   Perry Barr 86
   Solihull 7, 8, 9, 10, 12, 13, 19, 21, 23, 24, 27, 28, 29, 34, 40, 42, 44, 45, 48, 53, 61, 65, 66, 68, 73, 75, 78, 84–9, 93, 95, 96, 100, 102, 106, 108, 109, 110, 111, 113, 114, 121–2, 125–6, 129–30, 134–6, 143, 147–8, 155, 157, 159–62, 165, 170–72, 175, 177, 178, 182, 183, 185
   Tyburn Road 86
Land Rover models
   Series I 8–33, 40, 41, 42, 58, 93, 101, 172, 173, 175
   Series II 19, 23, 33, 34–42, 49, 58, 64, 101, 109, 175
   Series IIA 37, 38, 41, 42–60, 64, 174, 182
   Series III and V8 42, 53, 54, 55–85, 87, 110, 182, 186

Forward Control 109/110in. 43–6, 50–52, 178, 184, 187
Ninety 67, 75–97, 100–1, 109, 110–14, 178
One-Ten 7, 67, 75–97, 100–1, 109, 110–14, 118, 120, 178–80
Defender 7, 67, 70, 85, 92, 95–109, 116, 118, 120, 125–6, 128, 129, 130, 142, 145, 147, 150, 154, 155, 159–62, 164, 171, 179–80
Discovery (original and 'Romulus') 7, 67, 70, 89, 93, 96, 99–100, 104, 105, 106–8, 110–37, 139–40, 142–3, 145, 147, 150, 155, 158, 159–60, 162, 175
Discovery II ('Tempest' project) 106, 108–9, 134–47, 161, 168, 171
Freelander ('CB40' model) 7, 106, 108, 109, 134, 136, 139–40, 143–5, 147–71
SD5 project 76–7, 83
Project Jay (also 'Discovery') 93, 112 - 115
NAS models 102–5
Cariba concept car 104
90SV 104
'Highlander' project (*see* Freelander) 149
'Cyclone' project (*see* Freelander) 149
120in. forward-control car 174, 184
'Rover 1' air-droppable lightweight 180–3, 185
Forward-control 101in. 183–6, 188
'Llama' project 186

'Perentie' model 180
Leyland Cars 90
Leyland Vehicles 93
Leyland Motors 37, 45, 53, 90
Lincoln 90
Lockheed Hercules aircraft 183
London–Sydney Marathon 131
Lorenz, Andrew 106

Mackie, George 189
Martin-Hurst, William 43, 70
Mazda (and models) 170
McGovern, Gerry 155
Mercedes-Benz (and models) 146, 163
Mercury Marine 70
Metalurgica de Santa Ana 42
MG Rover (and models) 90, 152
Mini, new generation 8, 160, 161, 164
Mini Moke 180
Ministry of Defence (and British armed services) 7, 28, 35, 61, 175–86
Mitsubishi (and models) 65, 113–14, 116, 122
Morgan Plus 8 70, 123
Morris (and models) 8, 20, 105
Motor 21
Motor Shows
   Amsterdam 19
   Geneva 19, 129, 165–6
   NEC 145

Nissan (and models) 22, 65, 116, 157, 168

Oldsmobile (and models) 70

Paris-Moscow-Beijing Marathon Raid 100
Penfold 173

Phoenix Consortium 90
Pischetsrieder, Bernd 134, 149
Pininfarina 56
Pogmore, Colonel 35
Pontiac (and models) 70
Poppe, Olaf 16
Porsche Boxster 150
Premier Automotive Group 90, 147
Puma helicopter 185

Queen, Her Majesty The 54, 172, 188
Queen's Flight 127

Range Rover 7, 8, 53, 55, 56, 58, 61, 67, 69–71, 73, 75, 76–83, 85, 89, 91–3, 96, 99–100, 102, 105–6, 109, 110–32, 134–6, 139–50, 154–5, 159–63, 171, 175
Reitzle, Wolfgang 149, 164
Riley (and models) 24
Road Research Laboratory 187
Road Rover 33, 37, 111
Rolls-Royce 35, 67, 175
Rover company 8, 10, 15, 19, 22, 29, 31, 34–7, 41, 43–5, 53, 55–8, 65, 67, 68, 69–70, 76, 82, 86, 90
Rover – Coventry factory 10
Rover – Longbridge factory 126, 130, 134, 161, 165
Rover Group 90, 93, 95, 106, 126, 134, 143, 148–54, 160, 164, 167
Rover models
  M-Type 10
  Metro 114
  P3 16–20, 45
  P4 26, 37, 45–6, 55, 111
  P5 37, 46, 47, 55
  P5B 53, 70
  P6 (2000 and 2200) 21, 44–5, 64, 68, 160
  P6B 53
  SD1/2300/2600/3500 65, 67, 70, 73, 76, 86, 159–61
  220GTi 126
  400 series 154
  600 series 154
  800 series 126, 130, 154
  75 family 166–7
  Rover-BRM race car 174
  120in. forward-control prototype 174
Rubery Owen 16, 185
Ryder, Lord 67

Saab 163
Safety Devices 102–5
Salmons-Tickford 24–6
Santana 42, 67, 75, 87, 91, 100
Sikorski S58 helicopter 180
Simpson, George 106
Smith, A.B. 53
SS-Jaguar (and models) 180
Standard (and models) 10, 20, 29, 31, 33, 45, 67, 180
Standard Banner Lane factory 10
Stokes, Sir Donald (later Lord) 37, 45, 67
Stoneleigh 54
Sunbeam-Talbot (and models) 24
Suzuki (and models) 104

Taylor, James 127
Thompson, John 16
Toyota (and models) 22, 65, 116, 152, 157, 162–3
Triumph (and models) 8, 29, 45, 67, 70, 76, 82, 86, 90, 105
TVR 70, 82, 123, 128

Unipart 93

Valmet 150
Vauxhall (and models) 157
Volvo 90, 149, 163
VW Beetle 56

Westland Wessex helicopter 127, 180–2, 185
When Rover met BMW (TV series) 150
Wilks, Maurice 8–13, 40, 43, 67
Wilks, Spencer 8–11, 29, 34, 40, 43, 67
Willys 12
Willys-Overland 29, 34
Woodwark, Chris 114